TEACHING
ENGLISH

TEACHING ENGLISH
A PRACTICAL GUIDE FOR LANGUAGE TEACHERS

GRAEME CHING

CANADIAN SCHOLARS
Toronto | Vancouver

Teaching English: A Practical Guide for Language Teachers
Graeme Ching

First published in 2019 by
Canadian Scholars, an imprint of CSP Books Inc.
425 Adelaide Street West, Suite 200
Toronto, Ontario
M5V 3C1

www.canadianscholars.ca

Copyright © 2019 Graeme Ching and Canadian Scholars.

All rights reserved. No part of this publication may be reproduced, stored in a retrieval system, or transmitted, in any form or by any means, without the prior written permission of Canadian Scholars, under licence or terms from the appropriate reproduction rights organization, or as expressly permitted by law.

Every reasonable effort has been made to identify copyright holders. Canadian Scholars would be pleased to have any errors or omissions brought to its attention.

Library and Archives Canada Cataloguing in Publication

Title: Teaching English : a practical guide for language teachers / Graeme Ching.
Names: Ching, Graeme, 1971- author.
Description: Includes index.
Identifiers: Canadiana (print) 20190172460 | Canadiana (ebook) 20190172517 |
  ISBN 9781773381367 (softcover) | ISBN 9781773381374 (PDF) |
  ISBN 9781773381381 (EPUB)
Subjects: LCSH: English teachers—Training of. | LCSH: English language—Study
  and teaching.
Classification: LCC PE1066 .C45 2019 | DDC 428.0071—dc23

Page layout by S4Carlisle Publishing Services
Cover design by Liz Harasymczuk

19 20 21 22 23   5 4 3 2 1

Printed and bound in Ontario, Canada

Canada

This book is dedicated to language teachers who want to be better at what they do, and to those who want straightforward answers to commonly asked questions.

CONTENTS

Preface   xiii

PART I   TEACHING LANGUAGE: AN OVERVIEW

Chapter 1: All about Teachers   2
  Meet the Teachers   2
  Discovering Our Assumptions   5
  The Perfect Language Teacher?   7
  What Does a Language Teacher Teach?   10
  What Does a Language Teacher *Really* Do?   12

Chapter 2: Learning about Learners   15
  Meet the Learners   15
  Who Studies English, and Where?   18
  Why Do People Study English?   18
  How Much English Do They Already Know?   19
  How Do Students Learn?   22
  What Will Students Expect?   27
  Learning about Learners   27
  Observing the Variety   29

Chapter 3: Learning from Others: Approaches and Methods   33
  Encountering a Variety of Approaches and Methods   33
  Grammar-First Methods   35
  Fluency-First Methods   39
  Comprehension-First Methods   50
  Learner-Centred Methods   56
  Teaching with Technology   57
  Reflecting on Approaches and Methods   60

Chapter 4: Planning Courses   66

    Setting Course Goals   67
    Planning with Textbooks   68
    Planning a Course from Scratch   77

Chapter 5: Planning Lessons and Activities   81

    Lesson Objectives: Giving Activities a Purpose   81
    Planning Activities   83
    Evaluating the Effectiveness of Activities   88
    Lesson Plans   90

Chapter 6: Class Management   95

    Planning and Preparation   95
    Welcoming Students and Creating Atmosphere   98
    Running an Activity   100
    Managing the Flow: A Matter of Choices   101
    Dealing with Errors   103
    Reflection and Development   107
    Other Best Practices for the Classroom   109

Chapter 7: Assessment   111

    Assessment: More than a Measure   111
    Assessment for Learning   112
    Assessment as Learning   113
    Assessment of Learning   114
    Portfolio-Based Assessment   115
    Assessment Tools   117
    Using a Rubric   122
    Remembering the Purpose   124

PART II   TEACHING LANGUAGE SKILLS AND SUBSKILLS

Chapter 8: Teaching Speaking   128

    "Conversational" English?   128
    The Teacher as Language Counsellor   129
    Topics and Tasks   130

Common Speaking Activities   132
Necessary Subskills   135
The Teacher's Role   136
Integrating Skills: Speaking in Various Contexts   138
The Reward   138

Chapter 9: Teaching Listening Comprehension   140

Listening Gaps   140
Intensive Listening Practice   142
Running a Listening Activity   146
Integrating Skills: Listening in Various Contexts   147
Extensive Listening   148
Feedback and Encouragement   149

Chapter 10: Teaching Reading   151

Addressing Reading Problems   151
Choosing and Adapting Reading Material   155
Activities That Promote Intensive Reading   156
Reading Lessons   158
Other Types of Reading Practice   160
Integrating Skills: Reading in Various Contexts   161
Finding Solutions   162

Chapter 11: Teaching Writing   164

Types of Writing Activities   164
One Topic, Many Tasks   167
Process Writing   167
Giving Feedback   170
Integrating Skills: Writing in Various Contexts   171

Chapter 12: Understanding and Teaching Vocabulary   173

Why Learn Vocabulary?   173
Defining Vocabulary   174
Semantics and Language Learners   175
Understanding Meaning and Usage   177
Teaching Vocabulary: General Tips   178
Vocabulary Lessons   179

Integrating Vocabulary in Various Contexts   181
The Reward   182

Chapter 13: Understanding Grammar   184

What Should a Teacher Know?   184
The Structure of Words   185
Word Categories (Parts of Speech)   187
Phrases   192
Clause Structure   194
Types of Clauses   197
Sentences   200
Looking Ahead   200

Chapter 14: Teaching Grammar   203

Why Teach Grammar?   203
What Kind of Grammar Do We Teach?   207
When Do We Teach Grammar?   210
Preparing to Teach Grammar   211
Controlled Grammar Practice   212
Authentic Grammar Practice   215
Grammar Lessons   216
Integrating Grammar in Various Contexts   218
Motivated for Grammar?   218

Chapter 15: Understanding Speech Sounds   220

Speech Sounds   220
Identifying Speech Sounds: The International Phonetic Alphabet   221
Vowel Sounds   223
Consonant Sounds   225
Speech Sound Patterns   229
Issues for Language Learners   231
Looking Ahead   234

Chapter 16: Teaching Sound Perception and Pronunciation   236

Which Pronunciation?   237
Sounds in Words   237
Sounds in Sentences   240

Pronunciation and Spelling   242
Word Stress   242
Sentence Stress   243
Sentence Intonation   245
Using Thought Groups   246
Integrating Pronunciation Practice in Various Contexts   248

Chapter 17: Linguistic Factors in Language Acquisition   252

Interlanguage   252
Language Transfer   254
Language Universals and Markedness   254
Developmental Processes   256
Patterns in Language Acquisition   256
Theory in Practice   260

Chapter 18: Intercultural Communication   263

Ayako's Story   263
Language and Culture   265
Cultural Norms: Communication   267
Cultural Norms: Social Interaction   271
Generalizations and Stereotypes   275
Intercultural Competence and Accommodation   276
We're All Different   278

Chapter 19: Frequently Asked Questions   281

Appendix 1A: Common Acronyms   286
Appendix 2A: Student Details   287
Appendix 2B: Common Frameworks for Describing Language Proficiency   288
Appendix 2C: Appropriate Instruction for Particular Language Levels   289
Appendix 2D: Sample Needs Assessment   290
Appendix 3A: Sample GTM Grammar Worksheets   295
Appendix 3B: Sample GTM Reading Activity   298
Appendix 3C: Sample Audio-Lingual Drills   299
Appendix 3D: Sample Communicative Lesson   303

Appendix 3E: Sample Content-Based Lesson   307
Appendix 3F: Sample Lexical Approach Activities   310
Appendix 7A: Commonly Used (International) Proficiency Tests   311
Appendix 8A: Common Discourse Markers   312
Appendix 8B: Sample Simulation and Role-Play Scenarios   313
Appendix 9A: Sample Listening Activities   314
Appendix 10A: Sample Reading Lesson   317
Appendix 11A: Sample Writing Lesson   321
Appendix 12A: Sample Vocabulary Lesson   325
Appendix 13A: Verb Tenses in English   331
Appendix 14A: Sample Grammar Lesson (Tense)   332
Appendix 14B: Sample Grammar Lesson (Conditionals)   336
Appendix 15A: IPA Vowel Chart for North American English   342
Appendix 16A: Sound Families for Common North American Vowel Sounds   343
Appendix 16B: Sound Families for Tricky Consonant Sounds   345

Glossary of Key Terms   346

Index   357

PREFACE

This book began as a simple attempt to fill a need. The main textbook that I was using in my TESL/TEFL courses was very good, but a few topics were not well covered, and a few others were not covered at all, so I began writing supplements. To my surprise, my students asked for more, and as the number of supplements grew, I began to joke that it would be simpler to just write a book.

My students agreed. They liked the idea of a book that was well organized, carefully written, and eminently practical—a book that was written not for academics but for language teachers in the real world.

And so the journey began.

Years later, and after numerous trial versions and hundreds of updates, the final product is a book that serves primarily as a training manual for new teachers but also as a reference for experienced teachers and administrators. Its objectives are straightforward:

- introduce the various contexts in which people learn language and the wide variety of methods used to teach language
- consider how learners learn and what conditions best facilitate their learning
- provide an overview of course design, lesson planning, class management, and assessment, including current debates on such topics
- provide a thorough overview of best practices for teaching language skills (speaking, listening, reading, writing), language subskills (vocabulary, grammar, pronunciation), and content
- introduce theory related to language acquisition and intercultural communication

This book does not subscribe to a particular approach to language teaching. Rather, it attempts to give an overview of a wide variety of approaches and methods in order to provide a broad set of tools that a teacher may draw from to meet the needs of a particular class or student. Nonetheless, my personal preferences will at times be evident when I advocate practices that I have found particularly effective.

The book is organized into two parts:

- Chapters 1 to 7 provide an overview of language teaching: What makes a good language teacher? Who are our students and what do we need to know about them? What methods can we borrow from to help with our planning? How do we plan a course? How do we develop lessons and activities? How do we manage the class and assess students' progress?
- Chapters 8 to 18 are more specific, addressing language skills, language subskills, linguistic factors in language acquisition, and intercultural communication.

In short, the first part provides a broad base of general knowledge, while the second goes into more detail on specific topics. (Chapter 5, for example, introduces lessons and activities, but chapters 8 to 12, 14, and 16 explain how to create lessons and activities related to specific skills or subskills.)

The writing style of this book is aimed at readers who have little or no previous training as language teachers. Relevant terminology is introduced where necessary (to prepare new teachers for further study or discussion of these topics), but academic jargon and unnecessary complexity are deliberately avoided. However, the writing is also unusually compact, so readers are advised not to skim for the general idea but to slow down and discover the many practical ideas offered here that might otherwise be missed.

As noted, this book can be (and has been) used as a reference for experienced language teachers, but it is perhaps best used as a systematic overview for new teachers—a broad survey that can be covered reasonably quickly (as a general overview) or more slowly (for more depth on each topic). In my own TESL/TEFL classes, I use the book by applying the same principle found within it: *Students learn best by doing.* Each topic, therefore, is covered in three steps:

1. *Inform*: readings, presentations, and demonstrations
2. *Reflect*: discussion, debate, and written reflection
3. *Practice/apply*: classroom activities, case studies, curriculum development, and other written or oral assignments

Regardless of how this book is used, my hope is that readers—whether new teachers or seasoned administrators—will find it more helpful and more practical than any book twice its length; if so, I will have accomplished my goal.

PART I
TEACHING LANGUAGE: AN OVERVIEW

CHAPTER 1
All about Teachers

Think back to the teachers you've had. Who were your favourites? Why? Were they good teachers or just fun? Did you learn a lot? Were you inspired by their classes? Did they help you believe in your own abilities? What made these teachers different from others?

Most of us believe we can recognize a good teacher when we see one, but when asked what makes a good teacher, we have trouble pinning down the answer. We're more likely to judge one teacher as "good" by comparing that teacher to another we thought was "not so good." Moreover, when we attempt to be "good" teachers ourselves, we tend to teach the way we were taught, adopting what we believe were good attributes in other teachers while avoiding those we didn't like when we were students.

Is there, then, a right way and a wrong way to teach? Is there only one right way to teach? Are there certain qualities that set some teachers apart? Are some people natural teachers, and if so, is there any hope for the rest of us?

MEET THE TEACHERS

Modelling our teaching on the styles of others is not necessarily a bad idea. After all, we frequently learn by observing what works and what doesn't. Why should learning about teaching be any different? Then again, we are sometimes quick to judge what we see and tend to do so based not on objective criteria but on our own assumptions.

The following provides short descriptions of eight teachers and their teaching styles. How does each compare with your image of what a teacher should be? What are their strengths and weaknesses? What surprises you about their methods, and what ideas might you consider adopting from them?

- *Teacher 1*: Henri has been teaching language in a high school for five years. He is very comfortable in front of a class, and his students seem to like him. In a typical class, Henri stands at the front of the room and addresses the class as a whole. He follows the textbook closely and spends much of his time explaining concepts (especially grammar) clearly and effectively while the students listen and take notes. Sometimes Henri asks questions to make sure the students are listening, and he often tells funny stories to keep the students interested. At the end of class, he gives students a grammar worksheet or a short reading for homework. Overall, Henri remains the focus of attention so that students are not distracted by each other and can effectively prepare for monthly tests.

- *Teacher 2*: Lisa has been teaching young adults for two years. She enjoys working with her students, but she doesn't like to be the centre of attention. In a typical class, she gives students an assignment from the textbook or distributes a handout, briefly explains how to do it, and lets the students get to work. The students then talk freely among themselves (in English and their native languages) while completing their written work, while Lisa retreats to the corner of the room to observe. She interrupts the students only when necessary. When the students complete the assignment, she goes over the correct answers, distributes another assignment, and continues the cycle.

- *Teacher 3*: Bob retired from the military in his early forties and decided to teach language overseas. He enjoys the strong work ethic and discipline he sees in his students, and he works them hard. Bob believes that practice makes perfect, so he drills his students in one grammar form over and over until they can use it correctly and with little or no hesitation; he then moves on to the next form. He has little patience for "new" ways of teaching that coddle students or try to make language learning fun or personal; after all, learning a language is hard work and should be treated as such. Bob's personal history and his take-no-prisoners attitude in class have earned him the nickname "Drill Sergeant Bob."

- *Teacher 4*: Antonia has been teaching children for just over a year. Her classes have six to eight students each, and each class meets twice a week. Her classroom is decorated with pictures, and there is soft music playing when the children enter the room. In a typical class, Antonia and her students sit around a mid-sized table. Antonia speaks only English and uses gestures and context to make her meaning clear. She uses flash cards to teach vocabulary (mostly nouns and adjectives) and then asks questions about the objects on the cards: *What colour is the bicycle? Do you like apples?* She teaches verbs by having the students perform the actions: *Jump! Sing. Touch your nose.* She also leads the class in various games such as bingo (with colours, letters, or numbers) or Simon Says. Overall, her classes are very interactive, fun, and fast-paced, and the students enjoy the positive, reassuring style of their teacher.

- *Teacher 5*: Monica has been teaching language for three years, and she thoroughly enjoys interacting with her students. Because her class of adult ladies has only seven students, she has them sit with her around a large table. In a typical class, Monica initiates a conversation by asking a question or introducing a topic; she then encourages the students to participate. The students are generally hesitant at first, but Monica is patient, and the students gradually become eager to join in. At times, Monica takes an opposing view just to keep the conversation lively, but for the most part she lets the students take the lead in the conversation and interrupts only to guide the conversation or to explain a word or idea that the students are not familiar with. Overall, both Monica and the students are relaxed yet engaged, and the conversation flows naturally.
- *Teacher 6*: Jane has been teaching a variety of ages and levels for two years. Because she is a very active and lively person, she likes to do a variety of activities in her classes, each of which works toward one or more objectives she has chosen based on the students' needs. For each class, she introduces a general topic or theme, using stories or questions to build the students' interest. She then introduces an oral or written **activity** with a brief explanation or demonstration and lets the students get to work. Sometimes she has the students work individually, but often she has them work in pairs or small groups. While they work, Jane moves around, monitoring their progress and assisting them, but she tries not to interrupt them unless necessary. At the end of the activity, she provides **feedback** and addresses any issues before moving on to the next activity.
- *Teacher 7*: Jim has been teaching adult immigrants at the intermediate level for two years. He enjoys his job, but his real passion is technology. He frequently takes his class to the computer lab to have them write short **blogs** or social media posts, practice grammar on free websites, practice listening with free video-based listening activities, or check out the latest language learning app or website that he has discovered. When back in the classroom, Jim frequently brings in videos or movie clips to introduce Western culture, and almost every in-class explanation is a video or slide presentation found online. Overall, Jim loves the idea of being the most tech-savvy teacher in his school, and he thinks of his classes as "teaching for the 21st century."

- *Teacher 8*: Monty has been teaching for four years and knows everything. For him, every class is a stage and he is the performer. He "wows" students with his stories and impresses them with his well-informed opinions. He engages students in debates on almost any topic and usually wins. As the dominant personality in the class, he is the centre of every activity and keeps the class enthralled at every moment. He jokes that his class is really a personality cult, and he knows that his antics keep students coming back for more. He evaluates students simply by watching them in class and ensuring they keep up; after all, he keeps their attention constantly, so they must be learning something.

☞ *Consider: Which teacher would you like to be? Which styles or ideas were particularly impressive? Which were not? Which challenged your assumptions about teaching?*

DISCOVERING OUR ASSUMPTIONS

If you are like most people (and most people are, by definition, like most people), you probably reacted to the teachers described in the previous section by expressing approval or by questioning their choices—but on what basis did you make these judgments?

Most of us have certain assumptions about teaching (and about everything else, for that matter), and until we discover our assumptions, we cannot really see objectively. Consider our first teacher, Henri, for example. Would you like to be in his class? Did you appreciate his ability to stay in control of the class, or did you think he maintained too much control? Did you think he talked too much, or is that simply his job?

What about Lisa? Did you envy her confidence in letting the students work on their own, or did you want to nudge her and tell her to get to work; after all, she is the teacher, so shouldn't she teach more?

Drill Sergeant Bob might have scared you, or you might have appreciated his strong work ethic and keen focus on the fundamentals. But shouldn't a language class consist of more than just grammar drills?

Antonia was constantly interacting with her students through non-stop activities and games. Was her style a bit too intense, or was it exciting and fun? Was her teaching style (mostly oral work, and total immersion) a bit scary for those of us who like to "see" the language we're learning?

Control or facilitate?
Speak or listen?
Explain or elicit?

Figure 1.1: Discovering Our Assumptions

Perhaps Monica made you feel at home with her easygoing style and natural conversation. If you like engaging topics and group discussion, her class might be ideal for you. Then again, shouldn't a class be more than just discussion? And is Monica really teaching, or is she just hosting a get-together of students?

If you like student interaction and variety, Jane's class might seem more appealing. Then again, you might wish for Jane to take more control of her class, or for a quieter, simpler classroom experience.

If you are a fan of technology, perhaps Jim's style was most interesting—but does Jim rely too much on technology? Could technology be used more effectively in his classes?

And Monty? Does he really teach, or does he just entertain? Is he anything more than just a legend in his own mind?

Your reactions to these scenarios and your answers to the questions we've raised will help you understand your assumptions about teaching.

Questions Worth Considering

- What is the role of a teacher in the classroom? The commander-in-chief, the source of all knowledge, and the focus of attention? Or is a teacher more like a facilitator, one who spends less time teaching and more time guiding students as they learn?
- How much control should the teacher maintain? Will the students get out of hand without a firm authority at the front of the class?
- How much should the teacher talk? How much should the students talk?
- What role do explanations play in teaching? Is teaching mostly the explanation of concepts the students need to learn, or is there something else the teacher should be doing?

- What is the role of the students? Are they passive recipients, waiting to be filled with knowledge? Should they stay quiet and listen, or should they play an active role? Are they responsible for learning, or is it the teacher's job to ensure they learn?
- Who or what should be the focus of attention? The teacher? The students? Something else?
- How should technology be used in the classroom? How should it be used outside the classroom?
- Should learning be fun so that students can enjoy the class? Or should it be difficult—no pain, no gain, right?

THE PERFECT LANGUAGE TEACHER?

Perfect language teachers are difficult to find, though from time to time we meet a few teachers who are excellent in all kinds of ways. What makes them excellent? The answers vary, as do the teachers themselves, but there are certain qualities that they tend to have in common:

- Excellent language teachers are nice people who use their own personalities to make students feel welcome and comfortable.
- Excellent language teachers genuinely care about their students and are more like guides or mentors than instructors.
- Excellent language teachers remember what it is like to be a student, and they show their students respect and empathy. They are tactful and professional in all they do, but also personable.
- Excellent language teachers do not dominate the class; rather, they manage the class as necessary and provide opportunities for students to learn.
- Excellent language teachers keep the focus on learning, not on themselves, their teaching, or their students. In doing so, they unify the class in seeking a common goal, and they relieve much of the pressure (on both themselves and their students) to perform.
- Excellent teachers are goal oriented. They have clear, realistic **objectives** for each **lesson**, and they design a variety of related activities to meet those objectives. In fact, objectives are the basis for almost every decision they make.
- Excellent language teachers keep explanations clear and concise, check for understanding, and then facilitate practice.

- Excellent language teachers use their voices primarily to encourage others to speak, and they know when to keep quiet.
- Excellent language teachers **monitor** their students, adapt on the fly as necessary, and provide necessary support (known as **scaffolding**) while the students work.
- Excellent language teachers regularly reflect on their teaching, are open to new ideas, and continuously try to improve.

personable?
empathetic?
professional?
genuine?

concise?
goal oriented?
flexible?
clear?

Figure 1.2: The Perfect Language Teacher?

☞ *Consider: Which of the eight teachers described earlier in this chapter is closest to being the perfect language teacher? Why do you think so?*

Poor language teachers, meanwhile, are self-centred and tend to dominate the class. They like to hear themselves speak, enjoying the attention they get as they entertain the class, and they rarely change their **methods**. They spend too much time talking and too little time listening, and they interrupt and even belittle students to get their own point across.

Most teachers, of course, are neither of these extremes. Consider, for example, our teachers—Henri, Lisa, Bob, Antonia, Monica, Jane, Jim, and Monty. They all have positive qualities, yet each could learn from the others.

Henri might be called a traditional teacher. He remains the focus of the class and does most of the talking because he believes this is what a teacher should do. He acts as the source of information; students, then, are receptacles (although he wouldn't say it quite like that). Henri is polite, professional, and likeable, but it doesn't occur to him that while the students might be learning about the language, they are not learning to use it.

In contrast, Lisa lets the students focus on their work while she stays out of the way. She believes that students learn best by working on their own, but she doesn't seem to realize that while they may become adept at completing worksheets, they are learning little else. In addition, the students don't really see much of her personality and interact very little with each other, so they soon become bored.

Bob believes he is focusing on the fundamentals, but in reality he is just narrow-minded in his refusal to try other teaching methods. His students will likely be able to construct sentences with particular grammar forms, but they will not be able to communicate effectively, and they will soon tire of the repetitive nature of Bob's classes.

Antonia is a lively person who has created a wonderful children's class. She has started with the basics—vocabulary and basic sentences—and she makes learning fun. Her style works well in the small classes she teaches, but she might have to adapt it if she is asked to teach larger classes, particularly if she wishes to give each student frequent chances to use the language orally.

Monica is a calm, sociable, and extremely likeable teacher who believes students will learn best by practicing their English in a natural and authentic setting. She likens her class to a meeting of friends over coffee, and her class is very popular among chatty, sociable students. Students who wish to improve their speaking above all else particularly enjoy her teaching style. Some students, however, wish to work on other skills as well, so they would like to have a wider variety of activities.

Jane strives to maintain a balance. Under her direction, each lesson is unified by theme but varies in terms of activities. She plays the role of facilitator, setting up activities and giving explanations where necessary, but otherwise letting students "learn by doing." She also provides valuable feedback so that students know where they are succeeding and where they need additional practice. While Jane's style of teaching might not be perfect for every class, it is very good for most classes.

Jim means well, and his passion for technology could certainly be put to good use, but we can't help but wonder if there is any overall plan to his teaching. Surely there is room for other methods, techniques, and activities that can work together with technology to achieve clear overall objectives that better meet the needs of his students.

Monty is the classic entertainer and egotist, and there are plenty of teachers like him. Most of them are untrained and have few teaching skills, so they rely on personality and entertainment to fill the void. Worse yet, while some teachers like Monty are fun to be around, others simply use their classes to feed their egos, particularly if they are naturally loud and obnoxious.

While each of these teachers has certain strong points (even Monty—he keeps the class interesting, if nothing else), Jane is perhaps the closest to our ideal. Unlike Henri, she runs the class without dominating it, and she puts the focus on the activities, not on herself. Unlike Lisa, she supports learning by assisting and giving ongoing feedback. Unlike both Lisa and Monica, she chooses a variety of activities in hopes of accomplishing specific objectives based on the students' needs. Overall, Jane tends to do exactly what needs to be done, and she avoids doing what doesn't need to be done.

☞ *Try: Of the eight teachers described near the beginning of this chapter, which three (in your opinion) are most in need of help? Suggest a few ways for each to improve.*

WHAT DOES A LANGUAGE TEACHER TEACH?

Language training professionals often speak of the **four skills** of language learning. A typical class is likely to integrate all four skills to some extent, though it may focus on some more than others, depending on what the students want or need. The four skills are as follows:

- *Speaking*: Because many language learners study grammar and vocabulary in school but rarely have a chance to use them in real life, they often want practice speaking. In a sense, they want to **activate** the English they've already learned but have rarely used. Other students may have learned very little English, but they want to put it to use as soon as possible, and this means being able to speak. The teacher's job, then, is to plan and run activities that encourage students to speak at a level they are comfortable with, and to create an atmosphere in which students feel confident enough to speak up. (For more on teaching speaking, see chapter 8.)
- *Listening*: Many students have previously learned English in classes that gave little attention to listening, while others have little experience with English at all. In either case, they often cannot understand fluent speakers, both because of unfamiliar pronunciation and because of speaking speed. The teacher's job, then, is to plan and run activities that allow students to practice authentic listening, gradually increasing the level of difficulty over time. (For more on teaching listening, see chapter 9.)
- *Reading*: Many adult students have developed strong reading skills at school, while others remain at a very basic level. Still others may not be interested in reading, as they wish to focus on speaking and listening. The ability to read, however, is an essential part of functioning in another language. The teacher's job is to provide appropriate reading

material and **tasks** that require students to make use of that material in ways that are authentic and relevant to the students' needs. (For more on teaching reading, see chapter 10.)
- *Writing*: Some students don't like to write because it is hard work; others surprise us with a depth and clarity not evident in their speech. In many cases, students appreciate the opportunity to write something down before they say it, as it gives them a chance to focus their thoughts before presenting them to the class. Teachers, then, can use writing as a tool to enhance other activities or as an activity in its own right. (For more on teaching writing, see chapter 11.)

Many language courses emphasize **integrated skills**—that is, they make use of all four skills to complete a given task or learn particular content, reflecting a belief that skills are best developed not in isolation but as each one supports and reinforces the others.

In addition to the four skills of language, teachers also focus on the **subskills** of language that enable the upper-level skills:

- *Vocabulary*: Without vocabulary, we cannot speak, understand, read, or write anything, and the sooner a student's vocabulary grows, the sooner the student can communicate more successfully. The teacher's job is not to be a walking dictionary, nor to assign long, boring lists of words to memorize, but to help students build their vocabulary through a variety of activities. (For more on teaching vocabulary, see chapter 12.)
- *Grammar*: Love it or hate it, grammar is an important part of teaching a language. Some teachers (and even some books) try to avoid it, but every time a student asks us why we say something the way we do, our answer will involve grammar. In addition, there is a strong argument to be made for including grammar instruction as part of a successful language learning program. (For more on teaching grammar, see chapters 13 and 14.)
- *Pronunciation*: Learning a language includes learning how to correctly produce, arrange, and modify particular sounds. Part of a language teacher's job is teaching these features and providing practice to make them familiar, resulting in accent modification and more accurate listening skills. (For more on teaching sound perception and pronunciation, see chapters 15 and 16.)

Specific-Purpose Language Training

Many English classes have a very general purpose: helping students improve their English for use in a variety of social situations. Their content includes topics from general life and society. These courses are generally referred to as ESL, EFL, or EAL. (See appendix 1A for a brief discussion of how these terms are used, as well as a list of other relevant acronyms.)

There are also language classes that focus on specific areas such as business, academics, tourism, and so on. These classes, together known as English for Specific Purposes (ESP), include the usual practice in speaking, listening, reading, writing, vocabulary, grammar, and pronunciation, but the content is more relevant to the particular focus.

For example, in many countries, courses in "business English" are very popular. The usual skills are practiced, but readings are likely to be about business situations, speaking classes may include business presentations, writing will often include letters and memos, and grammar lessons often include the difference between formal and informal usage. The content is also likely to include cultural differences in how business is done in other countries.

Another common example is English for Academic Purposes (EAP), offered to students preparing to study at a college or university where English is the language of instruction. These classes provide significant practice in writing (reports and essays), taking notes (from lectures), and reading comprehension (of academic material). They may also include a general orientation in "how to live abroad."

"Test-prep" classes, while also preparatory in nature, are narrower in focus: they prepare students to write standardized language exams that are required when applying to many colleges and universities or for work. These courses focus not only on the language itself but also on the nature of the test and how to succeed in writing it.

To these we can add many more. In each case, the methods are similar, but the content and activities are customized to suit the specific focus of the course.

WHAT DOES A LANGUAGE TEACHER *REALLY* DO?

Overall, a good language teacher spends surprisingly little time "teaching," at least in the traditional sense of standing at the front of the class and talking. Rather, good teachers create and maintain (or adapt) the conditions in which learning can take place and then facilitate learning by providing the needed support:

- They discover the students' needs, set **goals** for the course and objectives for each lesson, and plan lessons and activities to meet those objectives.
- They introduce the class topic to generate interest and activate students' prior knowledge.
- They briefly introduce and explain new material and activities.
- They get out of the way so students can learn by practicing, but at the same time monitor and assist as necessary.
- They give feedback and follow-up, along with encouragement and advice.
- They keep the class running smoothly while adapting to the changing needs of the students.

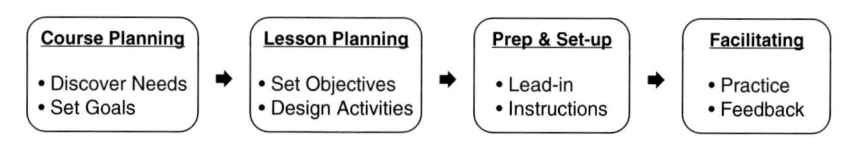

Course Planning	Lesson Planning	Prep & Set-up	Facilitating
• Discover Needs • Set Goals	• Set Objectives • Design Activities	• Lead-in • Instructions	• Practice • Feedback

Figure 1.3: What Does a Teacher Really Do?

Note that once the teacher sets up the activity, the focus is on the activity itself, not on the teacher. In other words, the teacher is often in the background, planning, organizing, and supporting the class activities while the students themselves carry out those activities. Think of it this way: *Whoever does the most learns the most.* Students, then, should be the busy ones in class, and in most cases, they should be doing most of the speaking—after all, they are the ones who need the practice. The teacher is there to organize, lead (as necessary), and facilitate that practice, and at times that means keeping quiet and staying out of the way.

☞ *Consider: Before reading this chapter, what was your image of a language teacher? What did you think a language teacher did? Have those ideas changed?*

QUESTIONS FOR REVIEW

1. Why do we say that a good language teacher spends surprisingly little time "teaching"?
2. In what sense is the teacher not the focus of the class? (What should be the focus?)

3. What "four skills" do language teachers often refer to? What else do language teachers teach? How might these be integrated?
4. What is meant by "specific-purpose" language training?
5. "Whoever does the most learns the most." Explain this statement in the context of language teaching.
6. This chapter implies that lecturing is likely a very ineffective teaching method for language classes. Are there any exceptions? (in language classes? in other classes?)
7. What might a language class, a dance class, and a math class have in common in terms of teaching style? How might this style differ from those used in other types of classes?

FURTHER READING

Sally Brown and Donald McIntyre's *Making Sense of Teaching* (Open, 1993) is a valuable resource for considering what good teaching looks like.

Tricia Hedge's *Teaching and Learning in the Language Classroom* (Oxford, 2000) provides a good overview of the various roles of the teacher. See her first chapter in particular.

Tom Keller's *The Various Roles of the Teacher in the English Classroom* (Grin Verlag, 2016) examines the various roles required of an English language teacher in order to facilitate students' success.

Jack C. Richards's *Teaching in Action: Case Studies from Second Language Classrooms* (TESOL, 1998) is an easy-to-read collection of case studies that examines and comments on a variety of teachers and classroom situations.

Bogum Yoon's *Teachers' Roles in Second Language Learning: Classroom Applications of Sociocultural Theory* (Information Age, 2014) examines the role of the teacher in the pre-16 language classroom in light of current socio-cultural theory.

CHAPTER 2
Learning about Learners

Picture a "typical" language class: Who are the students? Are they young or old? Why are they studying a language? Where and how often do they study?

Most of us have a certain image in mind when we hear the term *language class*, but we also know that language classes—and language students—can vary widely, and the differences are easily observed. As you read the descriptions below, ask yourself what you can learn by observing the students. For example, what are the students' backgrounds? Why are they studying English? How much English do they already know? What are their current strengths and weaknesses?

MEET THE LEARNERS

- *Student 1*: Hiromi is an office worker in her mid-twenties. She takes English classes at a private language school two evenings per week. Hiromi wishes to improve her English both for her job and for personal travel. Having studied English in school, she has a strong understanding of basic grammar and a vocabulary of at least a few thousand words. However, she finds it very difficult to have a conversation in English; she speaks it slowly and understands only a little of what is spoken to her. Her current teacher is a native English speaker who creates lessons that exercise all skills but with a particular emphasis on speaking and listening. As one of eight students, all in their twenties or thirties, Hiromi enjoys the class and knows that she needs oral practice, but she is much more comfortable with written work because she can "see" what she is learning.
- *Student 2*: Sung-Hoon is a 40-year-old engineer who studies English at work two mornings per week in a group of 12 co-workers. Because he shares the results of his research with colleagues in other countries, he must be able to write reports and give presentations in English. Having

previously studied English in school and university, he can read fairly complex documents in English, and he can speak in long sentences—though slowly, and he prefers to prepare in advance. He has more trouble, however, understanding what others say or interacting without preparation. His current class focuses on having students explain their work in discussions and presentations. Although Sung-Hoon knows he must improve his English, he doesn't care much for the class because he doesn't like discussions and would rather work on his own.

- *Student 3*: Mario is a 16-year-old high school student who studies English three times a week as part of his regular high school curriculum. His teacher follows the textbook closely, and a typical class consists of explanation of a grammar point followed by written practice. English is spoken very little in the class except when they do oral pronunciation activities, which generally consist of repeating after the teacher or after a recording. A few times a year, a native English speaker from another country visits the class, but the students cannot understand him. They are, however, quite well prepared for the standardized tests they will have to write at the end of the year. Mario, like many of his friends, does the work required but doesn't enjoy it; he'd rather be playing soccer or tinkering in his parents' garage.

- *Student 4*: Amelia is a 50-year-old musician who studies advanced English once a week with a group of friends. Like her classmates, she has always enjoyed English and speaks it very well. In fact, Amelia has a special gift: she can hear a sentence in an unknown language and repeat it almost perfectly. She learned English in school and then improved her skills by watching English TV shows and travelling to other countries. She is also able to read stories and magazines in English, though she sometimes struggles to understand the content. In a typical class, the students talk about whatever is new in their lives and then discuss a story or an article that they have read and written about for homework.

- *Student 5*: Aliya is an immigrant to a country where English is the local language. She studied English many years ago in school, but now in her mid-thirties, she has forgotten much of it. She attends a government-sponsored English class for immigrants where she is trying to "reactivate" the English she once knew. The class is at the high-beginner level, and students practice all **language skills** but with a particular emphasis on practical English for situations common to new immigrants. Aliya finds the class helpful, but because her husband frequently works

late and she is responsible for caring for their three children, she sometimes misses class and generally has little time to study on her own. As a result, she struggles to remember everything being taught in the class. Her progress is slow, and her motivation is dwindling.
- *Student 6*: Lucia is a 32-year-old accountant for her city office. She once spent three months in England to improve her English, and she can still carry on a basic conversation in most routine situations; however, she sometimes has to repeat herself to be understood, and because she rarely has a chance to speak English in her own country, she is worried that she will forget it. She attends private lessons once a week where she and her teacher sometimes follow a discussion-based textbook but often just talk about what is happening in their lives and in their city.
- *Student 7*: Ana is an eight-year-old elementary school student. She studies English in school, where they learn basic vocabulary, practice simple grammar forms, and write very short sentences. She also attends after-school classes with nine of her friends at a private language school, where they further practice what they've learned in school but with a much stronger focus on proper pronunciation and oral communication. Ana excels in school, earning very high grades, and she enjoys taking language classes with her friends, but aside from a few basic sentences, she cannot use English in any practical way.
- *Student 8*: Nellie, a young woman in her early twenties, recently arrived in a North American city as a refugee from a country in the midst of political chaos. She learned basic English from her grandmother as she grew up, so she can answer simple questions slowly, but she has never been to school and cannot read or write in any language. Even forming letters and numbers on paper is a challenge for her. She currently attends a class run by volunteers in her community, and though she can hold her own during a basic class conversation, she quickly becomes lost and frustrated when the teacher distributes handouts that she cannot read.

When observing these students, we notice something right away: there is probably no "typical" language student. They learn and practice English in a variety of ways and in various types of classes, and although they may have some attributes in common, they often differ in their reasons for learning a language, their level of motivation, their current ability to use the language, their level of confidence in using the language, and even their preferred ways of learning.

Discovering who language learners are and what makes them tick often involves observing them in class and asking the right questions. Some of the more common questions and typical answers are discussed in this chapter.

☞ Consider: What surprised you about the students described in this chapter? (Complete the chart in appendix 2A to compare and contrast their situations.)

WHO STUDIES ENGLISH, AND WHERE?

For many people, the word *students* brings to mind children or teenagers sitting in rows in a classroom, or perhaps those same students sitting around workstations in a classroom. Language students, however, come from all walks of life: they may be children or teenagers or adults, students or company workers or homemakers, labourers or professionals or executives. They may be young and cool, older and wiser, or just plain silly (regardless of age). They may sit in a formal classroom taking notes, or they may be huddled around a table in a coffee shop, passionately discussing current events. They may see learning as an academic requirement, a social activity, a method of self-improvement, or a necessity for work.

We also notice from these descriptions that many people who have completed their formal schooling probably do not identify themselves as students except in class; for this reason, we often use the term *students* to describe the individuals in a given class and the term **language learners** as a more general description of anyone who learns a language anywhere and in any way.

WHY DO PEOPLE STUDY ENGLISH?

As noted, not every language learner is a full-time student working to complete a required course. Many learners have very different reasons for studying and practicing a language:

- Some learners have personal reasons for attending a language class. They may plan to travel overseas, they may have an interest in other cultures and languages, or they may simply wish to study language as a form of self-improvement.
- Others have professional reasons for learning. They may be required to complete a course as part of a job, or they may have to present business proposals or research results to colleagues in other countries.

- Still others have academic reasons for learning. They may be required to pass a course for school or to write an exam as part of an application to study at university, or they may wish to publish their research in foreign journals.

The reasons for studying language are often as varied as the students, and discovering those reasons is an important step in planning a course. (See "Learning about Learners" later in this chapter.)

Personal   Professional   Academic

Figure 2.1: Why Do People Study English?

How Motivated Are They?

Whether adults or children, English language learners generally fall into three very broad categories: those who want to learn English and enjoy doing so; those who do not really want to learn English but do their best to learn because they should or must; and those who do not really want to learn English but attend classes (often with little intent to learn) only because they are required to attend or have social reasons to do so.

Among those who do not wish to learn English, some may be shy about speaking in another language, and others may simply not be interested—and yes, some might just be lazy. In each of these cases, an important part of the teacher's job is to help the students enjoy the class and perhaps even discover a personal reason to learn—in other words, to help improve motivation. (See "Welcoming Students and Creating Atmosphere" in chapter 6.)

HOW MUCH ENGLISH DO THEY ALREADY KNOW?

English is now required as part of the school curriculum in many parts of the world, and more and more countries are recognizing the need to speak English in the global community. As a result, many educated adults have at least some understanding of the language, ranging from basic vocabulary and short sentences to the ability to carry on a conversation with relative ease.

Nonetheless, there are also many adults who cannot use English effectively either because they haven't studied it or because they were taught with standardized methods that improved their knowledge of English (especially grammar rules) but not their ability to use it.

Unfortunately, there is no single, agreed-upon system for describing the language levels of learners. In fact, there are many systems, and they vary widely. They may define five, six, eight, ten, or even twelve different levels of proficiency, and they may even differ in the types of measures being used: some focus more on grammar, others on reading and writing, and still others on a variety of skills or abilities. (See appendix 2B for a list of common frameworks for describing language proficiency, and appendix 7A for a list of commonly used English proficiency tests.)

Each of these systems describes three or four broad proficiency levels, often categorizing students as being at the *beginner* level, the *intermediate* level, or the *advanced* level (terms used by many publishers of ESL/EFL textbooks). Each of these levels has sublevels, and though it can be difficult to define where one level ends and another begins, consider the following a rough guide, keeping in mind that each level represents a range:

1. *Low-beginner* students know little or nothing of the language.
2. *Beginner* students can copy basic text and use greetings, numbers, and simple words or **phrases**, but probably not full sentences (unless memorized). They can also follow simple instructions and answer simple questions about personal information.
3. *High-beginner* students can express basic needs and make simple or routine sentences, though with frequent errors and need of clarification. They can read and write short texts with limited vocabulary but have difficulty determining meaning when reading more than a few sentences. They can function in common social situations, though in a very basic way.
4. *Low-intermediate* students can handle most routine situations, though errors in grammar and pronunciation may cause need for repetition and clarification. They can engage in simple conversations and social situations (with some difficulty) and read a variety of basic texts. They can write short paragraphs, though the meaning may be unclear because of grammatical errors.
5. *Intermediate* students can speak and write well enough to communicate effectively in most everyday situations. Errors at this level are still common but less likely to impede comprehension.

6. *High-intermediate* students can speak and write about a wide variety of topics using fairly complex grammar. They are beginning to focus less on learning English and more on using English to learn other subjects. They can function in most high school classes without much difficulty. They fit into most social situations and can adapt their language as necessary.
7. *Advanced* students are fluent in English and use English to learn other subject material. They are beginning to understand nuance and style in their speaking and writing, and they are capable of using English to reason and persuade. Students at this level can study at the college/university level without much difficulty.
8. *Very advanced* students use and understand English at a level higher than that of many native speakers. They are often well-educated professionals who use English on a regular basis.

(For a description of appropriate grammar instruction at each of these levels, see appendix 2C.)

Finally, note that many adult learners join English classes as **false beginners**—that is, they appear to be at the beginner level, but they soon reveal a significant vocabulary and at least a basic understanding of grammar, both of which were learned in school but almost forgotten. They tend to progress quickly through the lower levels as they reactivate what they learned previously, but they "level off" by the intermediate levels.

Problems with Student Levels

In a perfect scenario, every class has the ideal number of students at precisely the same level, and they all improve in the same areas at the same rate. Of course, no such class exists. Even in classes based on the students' language levels, there are still issues that arise; worse yet, some classes may be formed on criteria other than language levels.

Most adult classes are formed on the basis of level. New students are given a **proficiency test** (or **placement test**, either formal or informal) and placed in an appropriate class. Even in this scenario, however, the grouping is not perfect:

- No matter how carefully students are tested, testing does not give a perfect indication of a student's level. Over time, this discrepancy will become apparent in class.

- Students at the same general level may have different strengths and weaknesses. Some students may be strong in speaking but weak in grammar, while others may be better at reading and writing.
- Even if students begin a class at approximately the same level, they will likely progress in different areas at different rates.
- Students at the same level may have different reasons for learning English and very different interests, making the choice of subject material difficult.

Moreover, students may be grouped together for reasons other than level. A small language school, for example, may wish to offer evening English classes to office workers but not have enough potential students for a wide range of classes, so students will be grouped with those of the nearest levels, resulting in a range of levels within each class; or if the school has significantly more students at one level than another, the classes may be rebalanced to even out the numbers, even if this results in students at different levels being in the same class.

Children are a different case. In most public schools and private language schools, children are grouped in classes according to age. As a result, there may be a wide range of ability and proficiency in any given class.

☞ *Consider: What levels are represented by the learners profiled at the beginning of this chapter? Which learners are stronger in one skill or another? How might that affect their participation in various types of class activities?*

HOW DO STUDENTS LEARN?

Which of the following is the best way to learn another language?

- Through a cognitive process—that is, by deliberately and thoughtfully learning complex rules and then applying them to produce new **utterances**?
- Through habit formation—that is, by memorizing patterns of language until we can use them automatically?
- Through intuitive acquisition or immersion—that is, by being exposed to and responding to significant amounts of **authentic language**, much like the way we learned our first language?
- Through skill development—that is, by learning and practicing language skills until we become proficient?

These four ideas, drawn from common theories of second-language acquisition, suggest that there is no clear consensus. In fact, over time, theorists, researchers, and instructors have designed, refined, implemented, and even modified numerous **approaches** to language teaching, many of which are still used today. (See chapter 3 for more information on approaches to language teaching, their underlying theories of language acquisition, and the teaching methods that are based on them.)

Amidst the variety, one point seems certain, or at least generally accepted: the ability to use a language is developed primarily through practice. Yes, there are still language details that need to be explained, but they are internalized most effectively when practiced, not simply heard or memorized. The cliché "practice makes perfect" may be an exaggeration, but good practice of the right kind does indeed lead to progress, particularly in a language class.

Class activities are, for the most part, just different forms of practice—speaking practice, listening practice, reading practice, writing practice, grammar practice, and so on. The teacher's job, then, is to prepare activities that facilitate practice, set them up in class, and manage them as necessary (whether by monitoring the activity, giving feedback, or simply staying out of the way). (For more information on activities and class management, see chapters 5 and 6, respectively.)

Note that if the focus of the class is practice through activities, then the teacher is not the centre of attention. Rather, the activity itself is central, and the focus is on learning, not teaching. This scenario also suggests *student talk* is more important than *teacher talk*; after all, the students, not the teacher, need the practice. A good general rule is that for a typical 20-minute activity, the teacher will spend only a few minutes setting up the activity and will then spend the rest of the time monitoring the students' progress and supporting them as necessary. (There are exceptions, of course. When practicing pronunciation or listening, for example, students will need to hear the teacher's voice more frequently.)

In addition, we must keep in mind that language learners are prone to **listening fatigue**. Listening to another language and trying to make sense of the content requires a level of attention and focus that can be maintained for only so long. Long explanations, then, even if they are interesting, are often counterproductive, resulting in confusion and loss of motivation; when possible, they should be replaced with activities that allow students to discover the content on their own.

☞ *Consider: Look back at the teacher profiles in chapter 1. Which teachers emphasize activities and student talk over teacher talk? How might the others improve?*

Variety in Learning

We must also remember that students learn in a variety of ways. In the past, theorists proposed that a given individual has a particular **learning style** and will learn best when that learning style is accommodated in the classroom.[1] While lists and descriptions of learning styles vary widely, some of the simpler ones include visual (learning by seeing), auditory (learning by hearing), and physical (learning through physical activity); others note preferences for collaboration, competition, or individual learning.

Some researchers have questioned whether learning styles are anything more than just personal preferences with no actual effect on learning.[2] They suggest that teachers should develop class activities not according to students' perceived learning styles but according to what best suits the skill or content being learned. They also suggest engaging multiple senses as appropriate; after all, every learner learns in a variety of ways, even if one way is preferred, and both skills and content are reinforced through multiple types of effective practice.

Consider, for example, a class in which students need to learn a list of new vocabulary. The items in the list can be presented visually (as a list of written words or as a series of images), aurally (read aloud), or kinesthetically (as a game that associates new terms with movement), but since new vocabulary must be encountered numerous times before being committed to long-term memory, wouldn't it make sense to employ visual, aural, *and* kinesthetic learning? And to engage learners both individually and in group activities?

Closely related to this topic is Howard Gardner's **multiple intelligences theory**, which broadened the concept of intelligence by suggesting various types of intelligence,[3] described here as they relate to language learners:

- *Verbal/linguistic intelligence*: Some people are good with words. Words seem to flow more naturally from them, and their expressions are often more creative and effective. Activities such as reading, storytelling, and creative writing will likely appeal to them.
- *Logical/mathematical intelligence*: People who are good at crunching numbers and solving logical problems through reason often enjoy science and engineering, but they are also likely to be good at understanding grammar and analyzing how language is used. They appreciate explanations that are logical and sequential, and they are likely to enjoy challenges that employ reasoning.

- *Visual/spatial intelligence*: Rather than merely listening to an explanation of a concept, visual learners prefer to see (or provide) a diagram, chart, map, or picture as well.
- *Body/kinesthetic intelligence*: People who are particularly good at physical activity often learn better and remember more when they are physically interacting with the space around them. They are likely to enjoy hands-on activities, field trips, and activities that let them move around.
- *Musical/rhythmic intelligence*: Some people are very good at discerning sounds, tone, and rhythm, and they are quick to recognize sound patterns. They learn well by listening, and they may employ music or rhythm in their learning.
- *Interpersonal intelligence*: Some people are naturally sociable. They communicate well, work well in groups, and may even solve problems between others. They learn best by working with others and often enjoy discussion and interaction.
- *Intrapersonal intelligence*: People who have a very strong understanding of themselves, their responses, and their motivations often show self-discipline and work well alone. They enjoy journalling and reflection, and they like to have choice in how they learn.
- *Naturalist intelligence*: Some people have a special understanding of and appreciation for nature, and they are very observant to its details and patterns. They enjoy learning about nature and are particularly motivated and inspired by interacting with it.

This theory also has its critics, but even if we recognize that every individual has particular strengths or talents, we must resist the tendency to label students according to those strengths because, as noted, every learner learns in a variety of ways (even if certain strengths are apparent). Once again, our choices when planning lessons should reflect what is best suited to the skill or content being learned and should include activities that appeal to a variety of preferences and strengths.

Factors That Affect Learning

Having noted that learners often have particular preferences that may or may not affect how (or how well) they learn a language, we should also note the factors that are likely to have a very real impact on language acquisition:

- *Age*: While there remains debate about the extent to which language acquisition ability is affected by age, we know for certain that native-like pronunciation is much more feasible for young learners. (The suggestion that an individual's ability to learn language declines after a particular age, normally around puberty, is known as the **critical period hypothesis**.)
- *Natural strengths*: Learners naturally vary in their strengths and weaknesses. For example, some easily distinguish and reproduce new sounds, while others continuously confuse them; some are quick to understand grammar forms, while others struggle to make sense of them.
- *Formal education*: Learners who have little or no formal education are less likely to have the basic skills, study habits, and understanding of common structures (of language, of writing) that educated people take for granted.
- *Motivation*: Highly motivated learners are, of course, much more likely to succeed in acquiring a language, and those with intrinsic motivation (i.e., a genuine interest in the language) are even more likely to be successful than those who have extrinsic motivation (e.g., the desire for good grades or approval). Note, however, that extrinsic motivation can lead to careful study, which can spark genuine interest and thus lead to intrinsic motivation.
- *Affective factors*: A learner's attitude toward the learning process can have a significant impact on language acquisition. In particular, anxiety, and especially fear of failure or embarrassment, can be detrimental to success.

There are also socio-cultural factors that affect language acquisition.[4] The following are particularly influential:

- *Perceived value*: The more that language learning is valued by the learner's culture, the more likely the learner will be successful in acquiring the language.
- *Perceived cultural distance*: The closer the learner feels to the **target language** culture, the more likely the learner will be successful in acquiring the language.
- *Opportunity for interaction*: The more opportunities the learner has to interact with more advanced users of the target language, the more likely the learner will be successful in acquiring the language.

This last factor comes from **social interactionist theory**,[5] which suggests that language acquisition is aided by social interaction with others who are more linguistically advanced in the target language and who can provide support in language development.

☞ *Consider: Review the learner profiles at the beginning of this chapter. What do we know about their preferences and other factors that might influence how they learn?*

WHAT WILL STUDENTS EXPECT?

A teacher who carefully considers the needs of students may be well prepared for class, but will the students in the class be prepared for the teacher? After all, students generally have certain expectations even before they step into the classroom: some expect the teacher to firmly lead the class from the front of the room and may even expect the teacher to do most, if not all, of the talking while students sit and take notes; others may expect to be active participants in the class, using the language authentically in order to learn it.

Overall, students often expect to be taught in the ways they have previously experienced. For some, the suggestion that the teacher should not be the centre of attention may be highly unusual. Part of the teacher's job, then, is to discover the students' expectations and to help them adjust to newer styles of class management, often by explaining the benefits and creating a positive, inclusive atmosphere. Some students will find it a challenge to speak up in class, as they are accustomed to speaking only when spoken to; others will find an activity-based class "busier" than a traditional class where they simply sat and took notes. Overall, though, students who are used to dry grammar explanations and stale dialogues will be delighted by a more interactive classroom in which language is used to communicate something interesting and meaningful.

LEARNING ABOUT LEARNERS

Students' backgrounds, reasons for learning, motivation, current language levels, and expectations are all helpful details when planning a class—but where do we find these details? Unfortunately, students don't come with manuals that explain everything we wish to know about them, and simply observing students to discover their needs often takes more time than we have available. To find our answers more efficiently, we can do a needs assessment.

A **needs assessment** is a method of discovering our students' needs, and if done well, it provides insight into how we can best meet those needs. It discovers not only the students' current language level but also their reasons for learning English, their past experiences with the language, their expectations, and any other details that might help us provide a better class experience for them.

Discovering Experience, Purpose, Motivation, and Expectations

Discovering the previous experiences, the reasons for studying, the level of motivation, and expectations of an adult student is generally straightforward. Simply ask questions such as these:

- Where have you studied language before? For how long? Why?
- What (kinds of activities) did you do in those classes?
- Did you enjoy those classes? Why (or why not)?
- What (kinds of activities) would you like to do in this class?
- Do you enjoy learning a language? Why (or why not)?
- Why do you want to study English? What is your goal for this class?
- Do you ever speak or write English at work? Do you use it for travel? For other reasons?

Such questions can be asked orally either in class or during individual interviews, or they can be given as a questionnaire. Oral interviews are best, however, as they allow us to adapt and reword the questions as necessary and to ask follow-up questions for further clarification; they also give us a general idea of the students' speaking and listening levels. Note, however, that we must take careful notes during the interview to capture the details before they are forgotten.

Discovering Language Level

Discovering students' current language levels is more difficult, and asking them is usually not helpful since most students will underestimate their ability (though a few will overestimate it). Worse yet, students who have completed an "advanced" language course at college may be surprisingly weak at speaking and listening and only slightly stronger in reading and writing, so asking about prior education is also of little help.

The best option here is some combination of written and oral work that will demonstrate students' overall ability and their particular strengths and weaknesses. Many textbook publishers provide online or paper-based placement tests matched to their textbooks, and though they tend to focus primarily on reading, writing, vocabulary, and grammar, they are nonetheless useful.

Alternatively, or in combination with provided placement tests, we can develop our own activities to help discover students' levels: an interview, small-group discussion, dictation, grammar exercises, a short writing assignment, a reading activity with comprehension questions, or any other type of activity that requires them to use their English. Ideally, each activity should become progressively more difficult so we can see at what level students begin to encounter difficulty—a dictation activity, for example, could begin with short, simple sentences and gradually move toward longer, more complex sentences with more difficult vocabulary; the speed at which the sentences are dictated could also increase.

For each activity, take detailed notes about each student's strengths and weaknesses in speaking, listening, reading, writing, vocabulary, grammar, and pronunciation, and use these notes not only to place students in appropriate classes but also to set appropriate objectives for each class.

For a good example of a basic needs assessment, see appendix 2D at the back of this book. Keep in mind, however, that no short-term assessment is perfect, and that a good teacher continues to observe students during class activities in order to confirm and refine these first impressions.

☞ *Consider: To what extent do the activities in appendix 2D represent a progression from beginner to higher levels (as described earlier in this chapter and in appendix 2C)?*

OBSERVING THE VARIETY

Returning to the students introduced at the beginning of the chapter—Hiromi, Sung-Hoon, Mario, Amelia, Aliya, Lucia, Ana, and Nellie—we can observe or surmise the following based on the limited information we've been given:

- Hiromi has chosen to study English for personal and professional reasons and is likely motivated to learn. She is probably a false beginner and will progress through the lower levels quickly. However, she may be shy about speaking up and will need to be encouraged in a warm, friendly class. She may also need to practice written examples before attempting oral ones.

- Sung-Hoon is quiet and thoughtful, and he is probably shy. He is an "English machine" when it comes to reading, writing, and grammar, but he needs more practice in listening to natural English. Because he prefers to study alone with his books, he will need a lot of encouragement in a class that requires speaking and presentations.
- Mario is a typical (or perhaps stereotypical) male high school student. He will do okay in his class because he knows he must, but he would do better with more practical, interactive, and hands-on activities. Sheer determination will help him attain the necessary score on his standardized test, but he will be unable to communicate orally without extensive practice—which his high school classes are unlikely to provide.
- Amelia is uniquely gifted and a pleasure to teach. She will have no problem doing well in her class, but if she wants to round out her abilities, she will need to focus more on reading comprehension and perhaps on complex grammatical structures as well. Without a lot of encouragement, though, she is more likely to focus on her current strengths, not her weaknesses.
- Aliya is another false beginner, but she has been out of school for many years and doesn't have much time to commit to learning English. For this reason, she will need plenty of encouragement, and the teacher will need to review new material regularly. In addition, the teacher's focus on practical English for common situations will help meet immediate needs, but it will be effective overall only if combined with long-term goals for gradual improvement in all areas of the language.
- Lucia's overall goal is language retention. She will likely be happy with a variety of activities that make use of the English she already has, as well as a few that challenge her to move beyond her current level. She is also likely to expect much more oral interaction (especially conversation) than grammar or writing; such a focus is fine, but the teacher may need to remind her that language skills reinforce one another, so none should be neglected.
- Ana is a typical young student who supplements her grammar-based school lessons with after-school classes. In this case, her after-school teacher has wisely chosen to focus on oral practice. Ana enjoys both classes, but her parents may need to be convinced that the after-school class is worthwhile; after all, if Ana is going to be successful, she needs very strong grades on her grammar and reading tests in school, and her parents may question the usefulness of oral activities and games.

- Nellie can keep up during oral activities, but her inability to read or write at even a basic level puts her at a distinct disadvantage; not only are written activities incomprehensible to her, but she must memorize everything she learns, as taking notes is not an option for her. Worse yet, the study skills and classroom skills that others take for granted are unknown to her. She will need a lot of encouragement as well as some extra tutoring to help her catch up.

The variety of students, needs, and expectations described here is not unusual, and discovering those needs is particularly important for planning classes; but that same variety is also what makes a class interesting.

QUESTIONS FOR REVIEW

1. Why is it important to learn the reasons that students are enrolled in a language class?
2. Is there one standard system for defining the levels of language learners? Explain.
3. What is a false beginner?
4. What problems might arise when grouping students by level?
5. In a given class, how do we deal with the variety of strengths, weaknesses, preferences, and other factors that affect how students learn (or wish to learn)?
6. How might students' expectations (for a language class) differ from our own? Why is it important for a teacher to understand these differences?
7. What is the purpose of a needs assessment, and why is it important?
8. When discovering students' backgrounds, reasons for learning, and expectations, why are oral interviews generally better than written questionnaires?

FURTHER READING

Carol Griffiths's *Lessons from Good Language Learners* (Cambridge, 2008) is a collection of essays by well-known scholars and addresses what makes good learners effective.

Nancy Hadaway, Sylvia Vardell, and Terrell Young's *What Every Teacher Should Know about English Language Learners* (Pearson, 2008) aims to help teachers understand the needs of language learners in the school system.

Tricia Hedge's *Teaching and Learning in the Language Classroom* (Oxford, 2000) provides valuable insight into learners and learning in the second-language classroom. See her first and third chapters in particular.

Pérsida Himmele and William Himmele's *Four Things Every Teacher Should Know about English Language Learners* (Language and Cognition Resources, 2016) also aims to help teachers understand the needs of language learners in the school system.

See also this book's companion website for links to relevant websites.

NOTES

1. Frank Coffield, David Moseley, Elaine Hall, and Kathryn Ecclestone provide a very thorough treatment of this topic in *Learning Styles and Pedagogy in Post-16 Learning: A Systematic and Critical Review* (Learning and Skills Research Centre, 2004).
2. Tesia Marshik gives a brief but informative TED Talk that challenges the popular understanding of learning styles: "Learning Styles and the Importance of Critical Self-Reflection," available at https://www.youtube.com/watch?v=855Now8h5Rs.
3. Gardner first described his concept of multiple intelligences in *Frames of Mind: The Theory of Multiple Intelligences* (Basic Books, 1983).
4. See Rod Ellis's *The Study of Second Language Acquisition* (Oxford, 2008).
5. Social interactionist theory and its key concept, the zone of proximal development, were developed by Lev Vygotsky and are described in "Zone of Proximal Development and Cultural Tools, Scaffolding, Guided Participation" in H. Rudolph Shaffer's *Key Concepts in Developmental Psychology* (Sage, 2007).

CHAPTER 3
Learning from Others: Approaches and Methods

In chapter 1, we met eight language teachers who varied widely in how they taught. Henri was very traditional, delivering information from the front of the class, while Lisa set students up to work on their own with little help and limited feedback. Bob acted as commander-in-chief, drilling students in grammar forms, while Antonia partnered with her young students, leading them in a series of interactive activities. Monica created a relaxed atmosphere and gave students freedom to speak freely on a variety of topics, while Jane facilitated a variety of activities and supported students as they learned. Jim relied on technology almost to the exclusion of anything else, and Monty, of course, was the egotist at the front of the room who had given very little thought to teaching methodology.

Although we are likely to choose Jane as closest to our ideal teacher for adult learners, and perhaps Antonia for young beginners, we must also realize that their teaching styles may not suit every student or every situation. What if a particular class has needs that are not easily addressed by their methods? Where do we turn for more ideas?

ENCOUNTERING A VARIETY OF APPROACHES AND METHODS

Language teaching isn't new. For as long as humans have encountered other humans who spoke a different language, they've made attempts to understand one another and learn each other's languages. Early attempts were likely very basic immersion experiences focused initially on vocabulary and short phrases, but later attempts were based on carefully considered approaches (the underlying assumptions and principles related to language and learning) and their resulting teaching methods. The 20th century, in particular, saw the development of numerous new methods, including some that might seem very familiar to us and a few that might seem a bit bizarre.

Over time, however, teachers and researchers have established a number of best practices (though many are still debated, of course), and as a result, three trends have been noticeable over the past few decades:

- Many of the more unusual methods are no longer used, or are rarely used, but certain principles, activities, and other ideas from them have been adopted for use with other methods.
- Many of the more popular methods have been modified to accommodate changing beliefs about how language is best taught and learned.
- Many language teachers do not subscribe to a particular method; rather, they pick and choose principles, activities, and other ideas from a variety of methods in order to meet the needs of their students.

For the remainder of this chapter, we will examine language teaching methods under four general categories:

- *Grammar-first methods* emphasize grammar teaching and controlled practice; they include the Grammar-Translation Method, the Audio-Lingual Method, and PPP.
- *Fluency-first methods* emphasize learning language by using it; they include the Direct Method as well as methods that fall under the Communicative Approach: Communicative Language Teaching, Task-Based Language Teaching, Content-Based Instruction, and the Participatory Approach.
- *Comprehension-first methods* emphasize extensive exposure to meaningful language before attempts are made to use it; they include the Natural Approach, Total Physical Response, and the Lexical Approach. (Note that although two of these include the word *approach* in their names, we will treat them as methods that fall under the Comprehension Approach to language learning.)
- *Learner-centred methods* emphasize ways to address learners' emotional, psychological, and social needs; they include Desuggestopedia, Community Language Learning, and Cooperative Learning.

We will also examine the use of technology and how it may support and enhance a variety of these methods.

```
Grammar-first          Fluency-first           Comprehension-first      Learner-centred
   │                      │                         │                       │
   ├─ Grammar-            ├─ Direct Method          ├─ Natural              ├─ (De)
   │  Translation         │                         │  Approach             │  Suggestopedia
   │                      ├─ Communicative          │                       │
   ├─ Audio-Lingual       │  Language               ├─ Total Physical       ├─ Community
   │                      │  Teaching               │  Response             │  Language
   │                      │                         │                       │  Learning
   └─ PPP                 ├─ Task-Based             └─ Lexical              │
                          │                            Approach             └─ Cooperative
                          ├─ Content-Based                                     Learning
                          │
                          └─ Participatory
```

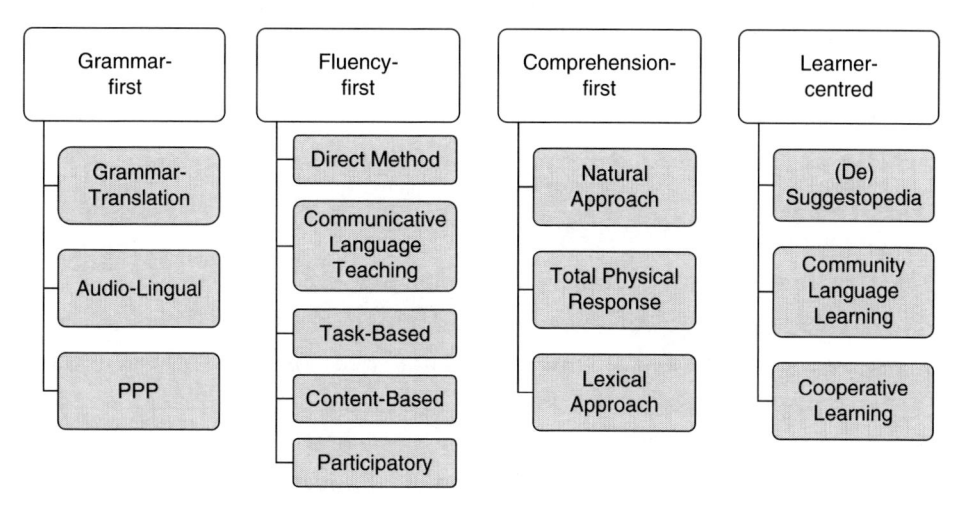

Figure 3.1: Language Teaching Methods

Our purpose, overall, is not to discover which method is best but to introduce a variety of principles, activities, and other ideas that will be useful to language teachers as they strive to meet the diverse needs of their classes.

GRAMMAR-FIRST METHODS

To a certain extent, almost every language learner follows a progression that begins with very simple grammar (a few words or phrases strung together) and gradually moves on to more complex forms. It is not surprising, then, that many language courses and textbooks are organized according to a typical progression of grammar: early lessons begin with the easier tenses (simple present, present progressive, simple past) and other basic grammar forms, while later lessons attempt to instill forms that pose more challenge.

Grammar is not the only factor in organizing a language course, but until the late 20th century, it was certainly the dominant one; yet grammar-first courses are also set apart by their tendency to focus on grammar instruction (either **explicit** or **implicit**) and grammar practice (written or oral) rather than actual use of the language for communication.

Classic Teaching: The Grammar-Translation Method

One of the more traditional ways to teach and learn language is the Grammar-Translation Method (GTM), also known as the Classical Method.

It is very academic, first used by scholars and students who wanted to read and write a classical language (i.e., Greek, Latin) and to translate to and from that language.

In its pure form, GTM is true to its roots, focusing on grammar, reading, writing, and translation, with little if any attention given to speaking, listening, or pronunciation:

- Students learn grammar rules and practice them by completing grammar worksheets that require them to fill in blanks, transform sentences (e.g., present to past tense, statement to question), or use the new grammar in some other way.
- Students learn vocabulary by memorizing lists of words along with their translations; they practice vocabulary by matching words with their definitions, synonyms, antonyms, or translations, and by using the new words in sentences.
- Students use new grammar and vocabulary by reading short passages and then answering related questions; the questions may include basic comprehension questions, questions that require students to make inferences, and questions that require students to relate the content to their own lives.
- Students may be required to translate portions of the passages or respond to them in written compositions of their own.
- **Accuracy** is considered key in this method; the teacher corrects mistakes immediately by reviewing the relevant grammar rule.

Because GTM is limited by its somewhat narrow focus, it is now rarely used in its original form. Nevertheless, variations of GTM are common in many parts of the world. In fact, a survey of current language courses in middle schools, high schools, and universities around the world will quickly reveal that the influence of GTM remains strong: numerous courses and textbooks continue to emphasize grammar rules and practice, memorization of vocabulary, and formal reading and writing activities. Yet many of these courses have expanded their focus to include a wider range of topics, various speaking and listening activities, and even pronunciation practice.

In spite of these updates, however, grammar, reading, and writing tend to take precedence over speaking and listening, likely for the following reasons:

- Reading, writing, and competence in grammar are thought to be more "academic" and worthy of study, so speaking and listening are often treated as add-ons.

- Reading skills, writing skills, and an understanding of grammar are easier to assess, especially in large classes.
- Students in many countries are more accustomed to written work.
- Academic courses are often designed to prepare students for written exams that emphasize reading, writing, and grammar.
- Language teachers and administrators in many countries are stronger in reading, writing, and grammar than in listening and speaking, and they naturally plan and teach from their strengths.

In addition, class management techniques from GTM also live on in many current academic courses:

- The teacher is in control of the class and does most of the speaking.
- Instructions and explanations are given in the students' first language.
- Meaning of the target language is made clear through translation.
- Evaluation consists mostly of formal tests, with a strong focus on grammar, reading, and writing.

While the effectiveness of these courses varies, most students who complete them are stronger in reading and writing than in speaking and listening, and they are often limited in their ability to communicate effectively. Nonetheless, GTM's strong focus on grammar and vocabulary provides a good foundation for later work in **fluency**.

For examples of GTM activities, see appendixes 3A and 3B.

Drilling It In: The Audio-Lingual Method

By the middle of the 20th century, the need to train large numbers of individuals (particularly US servicemen posted overseas during and after World War II) for basic communication in a foreign language led to the adoption of a new way to teach language: the Audio-Lingual Method (ALM).

The underlying theory of ALM comes from structural linguistics[1] and behavioural psychology,[2] in particular the belief that by forming certain habits through intensive practice, humans can be conditioned to respond automatically to certain stimuli—including language stimuli. As such, ALM makes extensive use of oral repetition and drills.

A typical lesson begins with a dialogue that acts as a model conversation and introduces common phrases and expressions. The teacher models the dialogue and uses gestures, pictures, and objects to make the meaning clear. Students then practice the dialogue several times to internalize the grammar and pronunciation. When they encounter problems, the teacher chooses from the following oral drills to help them:

- *Backwards buildup drill*: When students struggle to say a sentence or phrase, the teacher says only the final few words and has the students repeat; the teacher gradually adds more words, working backwards, with students repeating at each step until they say the entire sentence or phrase correctly.
- *Chain drill*: The teacher poses a statement or question to a particular student. The student responds appropriately and then poses the same statement or question to another student, who responds and then poses the same statement or question to yet another student, and so on.
- *Single-slot substitution drill*: The teacher gives a sentence and then a cue; a student must repeat the sentence, substituting the cue in its proper place in the sentence. In some cases, the student may need to make additional changes to the sentence to ensure it agrees with the cue. The process continues, with each cue targeting the same "slot" in the sentence.
- *Multiple-slot substitution drill*: This drill is similar to the single-slot drill, but in this case the cue will target a random slot in the sentence, so the student must determine where the cue fits.
- *Transformation drill*: The teacher gives a sentence in one form, and the student must return it in another, such as from present to past, affirmative to negative, or statement to question.
- *Question and answer drill*: The teacher asks a question, and the student must answer quickly and correctly. The question may target a particular grammar form or a particular social expression.

The drills must be performed accurately, so correction is immediate. (See appendix 3C for examples of these common ALM drills.)

Obviously, the repetition of basic grammar forms and drills can quickly become tedious, and ALM does not produce fluent speakers or a strong knowledge of the language. As a result, very few language classes still use ALM as their main method.

However, in spite of its shortcomings, this method is a valuable source of drills that can be used in combination with other methods. Such drills are helpful when students are learning new grammar forms and need immediate practice to internalize them. Furthermore, teaching grammar implicitly through practice is particularly useful for classes of young children who cannot yet think abstractly and will therefore struggle with explicit grammar instruction.

Three Steps: Presentation, Practice, Production

Closely related to other grammar-first methods is the **PPP** Method: Presentation, Practice, and Production.[3] Just as the title suggests, a PPP lesson is composed of three steps:

1. The teacher *presents* the language point (usually grammar) with a clear explanation and examples. (At this stage, the teacher does most of the talking, and accurate use of language is emphasized.)
2. The students *practice* the grammar point through oral drills or written worksheets, with guidance and correction from the teacher.
3. The students *produce* their own utterances using the target grammar, with minimal assistance from the teacher. (At this stage, the students do most of the talking [or writing], and fluency is emphasized, though accuracy remains important.)

While this brief explanation seems simple enough, these basic steps can be fleshed out to create a comprehensive, effective grammar lesson that emphasizes both accuracy and fluency. (For more information on creating grammar lessons, and on teaching grammar in general, see chapter 14.)

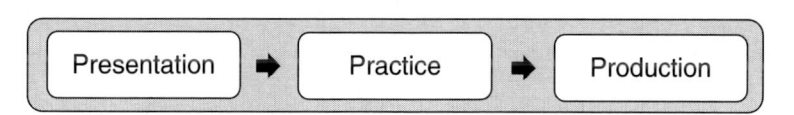

Figure 3.2: PPP Method Progression

☞ *Consider: What ideas or activities might we borrow from GTM, ALM, and PPP for use in other types of language classes?*

FLUENCY-FIRST METHODS

Language is most commonly used for communication, yet teaching methods such as GTM focus almost exclusively on academic study of a language, with very little attention given to its everyday use. The resulting gap left room for newer methods that aim to build students' fluency in the language by actually using it to communicate.

Learning by Using: The Direct Method

The Direct Method was developed early in the 20th century in response to the perceived shortcomings of GTM. Its goal is simple: enable students to think and communicate in a new language—without translating. Its methodology is also relatively simple: learn a language by using it, not by studying it.[4]

A class using the Direct Method is very interactive. The teacher works closely with the students and involves them in activities to practice using the target language. They begin by acquiring vocabulary, using demonstrations, gestures, visual aids, and **realia** to make meaning clear. As vocabulary is learned, it is used in oral questions and answers, basic conversation, and other activities that require students to communicate in the target language. When students make errors, the teacher attempts to have them self-correct.

Note the key factors that make this method more "direct":

- Vocabulary is learned through use, not by memorizing words and their translations.
- Grammar is learned through use, not by hearing explanations or studying rules.
- The class uses only the target language because the students must learn to directly associate an utterance with its meaning, not with its translation.

Note also that oral communication, including correct pronunciation, takes precedence. In a typical class, the teacher will introduce a particular topic (using a photo, a map, an object, a short reading, or some other type of prompt) and then ask questions to encourage students to discuss it. Later in the course, reading and writing are taught based on what students have already learned orally. Relevant activities may include oral reading, reading for discussion, dictation, sentence writing, paragraph writing, and other simple writing activities.

The Direct Method is effective for many students, but when used exclusively, it does present the following challenges:

- The emphasis on teacher-student interaction makes this method difficult to use in large classes.
- The lack of translation and grammar explanations may frustrate some adults who are used to a different style of teaching.
- Vocabulary is often limited (because abstract terms are difficult to learn without translation).
- Grammar, reading, and writing are not taught systematically.

In spite of these issues, the Direct Method is still widely used today (though often in combination with other methods). It is particularly exciting in the early stages of a course, as students enjoy using the language soon after they begin learning it, and it is well suited to children's classes, especially if the classes are small. (Children generally do not need or want grammar explanations, and they enjoy the interactive teaching style as well as the games and activities used to practice the language.)

Authentic Language: Communicative Language Teaching

While the Direct Method addressed the need for students to use the target language and not just learn about it, it did not solve a noticeable problem: students often produced language that was grammatically correct but sounded unnatural, largely because a few basic grammar forms were used in a wide variety of contrived social situations; and outside the classroom, they could not really use the language effectively at all.

Language teachers and course designers responded by developing the Communicative Approach, which has an overall goal of **communicative competence**. In other words, it aims to produce speakers who can use the language authentically and naturally in a variety of social situations.[5] Such speakers have not only grammatical competence but also **pragmatic competence**:[6] the ability to use the language effectively in ways appropriate to the **social context**. In particular, they are aware of how context contributes to the meaning of an utterance. Consider, for example, these expressions and their meanings:

- *Excuse me!* can be an apology or a request for someone to step aside.
- *How are you?* is generally used as a greeting, not a request for information.
- *Catch you later!* is a way of saying goodbye, with the implication that the speakers will meet again; it has nothing to do with someone being caught.

A speaker with only grammatical competence is likely to interpret these expressions literally, but someone with communicative competence understands the intended meaning by considering the expression in its social context.

One of the methods that grew out of the Communicative Approach is called Communicative Language Teaching (CLT). While its implementation varies, CLT generally emphasizes the use of authentic language and **language functions**[7]—the actions we perform when we speak, such as apologizing, asking for information, complaining, complimenting, expressing appreciation, expressing thanks, giving advice, greeting, inviting, promising, recommending, requesting, and so on. For each language function, students are introduced to a variety of grammar forms that can be used with the function and are alerted to which forms are appropriate in a given social situation, also known as a social context.

Consider a traditional, grammar-first class where students might learn the imperative form of the present tense with the following example: *Please give me a glass of milk.* In the days that follow, the students will be able to use this form in a variety of social contexts and with a variety of verbs, but they are likely to use only this form in each context, whether speaking to a classmate or ordering food in a restaurant.

In contrast, CLT focuses not on the grammatical form (imperative present) but on the language function: making requests. Students thus learn a variety of ways to make requests: *Please give me a glass of milk. May I have a glass of milk? Could I have a glass of milk, please? Milk, please!* The first example sounds unnatural in most contexts and possibly rude in some; the second and third might be used when visiting someone's home or ordering at a restaurant; and the final one might be used when getting impatient with a younger sibling during breakfast. Students are made aware of which forms are appropriate in which contexts, resulting in a more natural use of the language.

Note that grammar forms and vocabulary are not ignored in this method. Rather, instead of beginning with a particular grammar form and certain vocabulary, we begin with a language function and then introduce relevant grammar forms and vocabulary. In other words, grammar and vocabulary are drawn from the context in order to support use of the language function. The result, it is hoped, is that students will choose forms and vocabulary appropriate to the function and the social context, resulting in a more natural utterance.

In its attempt to enable students to use language naturally and appropriately in a variety of social contexts, CLT prescribes a few key principles:

- Classes are activity-based, so the teacher is a guide and a facilitator, setting up activities and providing needed support while the students use the language.
- Students frequently work in pairs or small groups in order to give each student numerous opportunities to communicate and interact with others.
- Class activities and lessons are designed around language functions, while grammar and vocabulary are derived from the context as needed, though also kept appropriate to the level of the students.

- Language skills are integrated into lessons, so students will practice the target language function through speaking, listing, reading, and writing activities.
- Communication is authentic, so students choose what to say and how to say it (in contrast to other methods that require a predictable answer in a specific form), and there is a genuine exchange of information rather than a canned answer.
- Class activities emphasize fluency (the ability to use the language smoothly, with little hesitation) over accuracy (the ability to use the language with correct grammar and vocabulary), so feedback consists of responding naturally in conversation, and mistakes are usually addressed at a later time if at all.
- Materials are authentic, or at least imitate **authentic materials**, so readings might come from (or imitate) newspapers, magazines, newsletters, restaurant menus, or websites; listening activities might come from (or imitate) everyday conversations, television shows, radio broadcasts, podcasts, or online videos; and other activities might include conversations, role plays, 20 Questions, or any other game or activity that requires authentic language use.
- The target language is used almost exclusively, even for instructions and explanations, though students' first language may be used if necessary for clarification.

Students generally enjoy CLT largely because they are actually communicating with one another, not just "practicing" language. This improved motivation, along with the focus on language functions and social contexts, generally results in a stronger ability to use the language naturally. However, like any other method, CLT has its challenges:

- It can be difficult to use at lower levels, where students have very little language to draw from.
- Its emphasis on fluency over accuracy (with little or no correction of errors) often results in speakers who can speak quickly but with many errors that eventually become ingrained and almost impossible to correct.
- The priority of language functions over language forms (grammar) may lead to serious gaps in the students' understanding of the structure of the language.

In response to these shortcomings, many teachers who use CLT have adapted it: they teach basic grammar and vocabulary (at lower levels) before emphasizing language functions, they introduce additional correction techniques within class activities, and they teach grammar explicitly and systematically.

We should also note that the emphasis on authentic language and minimal correction has at times resulted in "conversational English" classes that provide ample practice but little instruction, resulting in improved fluency but limited progress otherwise. However, this problem is not the fault of the method itself but of its implementation, and teachers who begin teaching this way often add additional structure and instruction as they become more comfortable in the classroom.

Although it is often modified and even supplemented with ideas and activities from other methods, CLT remains popular and is the basis of many language courses and textbooks available today.

CLT Lessons

A typical CLT lesson introduces a particular language function and then works through a series of activities that help students master that function, thus achieving the lesson's overall objective. A lesson on declining invitations, for example, might include the following progression of activities:

1. ***Lead-in***: The teacher will write the word *invitation* on the board and ask students how invitations are declined in their culture, and then might elicit an anecdote about an occasion when declining an invitation caused misunderstanding or even embarrassment.
2. ***Noticing***: Students will read a dialogue that provides a model of how an invitation is declined. Students will note vocabulary (including expressions) and grammar commonly used when declining invitations, and the teacher will clarify any that are new to the class. (Note that this step might include mini-activities, such as a short drill to help with pronunciation or grammar, or sample sentences to help students understand the natural use of new vocabulary. Overall, this step helps students understand the language used with the language function.)
3. ***Controlled practice***: Students will write and practice their own dialogue, using the original as a model, while the teacher provides necessary support. Alternatively, they might be given a new dialogue with the sentences out of order, and they will have to place them in the correct order and then practice them. In either case, their focus will be on practicing the language function while communicating effectively.

4. *Authentic practice*: Students will perform short dialogues or **role plays** that require them to decline invitations. While students may use their text and notes to prepare, the performance must use authentic language—that is, students will choose what to say and how to say it, without notes or other aids. (Other authentic activities include conversations, debates, free writing, or any other activity that allows students to choose what to say and how to say it; the best choice for a particular class depends on the language function and how it is best practiced.)

Language Functions

Noticing → Controlled Practice → Authentic Practice

Figure 3.3: A Typical Progression for CLT

See appendix 3D for an example of a communicative lesson. See also chapter 5 for more information on lesson plans, and chapters 8, 9, 10, 11, 12, and 14 for more information on teaching language skills and subskills, which are typically integrated into communicative lessons.

Getting It Done: Task-Based Instruction

The Communicative Approach is sometimes described as having a weak version and a strong version. The weak version, including CLT, provides opportunities for students to *learn to use* the language; the strong version requires students to *use the language in order to learn it*.[8]

Task-Based Instruction (TBI), also known as Task-Based Language Teaching (TBLT), is an example of the strong version. It is based on the idea that students learn language best when it is needed to accomplish a specific task such as planning an event, solving a problem, finding or providing information, or creating something. Key principles of this method include the following:

- *Language is necessary*: The task includes steps that cannot be accomplished without using the language to communicate.
- *Language is secondary*: The goal is not mastery of language forms but completion of the task.
- *Language is derived from the context*: New vocabulary and grammar forms are introduced only when needed to complete the task.

- *Meaning is made clear from the context*: Translation and simplification of language are not necessary.
- *Motivation comes from the task*: Students enjoy the challenge of the task, and language becomes a means to an end.

A class activity, then, or even an entire lesson, is built around a particular task. The task itself may be simple (requiring only an exchange of information) or more complex (requiring multiple steps), but as noted, it should always require significant communication between group members. The activities are often classified as follows:[9]

- An ***information-gap*** activity requires an exchange of information between the group members in order to complete the task. For example, students might work in pairs to draw each other's family tree, or they might exchange information to complete a chart or picture.
- An *opinion-gap* activity requires students to share their own opinions or feelings in order to complete the task. Students might work in a group, for example, to come up with a list of the best restaurants in town.
- A *reasoning-gap* activity requires students to use given information to solve a problem. For example, students might use a restaurant menu to plan a class meal within a given budget, or they might gather information on a particular topic and use it to create a poster, video, brochure, or website.

We should also note that a task may be *unfocused* (designed to elicit general communication) or *focused* (designed to elicit a particular grammar form).[10] In either case, in keeping with the belief that motivation comes from the task, the main focus should remain on the task itself, while language skills or grammar forms should be addressed only when needed for the task.

Finally, while a task-based class may consist of only an introduction, the task itself (often in multiple steps), and feedback, it may also include various additional activities designed around the main task:[11]

1. *Pre-task*: The teacher introduces the topic and builds students' interest, possibly with a demonstration or by facilitating a discussion; gives clear instructions; and reminds students of language that may be useful for completing the task. Students take notes and do whatever other preparation is needed before beginning the task.

2. *Task*: The students complete the task in pairs or groups, using only the target language to communicate. The teacher facilitates participation and provides assistance and encouragement.
3. *Report planning*: The student groups prepare and practice a brief report on how their task went. The teacher offers assistance as needed.
4. *Report*: The student groups take turns giving oral reports or reading written reports. The teacher gives brief feedback on each report.
5. *Analysis*: The teacher highlights relevant language that was used for the task and the reports.
6. *Practice*: The teacher prepares language practice activities based on the needs that became evident during the class. The students complete these activities.

Some instructors add an additional step that encourages students to reflect on their experience: what they accomplished, what role they played, and what challenges they faced. This step may include discussion, debate, role play, writing, or other activities that facilitate careful reflection, and it is intended to help students become more intentional in their learning.

While well-planned, interesting tasks can improve student motivation and engagement, this method shares a flaw common to fluency-first methods: the emphasis on fluency over accuracy tends to result in speakers who can use the language comfortably but with frequent mistakes. However, the teacher's feedback and resultant practice activities can help minimize these issues, and in any case, task-based activities can be effectively used with most other methods.

Dual Purpose: Content-Based Instruction

We noted above that the strong version of the Communicative Approach requires students to *use the language in order to learn it*. **Content-Based Instruction** (CBI), also known as Content and Language Integrated Learning (CLIL), takes this idea even further by requiring students to use the target language to learn other subjects; in other words, it combines learning language with learning content. The content is often academic, such as geography, history, current events, or even math, but it could also be content related to more personal interests.[12]

This approach is commonly used in academic settings. In many cases, the teacher uses a standard curriculum (similar to the curriculum used for first-language students who study the same content) but adopts specially designed materials and teaching methods (together known as *sheltered instruction*) in order to make the content more accessible to the learners. In other cases, and particularly where language learners are in the same class as learners using their first language, the course content is taught normally, but second-language students also attend a linked language course for additional support. This latter arrangement is known as the *adjunct model*.

The overall objective of content-based courses is dual in nature: students learn both content and language. To achieve this end, these courses follow a few basic principles:

- Specific learning objectives are related to both language and content, but language objectives are determined by the content, not added to it.
- Content is used as the starting point for class planning and activities, so any focus on vocabulary, grammar, or other language features is drawn from the content (not added to it).
- Language is used for learning specific content, not just communication, and is acquired through use when learning content, not through memorization or dialogues.
- The integration of content with language generates interest and improves motivation.
- Fluency is emphasized over accuracy, vocabulary is emphasized over grammar, and though all skills are developed, reading is generally prioritized (because reading is often the means by which content is acquired).
- The teacher provides language support to help the students discuss the content, but the focus is primarily on the content itself.

A typical content-based class is planned around a particular text and includes pre-reading activities, reading activities, and post-reading activities to help students master the content and be able to reproduce it in their own words. The activities are similar to or the same as those used in a normal academic class and may include relevant vocabulary activities, reading comprehension questions, graphic organizers (that require students to organize information into a chart), comparing and contrasting activities, **cloze** activities, a **dictogloss**, a discussion, a written response, or any other activity that helps students understand the content and acquire the knowledge.

While the advantages of CBI are numerous, two particular challenges tend to arise when using it: teaching and learning content is difficult at the lower levels, when students have minimal vocabulary and grammar to work with; and because this method favours fluency over accuracy, many students become reasonably fluent in the language but make many errors when speaking and writing.

These problems are easily addressed, however, by a few modifications: many programs favour language over content at the early levels and gradually move toward more substantial content as the students' language level progresses; and many instructors have introduced additional techniques for correction.

CBI Lessons

The progression of activities in a content-based lesson is based not on the language but on the content itself; in other words, the activities help the students gradually master the content. A lesson about the cultural significance of Thanksgiving in North America, for example, might look something like this:

1. *Lead-in*: The teacher will show various symbols of Thanksgiving, ask the students what they know about Thanksgiving, and then give a few interesting facts.
2. *Vocabulary and grammar*: Students will learn terms related to Thanksgiving, and any new grammar that is found in the reading. (Alternatively, this step could come after the reading and require students to guess the meaning of new vocabulary or grammar forms based on the context found in the reading.)
3. *Reading and related activities*: Students will read a short anecdote, article, or story about Thanksgiving and then complete activities about the content. (The best activities help students acquire the knowledge so they can recall it and use it in the future.)
4. *Writing*: Students will write a few paragraphs about Thanksgiving, perhaps as a personal reflection; in doing so, they must refer to specific details from the reading to ensure they remain focused on the content.

See appendix 3E for an example of a content-based lesson and chapter 5 for more information on lesson plans. See also chapter 10, as many of the ideas and activities found there are applicable to content-based classes.

Overall, CBI remains popular in many parts of the world, especially in academic settings such as language immersion classes where students study their usual school subjects but in another language. Students are attracted to the wide variety of topics and subjects available in a CBI class, and they generally gain a much broader vocabulary (related to the subjects they study) than they would with other methods.

Making It Personal: The Participatory Approach

While many students want or need to study specific content, not all need academic content. Immigrants new to their city or country, for example, would be better served by content that is relevant to their own lives. The Participatory Approach is designed to provide just that. Students themselves provide the topics, and the teacher develops the lesson around their identified needs. The overall objective is to empower students by giving them the language, literacy, and information they need to improve their everyday lives.[13]

A typical class begins with the teacher leading the students in conversation and asking them about their lives. Eventually, the teacher will identify a problem raised by one of the students; an individual in a class of recent immigrants, for example, might mention the difficulties associated with banking in a new language or finding a suitable apartment. The teacher will then have the students explore the topic and work together to come up with solutions.

☞ Consider: How might fluency-first methods be supplemented with activities from grammar-first methods? Why might we do so?

COMPREHENSION-FIRST METHODS

While fluency-based methods emphasize using language to learn it, the Comprehension Approach and its related methods suggest that students learn best when they spend significant time learning to comprehend a language before they attempt to speak it.

Keeping Quiet: The Natural Approach

One such method is call the Natural Approach.[14] Like the Direct Method, the Natural Approach emphasizes communication and vocabulary acquisition, but in this case, the students remain silent in the early stages while the teacher speaks to them and makes meaning clear through pictures, gestures, and other aids, and by using simplified language that is challenging but comprehensible to the students; translation, explicit grammar instruction, and correction are avoided. In addition, the class atmosphere and activities (such as stories and games) are designed to help reduce students' anxiety and increase students' confidence in order to promote more efficient learning. Students are not required to produce language of their own until they feel comfortable doing so and have built a significant inventory of vocabulary through extensive input. (A related method, called The Learnables, uses recorded utterances that students listen to while following along with accompanying pictures and tasks that make the meaning clear.)

In many ways, the Natural Approach draws from five hypotheses found in Stephen Krashen's theories of language acquisition:[15]

- The *acquisition-learning hypothesis* differentiates between *language acquisition* (a subconscious process by which a person acquires language through natural communication, not by study, much the way small children learn language) and *language learning* (a conscious process of formal learning about a language and how it works). Krashen suggests that only acquisition leads to fluent use of language.
- The *monitor hypothesis* suggests that knowledge of language rules enables learners to **monitor** the accuracy of their own language, but only acquired language enables a learner to fluently generate new utterances.
- The *natural order hypothesis* suggests that learners acquire the grammatical features of a language in a fixed, predictable order, similar to that of small children learning their first language (though Krashen rejects the idea that a course syllabus should follow this grammatical progression).
- The *input hypothesis* suggests that language is acquired by extensive exposure to **comprehensible input** (input at a level just a little higher than what the learner can easily understand).
- The *affective filter hypothesis* suggests that strong motivation, a high level of self-confidence, and low levels of anxiety are necessary for efficient language acquisition.

Overall, while the influence of Krashen's theories and the Natural Approach has been notable, the strong emphasis on language comprehension (rather than language production) has attracted criticism, and methods related to the Communicative Approach (which emphasizes language production) are far more popular today.

Moving to Learn: Total Physical Response

A method called Total Physical Response (TPR)[16] agrees that students should demonstrate strong comprehension of a language before producing utterances of their own, but it further suggests that learning is enhanced when associated with physical activity. The basic principles and activities of TPR are very practical and easily combined with other methods:

- The teacher gives instructions (such as simple commands) at a level just beyond the students' comprehension and makes meaning clear through demonstration, gestures, pictures, and so on. Students then respond by silently following the instructions.
- Correction is given by repeating the command and, if necessary, demonstrating the correct response.
- A set of commands is repeated until students are confident in their understanding. Novelty is maintained through variation in the order of commands, in the wording of commands, and in the speed at which commands are given.
- In later stages, students will take turns giving instructions.
- New commands are added as previous ones are mastered, and they gradually increase in complexity and difficulty.

Note also that TPR can be used to teach a variety of grammar forms and vocabulary through demonstration and repeated practice:

- Actions: *Swim. Jump. Dance. Walk. Laugh. Sing. Sit down. Stand up ...*
- Body parts: *Touch your nose. Touch your mouth. Touch your stomach ...*
- General objects: *Point at the chair. Point at the desk. Point at the wall ...*
- Singular/plural: *Touch your ear. Touch your ears. Touch your knee. Touch your knees ...*
- Prepositions: *Put the pen on the book. Put the pen under the book. Put the pen beside the book ...*

Although TPR is now dated and rarely used alone, it is useful as a supplement that adds a bit of variety to other methods, and it can be used with both large and small groups. It is particularly well suited to children's classes, giving the students an excuse to get up and move.

☞ *Consider: How might TPR be combined with the Direct Method and the Audio-Lingual Method to create an interactive curriculum for very young learners?*

Learning in Chunks: The Lexical Approach

The Lexical Approach, like other comprehension approaches and methods, suggests that students should receive abundant comprehensible input before attempting to produce language of their own, but the Lexical Approach goes further by suggesting that language is learned not by studying grammar forms or by practicing language functions but by identifying, analyzing, and experimenting with lexical chunks.[17]

A **lexical chunk** is a (more or less) fixed expression that occurs frequently in commonly used language. Lexical chunks are sometimes called *lexical phrases*, *lexical units*, or *prefabricated phrases*, and they include commonly used **collocations, phrasal verbs, idioms**, similes, and other multi-word units of meaning:

- Collocations are phrases made of **content words** that frequently appear together: *absolutely convinced, community service, highly popular, middle management, sense of humour, strong accent, terrible accident, weak tea.*
- Phrasal verbs are made of two or more words (usually a verb and a preposition) yet form a single unit of meaning: *call off, come up with, cover up, drop off, fall apart, get up, give up, hang out, take off, take out, turn into, turn off, turn on, work out.*
- An idiom is an expression whose meaning is not apparent from the literal meaning of its words: *back to the drawing board, beating around the bush, cost an arm and a leg, let the cat out of the bag, once in a blue moon, out of mind, out of the blue, put all your eggs in one basket, raining cats and dogs, spill the beans, the last straw, under the weather.*
- Similes are expressions that directly compare one thing to another: *as clean as a whistle, as cool as a cucumber, as dry as a bone, as funny as a barrel of monkeys, as happy as a clam, as hard as nails, as light as a feather, as strong as an ox, as white as a ghost, fight like cats and dogs, fits like a glove, slept like a dog, stuck out like a sore thumb.*

Proponents of the Lexical Approach suggest that natural, fluent use of a language depends on the speaker's ability to rapidly access a large inventory of frequently used lexical chunks, not an inventory of grammar rules and individual words. This assertion rests on a few additional, underlying assertions:

- Speakers construct many of their utterances using prefabricated phrases (lexical chunks).

- Learning these commonly used phrases is more efficient than learning individual words (whose meaning may differ when combined with other words) or grammar rules.
- Language is acquired not by learning small parts and combining them, but by observing larger chunks and experimenting with them.
- Language learners can understand and use phrases without understanding their parts or structure. However, over time, the ability to use them correctly is acquired by internalizing patterns through a process of observation (of lexical chunks), analysis (regarding how they are used), and experimentation.
- Most helpful are very common lexical chunks that are relevant to the learner.

The teacher's role, then, is to provide sources of authentic language input and guide students through activities that help them observe, analyze, and experiment with common lexical chunks:

1. Students observe the chunks by specifically identifying them in a given text. For example, students may be given a text with lexical chunks already highlighted as examples, and then given an additional text in which they must highlight the lexical chunks.
2. Students analyze how the lexical chunks are used, often through activities designed by the teacher:
    - Students consider other words or chunks that are commonly used with the ones they are learning.
    - Students compare or contrast chunks to similar expressions in their own language.
    - Students complete a modified cloze. (The teacher prepares the modified cloze by removing key words from lexical chunks in the text. Students must then fill in the blanks by supplying those key words from memory.)
    - Other activities that promote analysis. (See appendix 3F for examples.)
3. Students use or experiment with the lexical chunks to create new texts of their own.

The Lexical Approach generally emphasizes receptive skills (reading and listening) so that students can internalize common lexical chunks before attempting to use them. As such, many teachers advocate massive input via **extensive listening** and **extensive reading**. (For more information on extensive listening and extensive reading, see chapters 9 and 10, respectively.)

Lexical Chunks
Observe ➡ Analyze ➡ Experiment

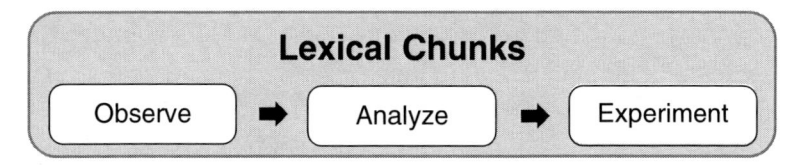

Figure 3.4: Lexical Approach Progression

Reactions to the Lexical Approach have been mixed. In particular, a few key issues have been raised and, to some extent, addressed:

- Native speakers use thousands of lexical chunks, and it is likely impossible for second-language learners to attain this level of proficiency; nonetheless, learning high-priority chunks seems to play a part in effectively and efficiently developing fluency in a language.
- Exclusive use of the Lexical Approach may result in students' overreliance on a limited number of fixed phrases, stifling their creativity and originality; yet overreliance on a limited knowledge of language is a feature of all methods in the early stages, and creativity and experimentation develop over time through additional learning.
- There is no linear progression to learning **language chunks,** so developing a linear syllabus seems artificial at best; yet learning lexical chunks is much like learning vocabulary: we begin with the simplest and most commonly used items and work from there.
- Commonly used lexical chunks should be taught, but not at the expense of other components of language learning (such as language skills).
- The Lexical Approach is really just a set of principles with no clear method, yet these principles can be applied to develop activities that can be combined with other methods.

This last point is insightful: the Lexical Approach might be most useful when combined with other methods that best meet the needs of the students.

Finally, it is worth noting that more recent work in the area of formulaic language has gone beyond lexical chunks (each of which is built around a word or meaning) to include other chunks of language,[18] including formulaic social expressions (fixed expressions with a particular social purpose) as well as grammar-based formulaic sequences, to name just two:

- formulaic social expressions: *You're welcome. Never mind. You have your point. What's up? You've got to be kidding.*

- grammar-based formulaic sequences: *Would you like* + [infinitive]. *I look forward to* + [gerund]. *I think* + [noun clause]. *I can't believe* + [noun clause].

☞ *Consider: Since lexical chunks are internalized over time and through use, much like vocabulary, which activities from chapter 12 (Teaching Vocabulary) might also be used with lexical chunks?*

LEARNER-CENTRED METHODS

The approaches and methods we've looked at so far consider how language should be taught or learned—by focusing on grammar, on fluency and functions, on content, or on comprehension—but others focus not only on the language but also on the learners. After all, learning a new language can be difficult and even stressful: some students are shy about speaking up in class, and others are concerned that they will not perform well on their assignments. Such anxiety can often hinder students' progress.

Two methods, Desuggestopedia[19] and Community Language Learning (CLL),[20] attempted to address these issues with very prescribed (and in some cases, unusual) techniques for the classroom, and while these methods are now rarely used, some of their ideas remain useful for creating a learner-centred classroom. Desuggestopedia, for example, aims to decrease students' anxiety by creating a classroom atmosphere and designing class activities that make students feel comfortable:

- The classroom is made welcoming through the use of comfortable seating, classical music, art, and decorations (such as posters) that encourage peripheral learning.
- The teacher is confident, positive, and encouraging, especially when correcting students.
- The teacher acts as a partner in the learning process and participates in class activities.
- Class activities are fun and include games, songs, drama, role play, movement, and humour, and even traditional activities are modified to be more interesting: a dialogue, for example, can be read multiple times using different emotions (though variety and novelty are preferred over repetition).
- Class materials often include indirect positive suggestions that encourage students in their learning. A reading comprehension activity, for

example, may use a reading about how students should believe in themselves and expect to succeed.
- Correction is gentle and encouraging, and it may even be done in private in order to avoid embarrassment.

In CLL, a learner-centred environment is created by building a strong sense of community, emphasizing student choice, and discussing the learning process. Activities focus on communication among students, and the teacher acts as a language counsellor who helps students (often through extensive use of translation) say what they wish to communicate. The teacher may also record and later transcribe conversations for use in future activities that draw attention to the language used.

Another method, Cooperative Learning, suggests that students learn best by working together (usually in small groups) toward common goals while being individually accountable. Each student is given a specific responsibility within the group, so the group's success depends on each individual's success; students therefore assist and encourage one another. The teacher designs and organizes these activities but also teaches social skills related to group work, cooperation, and encouragement.[21]

☞ *Consider: How might principles or activities from learner-centred methods be combined with other methods in this chapter?*

TEACHING WITH TECHNOLOGY

While no well-known, widely used, specific method has been developed around the use of technology, almost every method of language learning has been influenced by the explosive growth of technological options. Initially, acronyms such as CALI (Computer-Aided Language Instruction), CALL (Computer-Assisted Language Learning), and TELL (Technologically Enhanced Language Learning) were commonly used (or at least promoted), but they are less popular today simply because we now assume that technology is used in most classrooms and with most approaches to language teaching, so we no longer see a need to draw attention to it in that way.

The challenge of discussing the use of technology in the classroom is that technology keeps changing: many computer-based desktop programs have been replaced by websites and apps; blogs, once the dominant platform for user-created content, have largely been replaced by other social media sites and apps; CDs and DVDs have largely been replaced by online streaming services and cloud storage; and cameras, audio/video recorders, audio/video players, clocks/watches/timers, and, to some extent, even computers have been replaced by smartphones. Nonetheless, there are a number of helpful observations about technology that we can make without becoming outdated by next year.

Internet-Sourced Content and Practice

The Internet is a tremendous resource for teachers who use authentic content to create their own teaching materials. Gone are the days of literally copying, cutting, and pasting—or worse yet, retyping—print material from newspapers and magazines, or of trying to find that old, worn-out VHS copy of a much-loved video; the vast resources of the Internet are infinitely (or so it seems) more diverse and more convenient:

- Web pages with written content—such as online magazines, online newspapers, blogs, and even general websites—provide abundant source material that can be copied (while respecting copyright, of course) into a word processor and quickly edited for length and language level. (See chapter 10 for more information on creating reading material and activities.)
- Video sites, podcasts, and other online audio/video resources provide authentic content that can be used for extensive listening or to create listening comprehension activities. Some of these sites and apps even allow users to adjust the playback speed to a level that is suitable for the listener. (See chapter 9 for more information on listening materials.)
- Websites and apps designed especially for language learners provide recorded language lessons, as well as practice and testing in vocabulary, grammar, reading, listening comprehension, and sound perception; some even provide practice in speaking, pronunciation, and writing.

See this book's companion website for links to current Internet resources.

Other Technological Tools

Other basic, commonly used tools, whether physical or web based, are also helpful in the language classroom and beyond:

- Online dictionaries and translators are quick and convenient, and most students already have them on their smartphones. (Keep in mind,

though, that while translators are reasonably accurate for words and phrases, they are often very poor at accurately translating sentences.)
- Social media groups can be set up to facilitate announcements, class discussion, file sharing, and other interaction.
- Online word processors and presentation software, as well as blogs and social media sites and apps, are convenient ways for students to create and share their work or even collaborate on projects. They can also be used for personal reflection (on their experience using their new language, for example), commenting on one another's work, or even communicating with e-pen pals.
- The latest interactive whiteboards combine the advantages of a computer, a projector, and a whiteboard, but they are expensive; for those on a tight budget and using yesterday's technology, pointing a projector at a whiteboard and using actual dry-erase markers for markup is a low-tech compromise (and particularly useful when demonstrating a written exercise such as a grammar worksheet).
- Video chat apps can be used for face-to-face interaction over long distances, and even for online, personal language classes.
- Online proficiency tests can discover students' language levels and often feature adaptive testing—that is, they quickly and automatically adjust to the level of the student.
- Digital files (text, image, video, audio) and digital storage allow instructors to create an electronic **portfolio** of each student's work. (See "Portfolio-Based Assessment" in chapter 7.)

While it is tempting to list the "best" of these, they are constantly changing or even disappearing; an Internet search, recommendations from colleagues (including those who present at conferences related to language teaching) and students, and current online discussion forums for language teachers remain the best sources of information about the latest and greatest websites, apps, and other Internet resources for language learning.

Other Advantages and Pitfalls

Finally, there are two advantages to technology that are difficult to match:

- Flexibility: The use of technology in language learning is limited only by our imaginations. Almost any approach to teaching, any method, any type of skill practice, and any type of classroom can be enhanced with technology.

- Cost: Contrary to the very expensive desktop applications of the past, many apps and online services are free or very inexpensive, and while the devices needed to access them can be expensive, most students already have them. In fact, the rise in popularity of smartphones has almost eliminated what was once the most common barrier to using technology in the classroom and beyond: access.

While keeping these advantages in mind, we must also take care to avoid the most common pitfall when using technology in the classroom: using it for the sake of using it. Sometimes technology can be a distraction, a time filler, a time waster, or even a headache; and sometimes the older, non-technological methods and materials are better suited to what we wish to accomplish.

✓	Is its use relevant to the course goals or lesson objectives?
✓	Does its use facilitate students' success in reaching those objectives?
✓	Do students have the required skills to use it efficiently and successfully?
✓	What tech support might be needed? Is it available?
✓	Is it worthwhile in terms of time and cost?

Figure 3.5: Technology Use Checklist

It is up to us, as teachers, to ensure that technology serves the needs of our students and the objectives of the lesson, and does not detract from them.

☞ *Try: Search the Internet for "ESL practice" and check out a few of the sites. Which seem useful? How might they be used with the methods in this chapter?*

REFLECTING ON APPROACHES AND METHODS

Looking back at our eight teachers from chapter 1, we can see that Henri primarily employs the Grammar-Translation Method. Lisa has little methodology at all; she seems to draw from GTM but only in a very limited way. Bob seems to know only drills from the Audio-Lingual Method, and Antonia employs a version of the Direct Method supplemented with an atmosphere informed by Desuggestopedia. Monica thinks she is using a Communicative Approach, but her lack of structure and variety suggests that she is providing practice in "conversational English." Jane appears to draw primarily from Communicative Language Teaching but also borrows ideas and activities from other methods, as she should. Jim's method seems very limited: he's too focused on using technology. Monty, of course, doesn't really have a method, and if his boss knows anything about language teaching and is paying attention to what goes on in class, Monty soon may not have a job.

All of our teachers—even Jane—can learn something from the methods discussed in this chapter. After all, there is no language teacher whose teaching tool box is full. There is always room for new ideas and new activities, each of which can contribute to students' success in learning a language. Besides, the best teachers (and textbooks) mix and match aspects of various approaches and methods in order to meet the needs of their students. (In fact, we might say that we now live in the "post-method" age of language teaching.)

Low-beginner students, for example, need repeated practice with basic vocabulary and grammar before they can begin developing higher language skills, so drawing from a variety of methods is often best in the early stages:

- The Direct Method and TPR (especially for children) can be used to teach vocabulary, rehearse common phrases and chunks, and practice basic grammar forms.
- Simple Audio-Lingual drills can provide practice for basic grammar forms and pronunciation.
- Activities from GTM (especially for adults, who often prefer to "see" what they are learning) are ideal for practicing basic grammar, reading, and writing.
- Activities and ideas from Desuggestopedia and CLL can help create an atmosphere in which students feel comfortable participating.

High-beginner, low-intermediate, and intermediate students already have a good foundation in basic grammar and vocabulary and wish to move beyond the repetitive practice used at the lower levels. Their needs are nonetheless varied, so, once again, drawing from various methods may work best:

- Communicative activities can help students use the language more authentically and learn a variety of language forms for a given language function—not just the usual classroom English.
- Activities from the Lexical Approach can help students acquire useful phrases and expressions.
- Supplemental readings, activities, and worksheets from GTM can benefit students who need extra practice in reading and grammar.
- Occasional Audio-Lingual drills will provide quick, focused practice in a particular area of grammar or pronunciation.

- Problem posing and dialoguing (from the Participatory Approach) are useful for students (such as newly arrived immigrants) who face particular issues in everyday life.
- Readings and activities that are content based can help transition students from studying language to learning it by using it.

High-intermediate and advanced students have a fairly strong command of the language and prefer to use it to study a variety of interesting topics such as current events, literature, and foreign cultures, so many teachers plan a content-based course, though they supplement it with ideas and activities from other methods as needed.

There is, of course, no end to the number of ways we can use one method to supplement another, but the idea of "mixing and matching" need not refer only to a series of activities; we can also mix and match ideas to create a single new activity. Consider a class of young learners who need to review the basic tenses of common verbs. We could combine components from TPR with a question-and-answer drill and a substitution drill from the Audio-Lingual Method, resulting in the following:

Teacher: Ali, jump! (Ali begins jumping.) What is Ali doing?
Students: He is jumping.
Teacher: Ali, stop jumping. (Ali stops.) What did Ali do?
Students: He jumped. (or He stopped.)
Teacher: Tim and Christine, swim! (Tim and Christine pretend to swim.) What are they doing?
Students: They are swimming.
Teacher: Stop swimming. (They stop.) What did they do?
Students: They swam!

These various combinations are just examples, of course, and should not be seen as prescriptive; rather, teachers should consider the needs of their students, set clear objectives accordingly, and then choose what methods and activities would best meet those objectives, keeping in mind that there is no "best" method or one-size-fits-all solution.

☞ *Try: Look back through the various approaches and methods in this chapter and identify what aspects of each you might like to use. What influences your choices?*

QUESTIONS FOR REVIEW

1. What three kinds of questions are typically found in GTM reading activities?
2. Define and give examples of the following: backwards buildup drill, chain drill, single-slot substitution drill, multiple-slot substitution drill, transformation drill, and question and answer drill. (See examples in appendix 3C.)
3. What makes the Direct Method more "direct" and "natural"?
4. What is a language function? What is a social context (as defined in CLT)?
5. Describe a typical progression of activities in a CLT lesson.
6. What kinds of "gaps" are frequently used in TBI? Describe each and give examples.
7. What two models of CBI are commonly used? How do they differ?
8. Describe a typical progression of activities in a content-based lesson.
9. What is the source of content in the Participatory Approach? What is the overall goal?
10. Make a list of the principles and ideas used in learner-centred methods. Which ones would you use? When? How? Why?
11. What do we mean by saying that language teaching is now "post-method"?
12. Read through the sample activities, drills, and lessons in appendixes 3A to 3F. In what kinds of classes might these be used?

FURTHER READING

Overview

Diane Larsen-Freeman and Marti Anderson, *Techniques and Principles in Language Teaching* (Oxford, 2011).

Jack C. Richards, ed., *Approaches and Methods in Language Teaching* (Cambridge, 2014).

Communicative and Task-Based Methods

Rod Ellis, *Task-Based Language Learning and Teaching* (Oxford, 2003).

James Lee and Bill van Patten, *Making Communicative Language Teaching Happen* (McGraw-Hill, 1995).

David Nunan, *Task-Based Language Teaching* (Cambridge, 2004).

Dave Willis and Jane Willis, *Doing Task-Based Teaching* (Oxford, 2007).

Content-Based Instruction

Donna Brinton, Marjorie Wesche, and Ann Snow, *Content-Based Second Language Instruction* (Michigan, 2003).

Jana Echevarria, MaryEllen Vogt, and Deborah J. Short, *Making Content Comprehensible for English Learners: The SIOP Model* (Pearson, 2016).

Lexical Approach

James Nattinger and Jeanette DeCarrico, *Lexical Phrases and Language Teaching* (Oxford, 1992).

Using Technology

Gavin Dudeney and Nicky Hockly, *How to Teach English with Technology* (Pearson, 2007).

Gordon Lewis, *Learning Technology* (Oxford, 2017).

Graham Stanley, *Language Learning with Technology: Ideas for Integrating Technology in the Classroom* (Cambridge, 2013).

NOTES

1. ALM was initially developed by Charles Fries and is described in his *Teaching and Learning English as a Foreign Language* (Michigan, 1945).
2. B. F. Skinner's *Verbal Behaviour* (Appleton-Century-Crofts, 1957) was particularly influential in the further development of ALM.
3. PPP is listed here under grammar-first methods because of its initial focus on the accurate use of grammar, but it is often categorized as a weak communicative method because of its third stage, the production of authentic language.
4. Carl Krause's *The Direct Method in Modern Languages* (Scribner's, 1916) is one of the better known early treatments of the subject.
5. The concept of communicative competence is found in Dell Hymes's "Two Types of Linguistic Relativity" in *Sociolinguistics* (Mouton, 1966).
6. Jenny Thomas introduced the term *pragmatic competence* in her article "Cross-Cultural Pragmatic Failure" in *Applied Linguistics* 4, no. 2 (1983): 91–112.
7. CLT's concept of language functions is found in Michael Halliday's *Explorations in the Functions of Language* (Arnold, 1973).
8. The concept of weak and strong versions of the Communicative Approach comes from Anthony Howatt's *A History of English Language Teaching* (Oxford, 1984).
9. These "gaps" are described in N. S. Prabhu's *Second Language Pedagogy* (Oxford, 1987).

10. These are described in Rod Ellis's *Task-Based Language Teaching: Sorting Out the Misunderstandings* (Oxford, 2009).
11. Jane Willis describes these stages in her *A Framework for Task-Based Learning* (Longman, 1996).
12. See Bernard Mohan's *Language and Content* (Addison-Wesley, 1986).
13. The Participatory Approach was first developed by Brazilian educator and philosopher Paulo Freire.
14. The Natural Approach was developed by Tracy Terrell and Stephen Krashen and is described in their book *The Natural Approach: Language Acquisition in the Classroom* (Pergamon, 1983).
15. Krashen's theories are outlined extensively in his *Principles and Practice in Second Language Acquisition* (Prentice-Hall, 1987) and *Second Language Acquisition and Second Language Learning* (Prentice-Hall, 1988).
16. TPR was developed by James Asher and is described in his *Learning Another Language through Actions* (Sky Oats, 2009).
17. The Lexical Approach was developed by Michael Lewis and is described in his *The Lexical Approach* (Heinle, 1997) and *Implementing the Lexical Approach* (Heinle, 1997).
18. See Alison Wray's *Formulaic Language and the Lexicon* (Cambridge, 2002).
19. Desuggestopedia (originally Suggestopedia) was originally developed by Georgi Lozanov and is described in his *Suggestology and Suggestopedia* (translation; UNESCO, 1978).
20. CLL was developed by Charles Curran and is described in his *Counseling-Learning in Second Languages* (Counseling Learning Institute, 1976) and *Counseling-Learning: A Whole-Person Approach for Education* (Counseling Learning Institute, 1977).
21. See George Jacobs's "Cooperative Learning or Just Grouping Students: The Difference Makes a Difference" in *Learners and Language Learning*, eds. Willy Renandya and George Jacobs (SEAMEO, 1998).

CHAPTER 4
Planning Courses

When Jane first began teaching language, she developed a comprehensive needs analysis for her classes and discovered that her students had a wide range of experiences, abilities, and reasons for studying. While some of these classes were already underway (having been set up by previous teachers), others were new. Jane began mapping out their needs, with particular focus on their language level and their reasons for studying. Five of those classes nicely illustrate the variety Jane encountered:

- A class of eight low-beginner adults met two evenings each week to learn English for fun. They had previously studied English in school but retained very little.
- A group of 10 high-beginner adults were planning to immigrate to another country and wanted to improve their English as quickly as possible, as they were leaving in just six months, but their class met only twice per week. However, their placement tests indicated that they knew more vocabulary and grammar than they used when speaking.
- A class of twenty high-intermediate students, recently graduated from high school, met four times each week to prepare for study in an overseas college or university where the language of instruction was English.
- An intermediate class of university-educated business workers needed better English to participate in business meetings, conduct negotiations, and socialize with their colleagues from other countries.
- A group of research engineers had to present their findings to their colleagues, some of whom were in other countries. They all understood English at an intermediate or high-intermediate level, but in order to speak about their very specialized topics, they needed to learn specialized vocabulary, gain strong presentation skills, and develop an overall fluency in speaking.

Jane knew that to plan effective courses for her students, she would need to set clear long-term goals for each class based on their needs and their reasons for learning.

SETTING COURSE GOALS

In order to plan a course, we need to establish clear goals. In other words, we must determine the final destination—where we want our students to be by the end of the course. Without clear goals, we risk developing a course that might include numerous good ideas but results in little progress for our students.

Think of a language course like a road trip: if we don't keep our destination in mind, along with a clear idea of how to get there, we might spend of lot of time going in one direction or another, doing this and that, and perhaps even having fun, but we won't likely get where we want to go.

The goals we set for a course must be realistic and achievable, taking into consideration the students' current level and their particular needs as well as the amount of time they can commit to study. Consider, for example, the classes introduced above:

- The low-beginner students need the basics of the language, so Jane's goals for this class might include the ability to speak, write, and understand (when reading and listening) basic sentences using five hundred commonly used words (more if time allows) in routine social situations.
- The high-beginner students planning to move to another country need to strengthen the skills required for everyday life, so Jane's goals might include improved fluency in speaking, clear pronunciation, and better listening comprehension, as well as the ability to complete reading and writing tasks that will be relevant to their daily lives.
- The high-intermediate students preparing for college or university need to develop their academic skills, so Jane's goals for them include the ability to read difficult texts, write essays and reports, listen to lectures while taking notes, and discuss academic topics in small groups.
- For business workers who must participate in meetings, conduct negotiations, and socialize with their colleagues, Jane's goals are likely to include a high level of fluency when speaking, strong listening skills, an ability to adapt to different cultural expectations, and specific skills related to business meetings and negotiations.

- For high-level engineers who must present the results of their research to colleagues, Jane's goals are likely to include mastery of relevant vocabulary, strong presentation skills, and overall fluency when speaking about their very specialized topics.

Note that these **course goals** are broad and not necessarily measurable. To return to our road trip analogy, course goals describe the destination—not the roads that must be travelled, nor the stops along the way, nor even the mode of transportation. Those details will be determined later, as objectives—specific, measurable steps that move the class toward the goal. (See chapter 5 for more information on lesson objectives.)

PLANNING WITH TEXTBOOKS

Looking at Jane's five classes above, we note that the first four are not so unusual. In fact, it is very likely that she will be able to find textbooks to address the needs of beginners, false-beginner immigrants, students preparing for college or university, and business workers; but should Jane use textbooks, or should she design her own courses, customized to the uniqueness of her classes?

Textbooks: A Good Idea?

When Jane began planning her courses, one of her colleagues recommended a few textbooks that would be a good fit for her students. Another colleague, however, was adamant that textbooks are never a good fit; in his mind, every class is unique, but textbooks are standardized, so only the teacher can properly plan a suitable class. He further argued that textbooks provide too few models of real language and two few explanations of how conversations actually work, so students are unlikely to develop true communicative competence.

Jane considered her options, and after speaking to other colleagues, she decided to choose textbooks for most of her classes. Her reasons were as follows:

- No textbook will meet every need of a particular class, but with plenty of textbooks to choose from, there is often one that will meet most of their needs, and it can be supplemented with activities and lessons to meet the remaining needs.
- Two of her experienced colleagues were happy to discuss textbook options with her, including the strengths and weaknesses of particular books, and help her choose texts that suited the needs of her classes.

- A course is not simply a collection of lessons, but a *progression* of lessons working toward overall goals. Good course planning, then, requires a very high level of organization and a broad knowledge of the details that must be included. A good textbook already provides this progression and the details, so using such a resource can be very efficient for teachers.
- Jane was still one of the newer teachers in her school, and she didn't feel confident planning every course from scratch, even with help from her colleagues. She felt that choosing good textbooks for most of her classes would give her time to create materials for those times when a textbook wasn't sufficient.

Once Jane had decided to use textbooks for most of her classes, she asked the obvious next question: *What text, or even what kind of text, if any, would best meet the goals of each course?* To help Jane answer this question, we must consider three other questions: What types of textbooks are available, how do we choose a textbook for a given class, and how are textbooks best used?

Understanding Textbooks

A language textbook is a series of related lessons (often in the form of units or chapters, or contained within units or chapters) that gradually progress toward overall goals. Although all language textbooks are designed to help students learn a language, they vary in their purpose, their focus on language skills, and their methods.

Many teachers choose *general-purpose* textbooks for most of their classes. These textbooks are designed to help students improve their overall ability to use the language in common social situations, so the topics and activities are chosen to appeal to a wide variety of needs and interests.

Some classes, however, require *specific-purpose* textbooks for students whose needs are much more focused, often because they are learning a language for work, school, travel, or another specialized context. The purposes of such textbooks can vary widely, but they are always specific:

- Business English textbooks teach language relevant to the business world.
- Professional/vocational English textbooks provide students with language related to a specific profession, occupation, or industry.
- Test-prep textbooks are designed to increase students' knowledge of a language in order to pass a particular standardized test.

- EAP (English for Academic Purposes) textbooks are designed to improve students' ability to use the language for academic study.
- English for Tourism textbooks help prepare individuals for short-term travel.

In addition to their purpose, textbooks can be described by their focus on language skills. Many textbooks are considered *multi-skill* texts because they provide practice in speaking and listening, or reading and writing, or even all four skills. Some textbooks, however, focus primarily on a single skill (speaking or listening or reading or writing), while still others focus on a particular language subskill (grammar or vocabulary).

Finally, textbooks also vary in their approaches and methods, and they are often designed and organized according to specific principles:

- *Grammar-based* texts are organized by grammar and focus on accurate use of grammar.
- *Fluency-based* texts focus on successfully communicating meaning with minimal hesitation, even if the students' grammar isn't perfect.
- *Function-based* texts emphasize not only fluency but also natural language and authentic communication, with particular focus on language functions (i.e., what we do when we speak, such as describing, inviting, apologizing, asking for information, and so on).
- *Content-based* texts help students learn a language by using it to study specific content (often academic, such as history, geography, or math).

☞ Try: Examine two or three popular language textbooks (at your local library, for example). Then consider the details of each book: What level is it? What is its overall purpose? What skills and subskills are emphasized? What methods are used?

Figure 4.1: Understanding Textbooks

Common Types of Textbooks

At one time (more than a few years ago), most language classes used general-purpose, multi-skill, grammar-based textbooks. In a typical book of this type, each unit or lesson focuses on one or more specific grammar forms and includes both written and oral practice. A typical beginner-level textbook of this type is structured like this:

- Unit 1: Simple Present Tense of the Verb "To Be" and Subject Personal Pronouns
- Unit 2: Present Progressive Tense of Common Verbs
- Unit 3: Short-Answer Questions Using "To Be" (Simple Present) and Common Verbs (Present Progressive) with Basic Prepositions
- Unit 4: Simple Past Tense

The text continues by gradually moving through increasingly difficult grammar forms, with each unit providing a variety of activities to facilitate practice (through speaking, listening, reading, and writing) of its target grammar while introducing new vocabulary as well.

Note that although the text is organized by grammar, it must progress not only through increasingly difficult grammar forms but also through increasingly difficult skills practice: the listening activities in unit 12, for example, should be more difficult than the listening activities in unit 2, not only in terms of grammar but also in terms of speed and level of detail, just as the speaking activities in unit 12 should require a greater degree of fluency and detail than those in unit 2. In this sense, although grammar is the primary factor in the book's organization, it is not the only one.

Language teachers often find that a general-purpose, multi-skill, grammar-based textbook is useful for low beginners—those who need basic grammar and vocabulary just to get started in the language. Beyond the beginner level, however, grammar-based textbooks can seem a bit dry, and they tend to produce speakers of "classroom English." (We've all met language learners who use a limited number of grammar forms in every situation; their grammar may be correct, but their speech does not sound natural.)

Today, general-purpose, multi-skill, function-based textbooks are more commonly used. In a typical textbook of this type, each unit or lesson consists of a series of activities that facilitate practice of a common language function. The early units of a high-beginner textbook, for example, might look like this:

- Unit 1: Greetings and Introductions
- Unit 2: Basic Invitations (Making, Accepting, Declining)

- Unit 3: Describing Appearance
- Unit 4: Asking for Information

In each unit, the first or second activity is likely to provide an example of the language used for that function, the next activity will require students to use that language in limited ways, and later activities will require more authentic use of the language.

Consider, for example, a unit on invitations. The lesson may begin with a dialogue in which one speaker is inviting an acquaintance to a party. Students will read the dialogue and note any new vocabulary and grammar, which the teacher will clarify. Students will then practice the dialogue, taking note of the common ways of offering, accepting, and declining invitations, and of the language (i.e., vocabulary and grammar) used for each. The next activity might require students to write their own dialogue using the original as a model, and the final activity might require students to perform a role play that involves invitations. In this latter activity, the students must use the language authentically and naturally without the help of notes or the textbook.

Note the natural progression in these activities: from *noticing* the language used with invitations, to *controlled practice* of the language, to *authentic use*. Also note that such lessons are likely to provide a variety of expressions commonly used to perform the function, not just one standard grammar form (although the expressions used are chosen carefully to reflect the level of the text), and that language skills are integrated: students practice the language function through listening, speaking, reading, and writing activities.

The organization of content and activities is slightly more complex in this type of text. Although based on a progression through various language functions, it must also reflect a progression through various forms of grammar as well as increasing levels of difficulty for each language skill. Consider again the example used above:

- Unit 1 will focus on introductions, providing relevant vocabulary and grammar as well as relevant practice in speaking, listening, reading, and writing.
- Unit 2 will focus on invitations, providing relevant vocabulary and grammar as well as relevant practice in speaking, listening, reading, and writing.
- Unit 3 will focus on describing appearances, providing relevant vocabulary and grammar as well as relevant practice in speaking, listening, reading, and writing; but this content and practice should also be slightly more difficult.

- The remaining units will each focus on another language function and provide relevant vocabulary and grammar as well as relevant practice in speaking, listening, reading, and writing. Again, each aspect of each unit should reflect not only the focus of the unit but also the overall progression of the text.

This balance of language function progression, grammar progression, and skill progression can create a surprising level of complexity. Fortunately, many textbooks of this type include a detailed chart that goes well beyond a traditional table of contents, providing a thorough yet easy-to-follow snapshot of how the activities in a lesson are related and how skill practice in one lesson relates to skill practice in others. In essence, the chart provides a table of contents that can be read horizontally (to discover how a language function is treated in each area or skill) or vertically (to discover how each area or skill is developed over multiple units).

In some ways, function-based textbooks can be challenging for students because they use a wider variety of grammar forms at a given level; nonetheless, many teachers prefer function-based textbooks because they are more likely to produce speakers who use the language naturally.

Also popular are specific-purpose, dual-skill, fluency-based textbooks for learning business English. Some focus on speaking and listening, with practice related to business meetings, presentations, negotiations, interviews, and so on, while others focus on reading and writing, with practice related to memos, business letters, and other documents related to business. In both cases, specialized vocabulary and grammar forms related to formal English may also be taught.

Students preparing for academic study are likely to use specific-purpose, dual-skill, content-based EAP textbooks. A typical reading and writing EAP textbook, for example, is likely to be organized by content, with each unit providing readings on an academic topic followed by a series of related comprehension and writing activities. A speaking and listening EAP textbook, meanwhile, provides opportunities to learn academic content by speaking about specific topics, giving presentations, listening to recorded lectures while taking notes, and so on. In both cases, students use language to learn new content while sharpening their academic skills.

Finally, there are also textbooks that are still narrower in purpose, skills practice, method, or any combination thereof:

- A general-purpose vocabulary textbook introduces commonly used words, expressions, or idioms at a particular level and provides practice using them.

- A general-purpose grammar textbook provides user-friendly explanations of grammar rules followed by written and oral practice.
- A specific-purpose, dual-skill, fluency-based textbook that specializes in English for Tourism provides relevant practice in speaking and listening as well as necessary vocabulary and expressions.
- A specific-purpose, multi-skill test-prep textbook helps students prepare for a particular standardized test.

While these types of textbooks are among the most common, there are also many other types that may be better suited to the needs of a particular class.

☞ *Consider: Which type of textbook, if any, might be best for each of Jane's classes described above?*

Choosing Textbooks

Discovering the purpose, skill focus, and methods of a textbook can sometimes be as easy as reading the title, but to gain a more thorough understanding, we should read the introduction, closely examine the table of contents, and try a few activities in various units to be sure the text clearly meets the goals that we have set for a given course.

Looking back at Jane's classes described earlier, we can see that some choices are obvious but others are not:

- The low-beginner students need basic vocabulary and an understanding of the basic structures of the language, as well as practice using the language, so an intro-level, general-purpose, multi-skill, grammar-based textbook might be best for them.
- The false-beginner immigrants already have a basic understanding of grammar and a functional vocabulary, so they will likely be best served by a high-beginner, general-purpose, multi-skill, function-based textbook. However, because they will have immediate, practical needs as immigrants, Jane will likely need to prepare supplementary material to meet those specific needs.
- The students preparing for college or university have obvious academic needs, so Jane will likely choose a textbook that focuses on academic reading and writing, and will likely supplement it with additional material related to comprehending lectures, taking notes, and other relevant

skills. In addition, if the students must pass a standardized test as part of their application, they will likely use a text designed to prepare them for the specific test they must take.
- The business workers have fairly typical needs, but Jane will have to be careful to choose a text that focuses on oral communication in business, not on how to write business documents, in order to best meet their needs. A separate text on **intercultural communication** for business would also be helpful.
- The research engineers who must present their research to colleagues have very specialized needs. While there are textbooks designed for engineers and for business people, such texts are likely too general to be sufficiently relevant to the very specialized needs of this class.

With these considerations in mind, Jane finds a number of potential textbooks for each class and further narrows her choices by using a simple checklist to carefully examine each one:

- Is the text professional in appearance and well organized overall?
- Does the text provide skills practice that is appropriate to the class?
- Is the content not only relevant to the class but also interesting, with a variety of topics?
- Does the text follow a realistic progression to help students develop their skills and reach their goals?
- Is the language in the text realistic and authentic?
- Are the instructions clear and easy to follow?
- Does the textbook include supplementary materials such as a teacher's guide, audio and video materials, and online practice? How useful are these, and how do they affect the overall cost?

While no textbook meets all her criteria perfectly, Jane is able to find a very suitable textbook for each of the first four courses listed above.

Supplementing Textbooks

Even with suitable textbooks in hand, Jane realizes that her work is not finished; after all, a textbook's greatest strength is also its greatest weakness: it's already prepared. As such, it saves the teacher a lot of work, but it is designed for a "typical" class—and no two classes have identical needs. Once

Jane understands the degree to which a textbook meets her students' needs, however, she can begin to address this weakness by developing custom-made activities and lessons to supplement each textbook. Some of these she will be able to prepare in advance, but other needs will become apparent only once the course is underway:

- As students in the low-beginner class complete a particular lesson in their textbook, they might need additional practice before they feel comfortable moving on to the next lesson.
- The students in the high-beginner class may need specific knowledge relevant to life in a new country. They might also need additional practice to improve their speaking, listening comprehension, and pronunciation to the level they wish to achieve.
- The students preparing for university may also need specific knowledge relevant to their daily lives in a new country: food, shopping, currency, banking, transportation, and public services, for example, may be different from what they are used to.
- Students in any class who struggle with a particular grammar point may need supplementary activities such as worksheets, oral drills, or speaking and writing activities that provide further practice.

These are only a few of the many possible shortcomings that must be addressed, but in each case we note that Jane can choose from a variety of ways to supplement a textbook:

- *Extend an activity*: If students complete an activity but are not yet comfortable with the material, she can extend the activity by creating additional practice (such as additional questions in a speaking activity or reading comprehension activity, additional tasks in a listening activity, or additional sentences to manipulate in a grammar activity). Note that in this case, the additional practice should help students better achieve the original objective of the activity.
- *Repurpose an activity*: Sometimes part of an activity can be reused for a different purpose. The reading material in a reading comprehension activity, for example, can be reused for pronunciation practice or as a topic for speaking practice. (Note that in this case, material from the activity is reused for a different objective.)

- *Extend a lesson by creating an activity*: If students complete a lesson but are not yet comfortable with the material, Jane can develop additional activities to help them better achieve the lesson's objective.
- *Create a lesson*: If an otherwise good textbook does not cover a particular topic that the students need, Jane can create an entire lesson on that topic. (For more information on activities and lessons, see chapter 5.)

Ideally, a teacher will note the needs of their students, predict the shortcomings of the text, and prepare any necessary supplementary materials. This level of foresight is difficult for new teachers, however, so many teachers take careful notes during class and then create supplementary activities to address any shortcomings in later classes. In either case, by using a textbook and supplementary activities, we gain the strengths of both: the convenience of a professionally planned course with activities that progress naturally toward clear goals, and customized materials that more fully meet our students' needs.

☞ *Try: Choose three activities from an ESL textbook and extend them to provide more practice of the same kind. Then choose three other activities and consider how they might be repurposed for a different objective.*

PLANNING A COURSE FROM SCRATCH

Sometimes there is simply no textbook that sufficiently meets the needs of a class. In such a case, we may need to plan a series of lessons (for an entire course) that meet those needs. Doing so, of course, is significantly more work, but it may be necessary in a class with very specialized content or in a class of students who have very specific needs.

The first step in designing a course is discovering where the students are now (see "Learning about Learners" in chapter 2), and the second step is deciding where we want them to be by the end of the course—keeping our expectations realistic, of course. We can then begin mapping out the steps required to take them there.

Consider Jane's class of engineers, for example. She knows they need to present their research findings, but she needs more information in order to clarify how she can help them improve. After completing a needs assessment, discussing the students' needs both in class and with their supervisor, and interacting with students in meetings, Jane has made the following observations about their current level and needs:

- The students currently speak English at an intermediate or high-intermediate level, but they make frequent errors and are often hesitant when speaking.
- They have all studied a bit of "business English" already—though they are not really comfortable making presentations in English.
- They already know most of the specialized vocabulary they will need, but they often don't know how to pronounce those words or how to use them properly in context.

Jane then reworks her overall course goals to include more detail: *By the end of the course, students will be able to present their research findings with confidence, a high degree of fluency, few errors, strong presentation skills, clear pronunciation, and proper use of technical terms.* With these goals in mind, Jane begins to brainstorm ideas about how to achieve them over time:

- In each class, students will review five relevant technical terms. They will learn and practice the proper pronunciation, examine examples of each term in context, and write at least three sentences for each term using the context relevant to their work.
- In each class, students will review two or three common errors and how they are best avoided or corrected. Once taught, these errors will be revisited in future classes and students will be expected to self-correct with minimal prompting.
- Early in the course, students will spend part of each class discussing their research findings in small groups while Jane monitors and assists them. Their objective is to speak more naturally and to become more confident in speaking. They will also review basic presentation formats and procedures.
- Later in the course, each student will prepare and present at least three short presentations on their research. Jane will monitor each presentation and give feedback regarding fluency, errors, presentation skills, pronunciation, and accurate use of terms. Students will do additional presentations as needed.

Next, Jane begins to organize her ideas by writing a **course outline** (or **syllabus**). Her outline includes a detailed entry for each class, stating specific objectives, including which vocabulary will be learned, which errors will be addressed, which skills will be practiced, what discussions will be had or which presentations will be made, and so forth. Jane spends considerable time thinking carefully about what must be covered and in what order.

Finally, Jane begins to write the actual lesson plans. With her course outline in hand, she fleshes out the details to include an activity for each step in the process. A lesson early in the course, for example, will include a vocabulary activity (including pronunciation and usage) with supporting handouts, a common-errors activity with supporting handouts, an activity to introduce and practice specific presentation skills, and a small-group discussion activity with supporting guidelines and hints that the students may need. Jane consults dictionaries, business textbooks, online resources, and her supervisor in order to prepare the many details that make up these lessons.

Has Jane finished planning her course? Not quite. As the end comes in sight, Jane begins to notice areas where she can improve her course outline and her lessons. After all, many details become clear only after wrestling with many other related details, and Jane knows that revision is just as important as any other step in the process.

Jane's approach to planning this course includes basic steps that are typical of almost any type of course planning:

1. Carry out a needs assessment (see chapter 2) to discover students' current level (including specific strengths and weaknesses) and their specific needs related to language skills, content, and so on.
2. Formulate realistic, achievable goals for the course: Where do the students need to be by the end of the course? Refine as necessary.
3. Brainstorm ideas about how each aspect of the course goals might be met over the period of the course.
4. Organize those ideas by writing a course outline. The outline should include a detailed entry for each lesson: What will students accomplish in this class? What vocabulary, grammar, skills, and content will they learn? (Note that these details are essentially the objectives for each lesson.) Be sure the details are in the most natural order so that each class takes the students one step closer to the overall goals of the course.
5. Write the lesson plans for the course, using the objectives listed in the course outline. For each step, brainstorm ideas about how to help students move from their current level to the next step in the course outline. For each lesson plan, be sure to include all the necessary details related to activities, feedback, handouts, and so on. (For more details on lesson plans and objectives, see the relevant sections in chapter 5.)

6. Revise each aspect of the course in light of the discoveries made during the entire process.

Preparing an entire course is no small undertaking. It requires a clear understanding of the students' needs, a thorough knowledge of the course content, superior organizational skills, and lots of time—and in Jane's case, the help of a few trusted colleagues. It is nonetheless sometimes necessary, and the results can make the entire process both worthwhile and rewarding.

QUESTIONS FOR REVIEW

1. Why are course goals important? How do we choose them?
2. How might language textbooks have different purposes? Give examples.
3. How might language textbooks vary in their focus on language skills? Give examples.
4. How might language textbooks vary in their approaches and methods? Give examples.
5. Reread the above descriptions of the first two "common types" of textbooks. How are they similar? How do they differ? When might each be useful?
6. What is the greatest advantage of textbooks? What is their greatest weakness?
7. List and explain four ways to supplement a textbook. Give examples.
8. When might we need to design an entire course? What steps should we take to do so?

FURTHER READING

Kathleen Graves's *Designing Language Courses: A Guide for Teachers* (Heinle, 1999) is a comprehensive guide to course design.

I. S. P. Nation and John Macalister's *Language Curriculum Design* (Routledge, 2009) is a comprehensive and practical guide to curriculum design.

Jack C. Richards's *Curriculum Development in Language Teaching* (Cambridge, 2001) provides a thorough overview of course design.

Mario Rinvolucri's *Humanising Your Coursebook* (DELTA, 2002) provides practical tips for making textbooks more appealing in the classroom.

Tessa Woodward's *Planning Lessons and Courses* (Cambridge, 2001/2010) provides extensive help for planning both courses and lessons.

CHAPTER 5
Planning Lessons and Activities

We've all been in a class where the teacher introduced an activity that just didn't flow with the rest of the lesson. It might have been a fun activity to give the students a break, or it might have been used simply to fill the remaining time in a class that seemed like it would never end; in some cases, it may have flopped because the students simply weren't ready for it.

Activities that don't fit well with the rest of the lesson tend to have a common flaw: they were planned and designed without carefully considering the rest of the lesson, and as a result, they were not very effective.

LESSON OBJECTIVES: GIVING ACTIVITIES A PURPOSE

A good activity not only accomplishes something worthwhile but does so in the context of the lesson. In other words, each activity should serve the overall objective of the lesson.

We use the term **lesson objective** to describe what students will be able to do by the end of a particular lesson, just as we use the term *course goal* to describe where we wish students to be by the end of a course. Note the hierarchical relationship of these related terms:

- A course is a series of lessons, and a lesson is a series of activities.
- Course goals are broad and set with the long term in mind; they can be broken down into a series of smaller, specific lesson objectives, and each lesson objective is achieved by meeting a series of smaller activity objectives.

When developing an activity, then, we must keep in mind the objectives of the lesson, and when planning a lesson, we must keep in mind the overall goals of the course. After all, in order to decide what we want to accomplish in a given activity or lesson, we must consider what has already been accomplished and what we hope to accomplish in the future. If we keep this overall progression in mind, each activity becomes a step toward achieving the objectives of the lesson, and each lesson is a step toward reaching the goals of the course.

Consider this example: Jane is teaching a class of adult students who are transitioning from the high-beginner level to the low-intermediate level. They have more or less mastered the basic tenses (simple present, simple past, simple future, present progressive, past progressive) but are having trouble expressing themselves when speaking about multiple events in the past. Jane decides the past perfect tense would be a natural next step. Her lesson objective, then, is straightforward: *Students will be able to speak and write basic sentences using the past perfect tense accurately, naturally, and without excessive hesitation.*

☞ Consider: What kind of verbs does Jane use to express her lesson objective? How else does she define success?

Stating Lesson Objectives

A good lesson objective is stated in terms that clearly define what students will be able to do by the end of the lesson, and it does so using specific action words that are observable and measurable—words like *define, describe, explain, recall, identify, categorize, create,* or *solve,* rather than vague words like *know, learn,* and *accomplish.*

Choosing good action words is easier with a little help from what is known as Bloom's Taxonomy, a simple classification system for cognitive skills.[1] The revised version is shown in table 5.1 along with various verbs associated with each level. Note that a particular verb may be used at more than one level but with

Table 5.1: Bloom's Taxonomy (Revised)[2]

Creating	arrange, compose, construct, create, design, develop, formulate, manage, plan
Evaluating	argue, assess, defend, estimate, evaluate, judge, predict, rate
Analyzing	analyze, calculate, compare, contrast, differentiate, distinguish, organize
Applying	apply, demonstrate, dramatize, employ, illustrate, interpret, schedule, solve
Understanding	classify, describe, explain, indicate, locate, restate, select, summarize, translate
Remembering	define, duplicate, list, name, recall, recognize, restate, repeat, state

different expectations: the ability to write the past participle form of five verbs, for example, is very different from the ability to write five sentences using the past perfect form of those same verbs.

Looking back at Jane's lesson objective, we notice that it describes what students will be able to do by the end of the lesson, and it does so using specific action words such as *speak* and *write* along with specific details, not vague words such as *learn* or *accomplish*; with this strong, clear objective in mind, Jane can now begin preparing the steps (i.e., the activities) that will allow her students to reach it.

PLANNING ACTIVITIES

If a good lesson begins with a clear objective that guides the overall progression of the lesson, then each activity in the lesson should bring us one step closer to achieving that objective. For Jane's class, the objective of her lesson (as stated above) seems relatively straightforward, but her students will need significant practice at multiple steps (i.e., they will need to progress through various activities) in order to achieve it. Jane knows that they must first learn how to form the tense and then learn when to use the tense (keeping in mind that it is often used together with the simple past tense). She also knows that her students will need both written and oral practice to internalize the grammar and begin using it naturally. As such, she breaks down her lesson objective into specific steps, or activity objectives:

1. *Students will be able to write the past perfect form of given verbs.*
2. *Students will be able to complete given sentences using the past perfect tense with the simple past tense.*
3. *Students will be able to orally complete sentences using the past perfect tense with the simple past tense.*
4. *Students will be able to write five sentences about their weekend using the past perfect tense with the simple past tense.*
5. *Students will be able to authentically discuss their weekend using the past perfect tense with the simple past tense.*

With these steps in mind, Jane begins to plan and design one activity for each step toward her lesson objective:

1. *Using a brief explanation and multiple examples, show students how to form the past perfect tense. Have the students do the examples together and then*

complete a worksheet that requires them to fill in the past perfect tense of the given verbs.
2. Using a brief explanation and multiple examples, show students when to use the past perfect tense—in particular, how to use it together with the simple past tense. Have the students complete examples together and then complete a worksheet that requires them to fill in the appropriate tense (simple past or past perfect) in given sentences.
3. Lead students in an oral drill that requires them to supply the correct tense (simple past or past perfect) in the correct form.
4. Have each student write at least five sentences describing what they did the previous weekend. Each sentence must use both the simple past tense and the past perfect tense.
5. Have students work in small groups to discuss what they did the previous weekend. They must use both the simple past tense and the past perfect tense, and they cannot refer to their written work.

Note how each activity moves the students one step closer to the overall objective of the lesson. This point is particularly important: choosing an otherwise "good" activity that is unrelated to our lesson objective will likely be distracting at best and confusing at worst, while arranging well-chosen activities in an unnatural order is likely to be equally frustrating. Again, keeping our lesson objective in mind will help us choose the best activities and arrange them in the best order to achieve that objective.

Also note that each activity has a particular task that students must complete, and that successful completion of the task indicates that students have achieved the objective for that particular activity and are ready to move on to the next.

☞ Try: Re-examine the five activities Jane has outlined. What would success look like at each step? Would students be able to complete the latter activities without mastering the earlier ones?

Accuracy, Meaning, or Fluency?

Activities are often focused on accuracy, **meaning**, or fluency. A simple conversation activity, for example, might emphasize accuracy (students must correctly use the targeted grammar forms, vocabulary, or pronunciation when speaking), meaning (students must successfully communicate specific content, such as what they did on the weekend), or fluency (students must speak reasonably quickly, with little hesitation). Note that success looks different in each case because the activity's objective is different.

Consider again Jane's activities for her lesson on past perfect tense:

1. *Write the past perfect form.*
2. *Complete written sentences using the target tense.*
3. *Orally complete sentences using the target tense.*
4. *Write five sentences about their weekend using the target tense.*
5. *Discuss their weekend using the target tense.*

What is the focus of each activity? Do some focus almost exclusively on accuracy? on meaning? on fluency? Do some require more than one focus—a balance of sorts?

The first three are obvious: they focus on accuracy, requiring students to provide or use the target tense correctly. The fourth focuses on meaning, requiring students to write about what they did on the weekend, and the fifth likely focuses on fluency, requiring students to communicate (*without excessive hesitation*) what they just wrote about; but do the fourth and fifth activities not also require accuracy? After all, allowing students to use the target tense incorrectly in the later activities would undo much of their progress from the earlier activities.

This principle of balancing accuracy, meaning, and fluency applies to other teaching methods as well. Task-Based Instruction, for example, focuses initially on completing a task—a focus on meaning; but in later steps, students analyze the language that was used to complete the task—a focus on accuracy. Once that form is learned, however, it would be foolish not to insist on its accurate use in future tasks, even when the focus is once again on meaning.

The same principle applies to pronunciation. Once a sound or word is learned through activities that focus on accurate pronunciation, it only makes sense to require its accurate use in later activities, even if the main focus is on meaning or fluency.

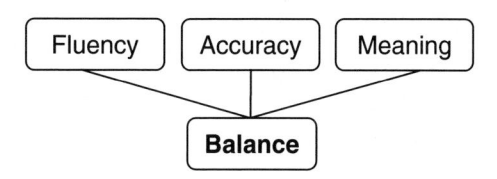

Figure 5.1: Balanced Focus

When planning an activity, then, we must consider whether our focus is accuracy, meaning, or fluency, or whether some sort of balance is appropriate. Without such balance, activities might reinforce errors that were previously addressed and affect the long-term development of the students. Consider, for example, how the language abilities of these students developed differently in the following very typical scenarios:

- Eryk studied English in a traditional class where most activities focused on accuracy. After many years of study, he has a strong understanding of grammar but cannot communicate naturally and effectively, and he is awkward in and frustrated by most social situations.
- Adelina studied English in a conversation class where most activities focused on meaning and fluency. She can now communicate relatively quickly but makes numerous errors. As a result, she doesn't feel integrated into English-speaking society, and at times her errors impede her listeners' understanding.
- Haji studied English in a class where activities focused on accuracy, meaning, or fluency, but they were always treated separately. As a result, he has a reasonably good understanding of grammar, and he can speak quickly, but he continues to make a lot of errors in his speaking and writing. Worse yet, those errors have become so ingrained over the years that they cannot easily be fixed. Overall, his situation is only slightly better than Adelina's.
- Zahra studied English in a class that included activities that balanced accuracy, meaning, and fluency; even when the focus was on meaning or fluency, she was expected self-correct (often with prompts from the teacher) when she made mistakes in areas already learned. Over time, she has eliminated most errors and has become comfortable speaking English in almost any situation.

The goal of most language learners is to be able to communicate effectively—that is, with a high degree of accuracy, clear meaning, and smooth delivery (i.e., fluency). Helping students achieve this goal requires a balanced approach to most activities. A conversation on a new topic, for example, shouldn't focus on meaning alone. Why not draw students' attention to new grammar and vocabulary appropriate to the topic (and to their level, of course)? Why not give feedback that not only praises students but also encourages accurate grammar, word use, and pronunciation so that students can more effectively express what they wish to say? (For more information on giving feedback in class, see "Dealing with Errors" in chapter 6.)

Supplementary Activities

In some cases, rather than creating an entire lesson, a teacher might create a single activity to supplement an existing lesson or a unit from a textbook. Here, too, the teacher needs to keep in mind the existing objective of the lesson or unit in order to better achieve it.

Consider, for example, a class of low-intermediate adults who have just completed a textbook unit on invitations. The objective of the unit seems reasonable: *Students will be able to accept and decline invitations in a manner common to Western cultures.* After completing the activities in the unit, however, the students understand the concepts but do not yet feel comfortable declining invitations. In fact, they tend to stumble over their words and turn red with embarrassment because they are not used to declining invitations in this way. It feels awkward for them.

The teacher makes note of this and wishes to create an additional activity to address these issues. What is her objective? To have students learn more about declining invitations? Of course not—they've already covered that. They need to improve their level of comfort and fluency when declining invitations in the Western manner.

Once she has this objective in mind, at least in rough form, the teacher must consider what students will do in order to achieve that objective. Should she provide additional readings about declining invitations? Should she have students memorize relevant key phrases?

She decides to do neither. After all, the students don't need more information about declining invitations, and they don't need prepared phrases; rather, they need practice declining invitations—lots of practice, if necessary, until they become more comfortable doing so. The teacher decides to have them prepare and perform role plays in which they are required to make and decline invitations. She will also monitor their performances and have students repeat them until the Western manner of declining invitations feels a bit more natural.

She fine-tunes the objective for her activity and writes it like this: *Students will be able to decline invitations comfortably and confidently in the Western manner.* Note that she doesn't change the original objective of the textbook unit but attempts to achieve it more fully by providing additional relevant practice that is well suited to her students' particular needs.

EVALUATING THE EFFECTIVENESS OF ACTIVITIES

As noted, an effective activity has a clear objective that moves students closer to the overall objective of the lesson, and it includes a task that provides practice in order to achieve the activity's objective. We also noted that if the task is carefully designed, successful completion of the task will demonstrate achievement of the activity's objective. With those ideas in mind, consider these examples and decide whether each is a good activity or not:

a)	Type of Activity: *Listening comprehension*	Student Task: *Complete the chart*
	Objective:	Students will be able to complete a chart with information derived from an audio recording.
	Activity:	The teacher plays a recorded conversation while students complete a chart according to what they hear.

b)	Type of Activity: *Grammar*	Student Task: *Complete the worksheet*
	Objective:	Students will be able to complete sentences using the past perfect tense.
	Activity:	The teacher briefly explains how and when the past perfect tense is used; the students then complete a worksheet on past perfect tense.

c)	Type of Activity: *Expressing opinions*	Student Task: *Discuss and report*
	Objective:	Students will be able to express their opinions about a news topic.
	Activity:	The teacher introduces an interesting topic from the news, clarifies key points and vocabulary, and then has the students discuss it in small groups. Later, the groups will report back to the class.

d)	Type of Activity: *Reading comprehension*	Student Task: *Answer written questions*
	Objective:	Students will be able to answer comprehension questions on a short reading.
	Activity:	Students read an interesting one-page magazine article and answer five short-answer questions about the content.

e)	Type of Activity: *Teacher explanation*	Student Task: *Listen*
	Objective:	Students will become more motivated in their study of grammar.
	Activity:	The teacher stands at the front of the room and gives a detailed explanation of why learning grammar is important.

Note that the first four activities include very specific tasks and that successful completion of the task will demonstrate that the objective of the activity has been achieved:

a) Students can complete the chart only if they understand what they are listening to.
b) Students can complete the grammar worksheet only if they understand how and when to use the past perfect tense.
c) Students can report back to the class only if they have adequately discussed the topic.
d) Students can answer the questions only if they have adequately understood the reading.

The final activity, however, does not include a clear student task (other than "listening"), nor does it include any way to determine if the activity achieves its objective. It is not a good activity, then, and perhaps not really an activity at all because students are not active—in fact, they may not even be paying attention.

Finally, we previously noted that *successful completion of the task will demonstrate achievement of the activity's objective*; this, of course, is true only if the task is well designed. Consider our examples once more:

a) If students can complete the listening chart without understanding the listening material, then the chart must be remade.
b) If the students can complete the grammar worksheet without really understanding how and when the past perfect tense is used, then the worksheet must be remade.
c) If the students can report back to the class without adequate discussion, then the requirements of the task must be reframed.
d) If the students can answer the questions without really understanding the article, then the questions must be rewritten.

An effective task, then, is set at an appropriate level and can be completed only if the students have achieved the desired objective of the activity.

☞ *Consider: When developing activities such as those listed in this section, how can we test their effectiveness before using them in class?*

LESSON PLANS

Objectives, activities, tasks—the many details of planning a lesson can seem almost overwhelming at times. Keeping track of the numerous decisions and details requires an overall plan—in other words, a lesson plan. A **lesson plan** is essentially an outline of what is planned for a class, with just enough detail to remind the teacher of what must be done, when it should be done, and how it should be done.

Many new teachers have a love-hate relationship with lesson plans. On the one hand, lesson plans take time to develop (though they get easier with practice and are done more quickly with a well-designed template). On the other hand, they help us carefully think through in advance the various details of a class, and they can relieve us of the stress of trying to remember what to do, when to do it, and how to do it. In fact, a good lesson plan is essential if we are to be methodical and effective in our attempts to meet our students' needs.

The details of a lesson plan will depend on what the lesson entails, but a typical lesson plan will include certain basic features: the lesson head, which includes general information about the lesson, and the lesson body, which includes the specific activities of the lesson.

Lesson Head

A good lesson head provides a quick overview of the lesson. It includes what the lesson attempts to achieve, how it attempts to do so, and other key information that teachers want to find quickly:

- *Objective*: Clearly state the overall purpose of the lesson—what will students be able to do by the end of the lesson?
- *Methods*: Briefly state the specific steps that students will take in order to achieve the lesson objective.
- *Preparation and materials*: Include in this list whatever the teacher must prepare, arrange, or collect in advance in order to be ready for the lesson.
- *Level*: What level is this lesson developed for?
- *Time*: Approximately how long will this lesson take?

Lesson Body

The lesson body gives the progression of activities that make up the lesson, along with the necessary details for each:

1. *Lead-in*: The lesson begins with an introduction (such as an **open-ended question**, a short anecdote, or a skit) that generates students' interest in the lesson and activates their prior knowledge about the content of the lesson. The lead-in to a reading lesson, for example, might ask students what they know about the topic, the genre, or both.
2. *Activities*: The bulk of the lesson plan is composed of specific activities that progress toward the lesson's overall objective. These activities are given in order, each under its own heading, with instructions for set-up, running the activity, monitoring it, and giving **assessment** and feedback. The particular order of activities will depend on the type of lesson. (See the following section, "Order of Activities." See also the relevant sections of chapter 6 for details on feedback and other issues related to class management.)
3. *Closing*: The final step in the lesson signals that the lesson is coming to an end, provides overall feedback, and addresses any other details that must be taken care of.

Order of Activities

The activities in a lesson plan are arranged so that each activity moves the lesson one step closer to the overall objective of the lesson:

- The activities in a Communicative Language Teaching lesson help students gradually master the target language function; in doing so, the lesson normally integrates all language skills and subskills, though speaking and listening may be given more attention (as appropriate to the target language function). (Review "CLT Lessons" in chapter 3 for more details.)
- The activities in a content-based lesson help students gradually master the target content; in doing so, the lesson integrates language skills and subskills, though reading and writing are often prioritized. (Review "CBI Lessons" in chapter 3 for more details.)
- In a lesson focusing on a particular language skill, the activities help students further improve that skill within a particular context. (See chapters 8, 9, 10, and 11 for more information on teaching speaking, listening, reading, and writing, respectively.)
- The activities in a vocabulary lesson help students understand and use a particular set of related words and phrases. (See chapter 12 for more details.)

- The activities in a grammar lesson help students gradually master a particular grammar form. (See chapter 14 for more details.)

Note that most good lessons integrate all skills; a communicative lesson, for example, helps students master a language function by providing speaking, listening, reading, and writing activities related to the function; a content-based lesson helps students master the target content through speaking, listening, reading, and writing activities; and even a vocabulary lesson can provide practice using the new word items with all four skills.

Another suggestion is to consider giving equal time in a lesson to each of four strands:[3]

1. *Meaning-focused input*: Students seek to understand the meaning of what they hear or read.
2. *Language-focused learning*: Students seek to acquire a grammar form, accurate pronunciation of a particular sound or related feature, correct use or spelling of new vocabulary, or the ability to use a particular feature of **discourse**.
3. *Meaning-focused output*: Students speak or write what they wish to communicate.
4. *Fluency*: Students seek to use the language smoothly and comfortably.

A very simple CLT lesson, for example, can easily incorporate all four strands:

1. Students will read and listen to a dialogue that models the target language function.
2. Students will complete activities that draw attention to and require correct use of certain grammar forms and vocabulary used in the dialogue.
3. Students will write their own dialogue using the target language function.
4. Students will practice their dialogues aloud two or three times.

☞ *Consider: How might other types of lessons include all four strands?*

Lesson Plan Checklist

When writing a lesson plan, consider using a simple checklist to evaluate the lesson's format and effectiveness:

- Overall:
  - ☐ Is the topic interesting and relevant to the students?
  - ☐ Is the language level appropriate for the students?
  - ☐ Is the lesson plan neat, error-free, and professional in appearance?
  - ☐ Are all necessary handouts attached to the lesson, and all explanations provided?
- Lesson head:
  - ☐ Are the lesson objectives, language level, and time clearly stated?
  - ☐ Is the materials/preparation section complete?
  - ☐ Does the lesson head function well as a quick summary for anyone previewing the lesson?
- Lesson body:
  - ☐ Does the lead-in generate interest in and activate prior knowledge of the topic?
  - ☐ Are the activities carefully chosen and fully developed to accomplish the lesson objectives?
  - ☐ Are all activities at an appropriate level?
  - ☐ Do the activities naturally progress in a logical order?
  - ☐ Do the activities include practice in all four language skills, if appropriate?
  - ☐ Are there techniques for meaningful evaluation and feedback during or after each activity?
  - ☐ Are the instructions clear, concise, and specific? Are they given as if spoken to the teacher? Does each step briefly explain not only what to do but also how to do it?
  - ☐ Does the lesson end with a sense of closure and provide students with an opportunity to give their feedback on the lesson?

Focused on Students

Finally, we should note that this traditional type of lesson plan is meant to be a helpful guide, not a set of boundaries. In other words, a good lesson plan provides direction, but a good teacher knows when and how to depart from the lesson plan if it becomes necessary in order to meet the needs of the students— needs that may become obvious only once the lesson is underway. This level of flexibility is essential if we are to provide the best experience for our students, and, like planning effective lessons and activities, it becomes easier with experience.

QUESTIONS FOR REVIEW

1. Why should each lesson be planned with the rest of the course in mind? Why should each activity be planned with the rest of the lesson in mind?
2. How do we choose appropriate objectives for a lesson? an activity?
3. How should a lesson objective be stated? What details should be included?
4. Why is the order of activities in a lesson important?
5. Why is a balance of accuracy, meaning, and fluency important when planning activities?
6. What should we keep in mind when designing supplementary activities? Why?
7. What makes a task effective? What might make a task ineffective? Give examples.
8. What is the purpose of a lesson plan? How much detail should it include?
9. What is the importance of a lead-in at the beginning of a lesson? What information should be included in it?
10. What does it mean to integrate language skills and incorporate the "four strands" when planning a lesson?

FURTHER READING

Brian Tomlinson's *Materials Development in Language Teaching* (Cambridge, 2011) is a thorough and accessible guide to developing teaching materials.

Tessa Woodward's *Planning Lessons and Courses* (Cambridge, 2001/2010) provides extensive help for planning both lessons and courses.

NOTES

1. The original Bloom's Taxonomy was published in *Taxonomy of Educational Objectives: The Classification of Educational Goals*, ed. Benjamin Bloom (Longman, 1956).
2. The revised taxonomy is found in Lorin Anderson's *A Taxonomy for Learning, Teaching, and Assessing: A Revision of Bloom's Taxonomy of Educational Objectives* (Allyn and Bacon, 2001).
3. The concept of the four strands comes from I. S. P. Nation's article "The Four Strands" in *Innovation in Language Learning and Teaching* 1, no. 1 (2007): 1–12.

CHAPTER 6
Class Management

When we speak of class management, what comes to mind? A frustrated teacher trying to control a class of rowdy eight-year-old students? A calm teacher, firmly in control, with all students listening attentively? A teacher who explains everything in the students' first language? A teacher who forbids the use of any language except the one being learned? A "talking head" at the front of the class drilling students in the fundamentals? A smiling, sociable teacher engaging students in a conversation about current events?

We noticed in chapter 3 that well-known methods of language teaching vary widely in their prescriptions for the classroom. Some methods are teacher centred while others are student centred; some require extensive use of the students' first language, others do not use it at all, and still others allow it in particular circumstances; some emphasize drills and repetition while others emphasize authentic language use; and some require students to be corrected immediately while others require little or no correction.

When choosing which ideas to adopt, we must think back to chapter 1, where we proposed that a teacher's job is not to control students but to facilitate their learning. If that is true, then perhaps class management includes less time giving orders and more time working in the background, making decisions and creating the conditions that best allow students to learn.

PLANNING AND PREPARATION

Effective classes begin with solid preparation based on clear objectives. Such preparation begins by envisioning what the class will look like and deciding what needs to be prepared before class begins. These decisions, of course, are made according to what best meets the objectives of the lesson.

In chapter 5, we saw that Jane developed a simple but effective objective for her lesson: *Students will be able to speak and write basic sentences using the past perfect tense accurately, naturally, and without excessive hesitation.* Examining this objective, we note a number of items that Jane must prepare: an introduction to past perfect tense that interests students and briefly explains the grammar, with examples; one or more worksheets for students to practice writing verbs and sentences in the past perfect tense; and guidelines and details for activities that require students to speak about themselves and others in the past perfect tense.

It may be tempting for Jane to prepare the worksheets and perhaps a handout for the introduction, but nothing else; after all, the rest is done orally, so she can do it on the fly, right? Fortunately, Jane knows that explanations done on the fly tend to be convoluted and unclear, so she will work out in advance how she will introduce each activity in a way that is simple yet complete, and because she is still a fairly new teacher, she will practice these explanations in advance.

This last point is extremely important but often forgotten: explanations can quickly become a source of confusion in a language class, so they must be carefully prepared and practiced to ensure absolute clarity.

Materials

In addition to written explanations and handouts, there are other materials that may make an otherwise dry topic come alive; simple props, for example, can help keep the mood light. In Jane's case, in addition to preparing written materials, she also decides to bring to class objects to help explain and practice the past perfect tense, including a book and a movie to use when demonstrating the sentence *I had already watched the movie when I read the book.*

Student Groupings

Do students work better alone, as a group, or in small groups or pairs? The answer, as always, depends on the activity and—more importantly—on the objectives of the activity. If, for example, the activity is designed to get students speaking, then dividing the class into pairs or small groups will give each student more opportunity to speak. If the objective is to have students master a grammar form by completing a worksheet, then working individually seems fine, though we may wish to have students compare answers with a partner or even explain the answers to each other. If the activity requires a short verbal or physical group response, then working as one large group may be the answer. The key, as always, is to be flexible and to choose the option that best suits the objectives of the activity. (Note also that using a variety of groupings helps keep the class moving and fresh.)

For her class, Jane will speak to the large group when she introduces the past perfect tense. Her students will then work individually to complete the worksheets before comparing their answers in groups of three. For the interactive oral practice, students will work as one large group. Finally, they will break into twos for the oral pair work.

Classroom Arrangement

A sea of desks and chairs spread in rows across the width of a classroom is generally not the best arrangement for a language class. After all, language is about communication, and communication works best when we can see each other's faces without straining our necks. For large-group work, then, a horseshoe arrangement is often ideal (if space allows), as it gives everyone a front-row view of everyone else.

Other activities may have different needs. For small-group activities, having students sit in groups around mid-sized tables (or smaller desks pushed together) is likely the best option, while for individual written work, almost any arrangement will do. For activities involving lots of movement or interaction, we may choose to push the chairs, desks, and tables aside and simply have students stand in the middle of the room or move around.

Overall, we need to be flexible and creative, using whatever arrangement works best for the activity and keeping students facing each other as much as possible when communication is important. (Keep in mind, however, that some scenarios, such as sitting on desks, may be considered disrespectful or even rude in some cultures. When in doubt, ask.)

Dealing with Differences

In a sense, every class has a range of abilities and levels, as well as a variety of strengths, weaknesses, needs, interests, and expectations. How do we deal with this?

Simply "teaching to the class" as a whole is probably not the best solution, even if it is the easiest. Since students have different needs, those needs must be met or the students will become discouraged at their lack of progress. Teaching students individually according to their needs, however, is simply not realistic if the class has more than a few students. There simply isn't time.

The solution is likely a form of **differentiation**: develop a lesson for the class and include activities that appeal to a variety of strengths and preferences, but also individualize some (though not all) components to suit the needs of the students. As part of a reading activity, for example, one student may give a written response while another gives an oral response; still another may answer comprehension questions, and some students may want additional homework in order to catch up to the level of the others.

The extent to which a general lesson is customized for individual students really depends on the teacher, the needs of the students, and, of course, the amount of time available (particularly for preparation). New teachers often find the perfect balance elusive, but over time they become adept at spotting needs in the class and quickly adapting to meet them.

☞ Try: Choose three activities from an ESL textbook and plan any necessary explanations, groupings, and seating arrangements for each.

WELCOMING STUDENTS AND CREATING ATMOSPHERE

As teachers, we sometimes forget that walking into a classroom can be intimidating for students, particularly if they are insecure about their own language abilities or if they are shy around other students whom they've only recently met. Part of the teacher's job, then, is to create a positive atmosphere that helps students enjoy learning—even those students who are not particularly motivated.

The process of building atmosphere begins as the students enter the classroom: Is the teacher happy to see them? Do the students feel welcome? Some teachers will play soft music in the background before class starts; others will stand at the door and greet the students as they enter. Overall, students appreciate a teacher who is friendly and welcoming, and who takes the time to get to know them personally, often through brief but friendly chats before class begins.

The atmosphere is then maintained largely by the attitude of the teacher: Is the teacher positive and encouraging? Does the teacher make activities fun, interesting, and relevant? Generally speaking, the teacher's attitude sets the tone for the lesson; if the teacher is friendly, positive, and encouraging, the students are likely to feel the same way and be more confident in approaching each activity; but if the teacher is dry, boring, or unfriendly, the students will find it more difficult to motivate themselves to learn.

We must also remember that some students find a language classroom very stressful, particularly if the target language is the only one being used. Even if they want to learn, they may be wound up with anxiety because much of the content seems incomprehensible. By keeping explanations simple, using frequent demonstrations and examples, and showing genuine concern for their well-being, we can help students avoid frustration and instead contribute to a positive atmosphere in which learning is more likely to take place.

Finally, we can create a positive class atmosphere by remembering that language is about communication, and that people are generally very communicative in the right circumstances. When we arrange seating to promote communication, choose topics that are interesting and relevant to the students, and develop activities that are interactive, the hard work of learning is transformed into something much more enjoyable.

Sometimes, though, a little creativity is needed to address a specific problem. In Jane's class, there is one student who likes to complain that he is tired and overworked. Most days, he does as little work as possible and contributes nothing positive to the class atmosphere. Jane's first instinct is to pull him aside for a little chat about his attitude; instead, however, she decides to use humour in an attempt to win him over. She jokes with him (using exaggerated gestures and expressions—his English, after all, is quite limited) that she too is tired and overworked, and that perhaps he can teach the class for her. He eventually laughs and begins to lighten up. After several classes like this, his general attitude changes for the better, and he is no longer a drag on the class atmosphere. (Note that Jane uses good humour to win him over; she does not use humour to mock him, belittle him, or alienate him in any way, which would likely result in souring the mood of the entire class.)

The way in which a teacher creates atmosphere depends largely on the teacher's personality. A fun, outgoing teacher may quickly win over the class through lively activities and a fast-paced class, while a quiet, dry teacher with a quirky sense of humour may take more time to connect with the students in smaller, quieter ways. In both cases, if the teachers genuinely care about their classes and students, and allow their personalities to flavour the class activities, the students are likely to respond in kind, resulting in a more positive atmosphere and a better learning experience for everyone.

☞ *Consider: Imagine that you are teaching a group of 10 teenagers at a private language school. Two of them are highly motivated and do well in every activity. Seven of them are somewhat motivated and will do what is asked, with acceptable results. One of them, however, slumps in her chair with her arms crossed and does very little work, and her attitude is affecting the class atmosphere. What will you do?*

RUNNING AN ACTIVITY

As we've noted already, teachers really have one main job—providing and maintaining opportunities for students to learn. For much of the time in class, this job involves running activities during which learning takes place. Although activities come in all shapes and sizes, running them generally involves a few basic steps:

1. *Introducing the activity*: As we saw in chapter 5, good teachers normally begin a lesson with a lead-in that generates interest and activates the students' prior knowledge of the topic. A lesson on declining invitations, for example, might begin with a skit or dialogue that illustrates the topic, or even a simple question about students' own relevant experiences.

    Because the activities that follow will further develop the same topic, there is no need to introduce the topic again; instead, the teacher should transition between activities by connecting the next activity with the previous one and explaining the next step. A role play at the end of a class on refusing invitations, for example, might be introduced as follows: *Now that we understand how invitations are declined, let's practice declining invitations so that it feels more natural.*

2. *Set-up, instructions, and explanations*: Giving instructions or explanations to an advanced class is relatively easy because the students can understand almost everything we say. Most classes, however, are not advanced, and students can easily become confused by unclear instructions or convoluted explanations. Teachers, then, should avoid the common trap of speaking without adequate preparation or overwhelming students with details. A few guidelines can help:

    a. Prepare in advance whenever possible. (Write out the details if necessary.)
    b. Explain only what needs to be explained, using short sentences and simple words, and give key words, examples, diagrams, and other visual aids on the whiteboard.
    c. Whenever possible, elicit the details instead of explaining them. Note the difference:
       - Explanation: *The simple present tense is used to describe something habitual or something that is generally true, while the present progressive tense is used to describe something that is currently in progress.*
       - Elicitation: *What is the difference? "I teach English. I am teaching English."*

Note that the explanation is likely to confuse students, while elicitation allows students to figure out the details at their own pace and in their own words.
   d. Give numerous examples.
   e. Distribute handouts related to the explanation. (Handouts are optional, but they are very helpful for any explanations that require more than a few sentences. Also note that in most cases, handouts should be distributed after the explanation so they will not serve as a distraction.)
   f. Quickly move on to practice, and when prompting students for an answer or correcting an error, be brief and positive.
3. *Running the activity*: Once an activity is running, the teacher's job is to circulate among the students and monitor their progress, providing feedback and assistance as necessary. Specifically, the teacher should help students achieve the objective of the activity, whether by clarifying instructions, reviewing a key point taught just before the activity, correcting errors, or simply staying out of the way.

   Note that feedback and assistance are most valuable during (not after) an activity, particularly when addressing problems or errors that impede students' progress toward the objectives of the activity. (Some types of errors, however, can be dealt with later or even not at all. See "Dealing with Errors" later in this chapter.)
4. *Closing the activity*: Every good activity must end at some point, whether according to the clock, the teacher, or the expressions on the students' faces. If the activity comes to a natural end, we may signal this by thanking everyone for their hard work. If the activity is still well underway but time is running out, we may wish to announce the approaching deadline ("Two more minutes!") to encourage students to begin wrapping things up. In either case, it is good to say something to give students a sense of closure and to end on an encouraging note.

   Depending on how much feedback we gave students during the activity, this may be the time to give additional feedback on their performance, or to address general issues with the class, before moving on to the next activity.

MANAGING THE FLOW: A MATTER OF CHOICES

There are some teachers who under-manage a class—they distribute worksheets or briefly set up activities and then disappear. Many teachers, however, have the opposite problem—they over-manage the class and get in the way, usually by talking too much.

Remember, language skills develop through practice, so the teacher's job is to enable practice and support it; beyond that, the teacher's job is largely peripheral. It includes introducing and setting up the activity; giving support, guidance, and feedback as needed (and only as needed); and wrapping up the activity before moving on.

It is worth noting that this peripheral role may come as a surprise to students who expect the teacher to be the focus of the class. For this reason, the teacher in a new class may need to play a strong role initially and gradually give more control to the students as they become more comfortable with an activity-based class rather than a teacher-led class.

Dealing with Issues and Making Decisions

In the midst of managing activities, the teacher may have to deal with a few classroom issues. For example, a student arrives 15 minutes late and in the middle of the first activity; worse yet, it is not the first time he is late. Another student insists on speaking her native language in the group, and she has a habit of doing so.

In dealing with such issues, the teacher is frequently called on to make immediate decisions. The ability to make good decisions on short notice comes with experience, but in the meantime, making such decisions is easier if the teacher considers in advance how certain situations might be handled. (This is not to say that we can predict every issue that might arise in class, but by preparing for some, we will be better equipped to deal with others.)

Some decisions are a matter of policy. If, for example, the school has a policy about students arriving late for class or speaking their native language in class, then the teacher will need to encourage the students to respect that policy and may need to take action to enforce it. Be aware, however, that rules that exist as policy may not be regularly enforced, so a new teacher who suddenly enforces them may stir up more trouble than expected. (It is helpful for new teachers to discuss such issues with a supervisor before acting on them.)

Note also that some classes may not have a late policy at all. Companies, for example, may hold language classes during working hours, and a student (i.e., a company employee) may be involved in a project or a meeting and may not be able to leave their work precisely when class begins. In this case, it is the teacher's job to manage the late student's arrival with the least possible disruption to the class while making the late student feel welcome.

Other decisions are a matter of purpose. Allowing students to speak their first language may be disruptive if the focus of the activity is fluency, but it may be helpful to allow limited use of the students' first language if the objective is to understand something not easily explained. For example, a student explaining what he did on the weekend should use only English, but students helping other students understand a difficult grammatical concept may wish to use their native language. As always, the choice depends on the objectives of the activity.

Consider another situation that requires a decision: an activity that was planned for 20 minutes has been running for 30 minutes and shows no sign of slowing down. Does the teacher stop the activity immediately? Or announce that there are two minutes left in the activity? Or ask the students what they prefer?

Of course there is no simple answer except this: it depends on the situation. What will be gained or lost by stopping the activity? Which choice will best serve the objectives of the class? (Once again, having clear objectives established in advance makes such decisions easier.)

DEALING WITH ERRORS

We noted previously that certain types of feedback should be given during an activity, while other types should be given later, if at all. Feedback related to errors is particularly tricky, and opinions on the matter vary widely:

- Some teachers advocate correcting every mistake as soon as it is made. This "old school" approach suggests that mistakes will be reinforced if not immediately corrected. While there is some truth in this, we also know that it is probably not possible to correct all mistakes immediately, as there are simply too many, and that overcorrecting can hinder the flow of the conversation and possibly discourage students from speaking. Moreover, when one teacher oversees students speaking in multiple small groups, correcting every mistake is impossible.
- Other teachers advocate only positive feedback and encouragement, believing that immediate correction is harsh and demotivating, and that a softer, gentler approach is necessary to encourage students to speak up. However, this approach tends to inadvertently reinforce mistakes and often leads to broken, awkward language. Moreover, correction (even immediate correction) can be helpful and even encouraging if the teacher takes the position and tone of a helper rather than a judge.

- Still other teachers attempt a compromise, focusing on only major errors (such as those that make an utterance incomprehensible). Corrections may occur during an activity if the interruption is not awkward (such as during a one-on-one conversation) or after the activity if an interruption would be awkward (such as during a role play).
- Finally, some teachers (and many teacher-training textbooks) advocate immediate correction in accuracy-focused activities and delayed correction in meaning-focused or fluency-focused activities. However, as we saw in chapter 5, this approach ignores the fact that many activities should aim for a high degree of accuracy even if their focus is on meaning or fluency.

These approaches to correction are the most common, but of course there are numerous variations, and every teacher has reasons for choosing one approach over the others. In the end, however, there are three questions that teachers must carefully consider:

1. *Which errors do we correct?* Since we cannot (and probably should not) correct all errors, we should limit our focus by establishing specific types of errors[1] that require our focus:
    - Errors that impede comprehension, such as unintelligible pronunciation, a misused word, or a grammatical structure that simply doesn't make sense, must be dealt with to ensure the students' meaning is successfully communicated.
    - Errors that make the utterance socially awkward—such as inappropriate slang, vulgar language, or language that is racist or sexist—must be addressed so that students can avoid potentially awkward or embarrassing situations in the future. (Note that such errors are often made innocently, having been learned through movies, television, and acquaintances.)
    - Errors in areas recently learned should be addressed in order to reinforce what has recently been taught.
    - Errors that the student makes frequently should be corrected in order to break old habits and form new ones.
2. *When do we correct errors?* The most unobtrusive time to correct student errors is "never" but such an approach is not very effective; at the other extreme, correcting every error immediately may be so obtrusive that it is more discouraging than effective. Balance, of course, is the key.

- Immediate correction is the most effective and should be used whenever possible (though certainly not to the point of overwhelming the student). Students who have something meaningful to say will be happiest when they can say it correctly, and they are more likely to make note of a correction when it helps them express what they wish to communicate. In fact, when done correctly (see point 3 in this list), immediate correction is not intimidating and can engender a sense of satisfaction and accomplishment among students.
- Some activities, such as role plays and debates, have a natural flow that should not be interrupted. In these cases, we can make note of common or noteworthy errors and address them at the next natural pause in the activity, or even at the end of the activity.
- There are some instances where little or no correction may be appropriate. When dealing with a student who has very low confidence, for example, or who reacts poorly to correction, an activity with no correction may be required in order to build the student's confidence. Note, however, that such circumstances should be considered exceptions, and that quietly offering the student individual help may be necessary.

3. *How do we correct student errors?* Many teachers hesitate to correct students immediately because they do not wish to interrupt the flow of the conversation or activity, but as we know from our everyday interactions, certain types of tactful interruptions are part of the natural flow of conversations. These can be used to correct student errors with varying degrees of effectiveness:
    - *Recasting* is the act of repeating the student's utterance in corrected form: for example, when a student says, "He seed a moose," the teacher replies, "He saw a moose." While **recasting** is better than not correcting at all, its effectiveness is limited because students often see a recast as clarification or confirmation of meaning, not as a correction of an error. Nonetheless, recasting is an effective way to correct vocabulary or pronunciation with minimal interruption, or to deal with errors beyond the student's level (when there is need to correct such an error).
    - *Requesting clarification* requires the student to restate what was just said. However, the student may simply reword the utterance for clarification without recognizing the error.

- *Repeating* the student's error as a question with emphasis that draws attention to the error will cause the student to reconsider what was said. For example, when a student says, "He seed a moose," the teacher asks, "He *seed* a moose?" with particular emphasis on the error.
- *Echoing* the student's sentence up to the error also draws attention to the error and requires the student to correct it. For example, when a student says, "I went to supermarket yesterday," the teacher replies, "You went to …" and waits for the student to self-correct.
- *Metalinguistic clues* are prompts such as "Tense?" or "Article?" that draw attention to the type of error made and require the student to correct it.

Regardless of the method, we can always be positive and encouraging, focusing not on the error but on how to make it right. In addition, we should be sure the student gives or repeats the correct form, not only to reinforce the form but also to give the student the satisfaction of having said it correctly; we can then follow immediately with affirmation.

For more information on giving feedback during certain types of activities, see the relevant chapters on speaking, listening, reading, writing, grammar, and pronunciation.

Which Errors?	When?	How?
• impede comprehension • socially awkward • recently learned • habitual	• immediately • end of activity • separately	• recast • request clarification • repeat as question • echo up to error • metalinguistic clue

Figure 6.1: Dealing with Errors

Cultural Considerations

Finally, keep in mind that some students may come from cultures where being "wrong" brings shame. They may be hesitant to speak up for fear of making an error, and they may be even more hesitant after being corrected in public.

To deal with these issues, have a frank and open conversation about the students' attitudes toward errors and correction. Explain to them why errors are okay, why they should be corrected, and how you will help them correct their errors.

In addition, be careful not to correct some students more than others, as they may be sensitive to the underlying suggestion that they make more mistakes. If this is the case, consider additional private correction or delaying correction until later, when the source of the error is no longer obvious.

Finding the correct balance in giving feedback takes time and practice, but it is a balance worth finding and one that students will help us find. If we ask them how much and when they would like to be corrected and explain to them that our goal is to help them communicate effectively, we will likely find a balance that works reasonably well and can be tweaked over time.

REFLECTION AND DEVELOPMENT

We noted above that managing a class is often about making decisions: *What should we prepare in advance? How should we group the students and arrange the classroom? How do we make students feel welcome? How do we introduce an activity and give instructions? How long should the activity run, and how should we close it? What kind of feedback should we give, and when?*

We also noted that there are no simple answers to many of these questions; in fact, the answers depend on the circumstances of the class and the activities, and our ability to make effective choices will improve over time—but this improvement does not happen automatically. Rather, we improve most when we carefully reflect on the choices we've made and on the results of those choices, all while looking for better solutions. We can begin our reflection by asking a few basic questions after a given class:

- *Did the students feel welcome? Did they seem comfortable in class? What might be done differently next time?*
- *Did the students achieve the lesson's objectives? Were those objectives realistic? Were the activities effective in helping students progress toward the objectives? What might have hindered students' performance in class?*
- *What can be done to help those students who struggled more than the others?*
- *What else might improve the chances of students' success?*

We can also consider longer-term decisions and their effectiveness as they relate to our students' success:

- *Are the students achieving the long-term goals set for the course? Were those goals realistic to begin with? Were any lessons or activities ineffective as part of the long-term progression?*

- *Does the course include sufficient review of new material to help students retain it and use it naturally?*
- *What else can we do to help students reach the course goals?*

In the midst of this, we must also reflect on our own progress: *Are we becoming better teachers? What are our strengths and weaknesses, and how have they changed?* Reflection can be difficult, however, without a mirror—that is, without an accurate image of ourselves from an outside perspective. Here are a few ideas we might try:

- *Ask students for feedback*: Keeping in mind that students will generally say kind things whether we deserve them or not, we should ask open-ended, objective questions about what the students liked or disliked, what they found helpful or unhelpful, and so on. (Note that yes/no questions such as *Did you enjoy this activity?* are not at all helpful because students will usually say *yes* without thought or further feedback.)

    Also keep in mind that students are much more likely to give honest feedback when the focus is on their learning and not on our teaching, and that honest feedback gives us valuable insight into what works well in our classes and how we can improve future classes.
- *Ask colleagues for feedback*: It is very helpful to have a supervisor or another teacher observe our classes and comment on our methods and overall style, with specific suggestions for improvement.
- *Observe our own teaching*: Making and reviewing a video of our own teaching is often a very humbling experience as we discover our own quirks and oddities, but it is very useful.
- *Observe other teachers*: Noting how other teachers do things differently and discussing their choices can be very insightful, particularly if we make a list of new ideas we would like to try in our own classes.
- *Keep a teaching journal*: At the end of each class, record one positive element of the class (to do again), one negative element of the class (to change or avoid in the future), and perhaps a question or problem that needs an answer.
- *Continue learning*: Books, conferences, websites, and videos are all good sources of teaching tips and ideas that we can draw from. (They are most helpful when we keep an open mind and remember that we still have a lot to learn.)

OTHER BEST PRACTICES FOR THE CLASSROOM

There are numerous other techniques and hints that are always good to remember when teaching language. Here are a few basic ones to keep in mind:

- *Keep explanations short*: Use short sentences, and pause between sentences to allow students to process the information. Also use the whiteboard, handouts, and visuals to help students understand. Whenever possible, elicit the information from students so that it will be presented in their words and at their pace. (Remember, they are processing both the language and the content, so they can become overwhelmed very quickly.)
- *Learn to keep quiet*: The teacher's voice can often be a distraction rather than a help, so avoid running commentaries during student activities and resist the temptation to finish students' sentences for them. When they are stuck, simply give them a hint.
- *Check frequently for understanding*: Avoid asking simple questions such as *Do you understand?* because students will almost always answer *yes*. Instead, ask open-ended questions, such as *What was most difficult?* or have students give explanations back to you.
- *Revisit new material*: Use new grammar forms and vocabulary again in future classes to help students commit them to long-term memory.
- *Negotiate class rules with students*: For example, what are the consequences for using their first language during an activity when it is not allowed?
- *Limit first-language use*: If you speak the students' first language, do not use it, and refuse to "hear" it, unless there is good reason for it to be used. Encourage them to use the language they are learning as much as possible.
- *Avoid favouritism*: Don't focus on the student who is the brightest or the most interesting. Focus on the group, and pace the class according to their overall progress, not according to the pace of the faster students.

QUESTIONS FOR REVIEW

1. Why is it important to prepare instructions in advance?
2. Why might we use different student groupings and seating arrangements for different activities? What factors should we consider when deciding these?

3. How do we deal with different levels, different needs, and different interests in a class?
4. What are some ways we can improve student motivation and help students enjoy learning?
5. How might we introduce an activity? How might we transition between activities? Give examples.
6. How can we make instructions and explanations easier for students to understand?
7. What is the teacher's main role when running an activity (once the activity is running)?
8. What three questions should we ask ourselves when giving feedback to students? What are the options for each?
9. Why is it important, as teachers, to reflect on our teaching? How might we do this?
10. How do we get meaningful feedback from students who are always overly agreeable?

FURTHER READING

Gary Chambers's *Motivating Language Learners* (Multilingual Matters, 1999) discusses social and academic factors that influence students' attitudes and perceptions.

Carolyn Evertson and Carol Weinstein's *Handbook of Classroom Management: Research, Practice, and Contemporary Issues* (Lawrence Erlbaum Associates, 2006) provides a thorough overview of the field along with practical advice.

Janet Gianotti's *Voices of Experience: How Teachers Manage Student-Centered ESL Classes* (Michigan, 2015) provides practical advice on basic class management.

Jim Scrivener's *Classroom Management Techniques* (Cambridge, 2012) offers practical techniques for effective class management and avoiding problems.

Harry Wong and Rosemary Wong's *The Classroom Management Book* (Wong, 2018) offers very practical advice and suggestions for creating a successful learning environment.

NOTE

1. My explanation is influenced by the work of Marianne Celce-Murcia and Sharon Hilles in *Techniques and Resources in Teaching Grammar* (Oxford, 1988), 19–21.

CHAPTER 7
Assessment

Remember Monty? He was the entertainer and egotist masquerading as a teacher. Six months after he began to teach, some of his students loved his classes, but others were less enthusiastic—in fact, they began to question if his classes were right for them. Their main complaint was that although their listening skills had improved, their overall ability to communicate had not.

When confronted by his employer, Monty gave assurances that everything was fine, but when questioned further, he could speak only in general terms about his classes, and his claims of being an effective teacher and of his students' progress rang hollow when he could give no evidence of either.

Fortunately for Monty, his employer recognized certain strengths in him and decided to provide further training. The goal was simple: if Monty could learn to assess his students' progress and discover how he might better help them reach their learning goals, both he and his students would benefit.

ASSESSMENT: MORE THAN A MEASURE

The word *assessment* often brings to mind memories of tests, essays, exams, presentations, and projects, along with the resulting grades that brought relief, satisfaction, or disappointment. Assessment, however, is more than that. In chapter 2, for example, we noted that a needs assessment is a useful tool to help us discover who our students are, what they know, why they are in the class, and what they would like to learn. Moreover, we constantly assess our students' abilities and needs as we monitor their progress during class activities.

Assessment, then, shouldn't be limited to a formal measure of the students' progress at certain points in the course. Rather, it should be ongoing, and when used correctly, it serves as a tool that helps us at many steps along the learning process:

- It can measure students' overall proficiency in a language, or in a specific skill, at a particular point in time. (This type of assessment is often used for placing students in appropriate classes, or for standardized testing required for future academic study or job promotion.)
- It can measure achievement—the degree to which students have mastered recent material—so that a grade can be assigned (if required).
- It can help us determine students' progress since the previous assessment period and their progress in achieving the course goals.
- It can assess students' strengths and weaknesses in order to help instructors plan future classes that are relevant and effective.
- It can provide opportunities for students to demonstrate their skills and knowledge, thus increasing their level of engagement.
- It can provide a measure of the effectiveness of our teaching methods in a given class or over a longer period of time.

ASSESSMENT FOR LEARNING

We noted in previous chapters that a teacher should monitor students' progress during an activity to ensure they are moving toward achieving the activity's objectives. This type of monitoring is known as *assessment for learning*, or **formative assessment**. In effect, the teacher is regularly monitoring and assessing the students' performance in order to provide assistance and feedback, and to determine the next step in the learning process. By focusing on how to address students' strengths and weaknesses, formative assessment encourages and facilitates the learning process rather than simply measuring its outcome.

Formative assessment may be *informal* (general classroom activities monitored by the teacher) or *formal* (a test, an assignment, or a project that is graded), but it generally has certain features that make it an effective tool in any classroom:

- It is used during the learning process, not simply at the end of it.
- It clearly identifies what constitutes good performance in an activity or assignment.
- It includes timely, specific *qualitative feedback* (not simply a grade) that describes the student's strengths and explains what is required for the student to improve.

- The feedback is used to modify the teaching approach, the learning activities, or both to better suit the needs of the students.

In some types of language classes, informal formative assessment might be the only type of assessment used. A class of adults studying for personal reasons, for example, may never have tests or exams. Instead, the teacher will constantly monitor their progress in class and adjust the content, pace, and activities accordingly. However, because students like to "see" their progress, teachers may keep copies of students' work (or even videos of class activities) in order to compare them to work done at a later date. The results tend to be very enjoyable for both students and the teacher. (See "Portfolio-Based Assessment" later in this chapter.)

In an academic setting, however, teachers are generally required to submit a formal grade for each student in the class. Formative assessment in this case is likely to be more formal, including tests and assignments that are graded; nonetheless, the basic principles still apply: assessment occurs throughout the course and includes qualitative feedback to help the student and teacher make decisions about how the learning process should proceed from that point.

ASSESSMENT AS LEARNING

Closely related is the concept of *assessment as learning*; it can also be used for formative assessment, but in this case, the assessment is done by students themselves, mostly in the form of providing feedback to themselves and to each other. The teacher provides a supporting role, guiding students as they set personal goals, ask questions about their own learning, and choose next steps in their learning.

Consider, for example, the assessment of student presentations. The teacher might provide students with a detailed **rubric** to assess themselves as well as their peers; alternatively, the teacher and students might work together to create the rubric. Students could then use the feedback from the rubric to determine next steps in improving their presentation techniques.

The teacher's role here is key. Good feedback is likely only if the students are given the right training, tools, and guidance. (See "Using a Rubric" later in this chapter for more information.)

This combination of self-assessment and peer-assessment has two purposes: first, as the students assess their own learning, they are in fact continuing to learn the content or skill that is being assessed; second, they are also learning about learning, and (ideally) becoming reflective, self-monitoring, and more self-sufficient as learners.

ASSESSMENT OF LEARNING

In contrast to formative assessment is **summative assessment** (sometimes called *assessment of learning*). Summative assessment aims to provide an objective measure of what has been learned up to a given point in time. It is used at the end of the learning process, not during it.

In language classes, summative assessment may take the form of a test or exam that measures the students' grammar, vocabulary, and language skills. The best form of summative assessment for a given class depends on the objectives of that class. For example, if the general objective of a class is to improve students' speaking and listening skills, then an oral interview might be a valid form of assessment, but a grammar test would not be. However, if the objective of a class is to eliminate common grammatical errors, then a grammar test (written or spoken) that requires students to correct common grammatical errors might be a good option.

Summative assessment usually results in a score or grade that is meant to reflect the student's knowledge or ability. It sometimes includes qualitative feedback as well, but that feedback is often of limited use because it comes at the end of the learning process and the course is finished or the class is ready to move on to new material.

Summative assessment is often criticized for precisely that reason: it does too little, too late. It simply measures the results of the learning process without serving or informing that process. Nonetheless, summative assessment remains common in academic language classes where teachers employ traditional teaching methods and classes are too large to allow significant opportunity for the teacher to interact individually with students.

Achievement versus Proficiency

Summative assessment used in classes usually measures *achievement*; in other words, it measures the degree to which students have acquired the knowledge or skills taught in class.

In contrast, many standardized language tests measure *proficiency*, not achievement; in other words, they measure the ability to use language in real-world tasks by comparing the individual's performance to a set of predetermined criteria. Such tests are used in a variety of situations:

- Colleges and universities often require evidence of language proficiency as part of the application process. Standardized tests such as IELTS and TOEFL, offered by private companies, measure an individual's ability to use academic English; the results are given as an overall score as well as a score for each language skill.
- Companies sometimes require prospective employees to provide evidence of language proficiency, and in some cases require employees to meet certain language requirements as part of their promotion process. A standardized test such as TOEIC gives a score to reflect the individual's ability to use English in an international work environment.
- Certain schools, colleges, universities, companies, other organizations, and even countries have developed their own standardized language proficiency tests.

The latest generation of standardized proficiency tests are computer based or Internet based, and most measure the student's speaking, listening, reading, and writing skills, as well as their grasp of grammar and vocabulary. Such tests are a very efficient method of ranking the relative abilities of a large group of students. However, their accuracy in measuring such abilities is sometimes questioned, and they are frequently criticized for measuring a student's ability and readiness to take a test rather than the student's overall ability to use the language effectively. (See appendix 7A for a brief description of common standardized tests as well as a comparison of their scoring systems.)

PORTFOLIO-BASED ASSESSMENT

Portfolio-based assessment is meant to reflect students' progress over a period of time. Each student contributes work to a personal portfolio, which is essentially a collection of samples of the student's work. The samples chosen represent not only the student's best work but also the student's typical work, and they are arranged chronologically so that the portfolio gives an accurate and realistic impression of the student's progress, over time, in each language skill and content area.

Because the samples are chosen as representative of the student's work, the content of one student's portfolio may differ from that of another student's. In this way, assessment is customized for each student and gives a more thorough and accurate picture of the student's progress.

A portfolio may take the form of a file folder, a shoebox, a shelf or drawer, or an electronic folder on a computer, USB drive, or online storage provider.

Each student's portfolio should contain the student's original needs assessment (from the beginning of the course) and the student's original goal statement (a specific and realistic statement of what the student hopes to achieve in the course), as well as a collection of samples of the student's work, arranged chronologically, to demonstrate the student's progress in various skills or content areas. Such work might include the following:

- work that demonstrates speaking skills, such as audio or video recordings of the student's conversations, presentations, speeches, or other speaking activities
- work that demonstrates listening skills, such as completed worksheets from listening activities, or recordings of oral interaction in which the student must accurately comprehend another speaker in order to respond appropriately
- work that demonstrates reading skills, such as written answers to reading comprehension questions or written responses to assigned readings
- work that demonstrates writing skills, such as journal entries, written responses to class conversations or readings, creative writing, letters, or other written work
- work that demonstrates understanding of the content that was learned, such as reports, presentations, or tests

A portfolio should also include the instructor's qualitative feedback on these items, ideally in the form of rubrics that give specific details on the student's strengths and on how the student might improve.

The time required to collect and organize such content and feedback is, of course, significant, and in practice, portfolios are often weighted toward written work simply because it is easier to collect; nonetheless, with the popularity of smartphones and digital storage, making audio and video recordings of student work has never been easier.

Finally, portfolios may be either informal or formal. Informal portfolios contain samples of work from everyday class activities, while formal portfolios contain only work that was produced under specific, test-like conditions where the student must perform specific skill-based tasks at a specific time with no help from others. In either case, there are certain best practices that help ensure the success of this form of assessment:

- Samples of the student's work are chosen by the teacher and the student; the most useful samples provide clear evidence of the student's level of competence in a specific skill or content area.
- The activities on which the portfolio contents are based must be designed at an appropriate level for the student.
- The portfolio must be systematic and organized to show progress in each language skill and content area over a period of time.
- Portfolio content should be reviewed periodically by the teacher and the student together, reflecting on progress made and next steps.

This last point is key. If a student's portfolio is reviewed only at the end of the course, it becomes part of a summative assessment, but if it is reviewed regularly, it becomes part of the formative assessment of the student, thus providing valuable and timely feedback that can help the student improve.

Moreover, portfolios are useful not only for assessing progress over time, but also for helping students recognize their own progress by comparing recent work to earlier work, and for providing concrete evidence of progress when it is required by administrators, parents, or other interested parties.

ASSESSMENT TOOLS

Accurately assessing a student's level and progress needn't be a daunting task. In fact, most forms of assessment are very similar to the activities we regularly do in class, and the same principles apply:

- Always keep the course's long-term goals in mind. If the students have spent much of their time working to improve their reading comprehension, then their assessment should reflect this, and it should not assess skills that received little or no attention in class.
- The activity and its expectations must be set at the appropriate language level for the class. A speaking activity for a beginner class, for example, should not require complex sentences, and any oral or written prompts must also be at the appropriate level.
- For each activity, the student task should be carefully designed such that successful completion of the task will demonstrate achievement of the activity's objective. (See "Evaluating the Effectiveness of Activities" in chapter 5.)

These principles are closely related to the concept of **validity**, which is the degree to which an assessment tool (such as a test or assignment) accurately measures what it is intended to measure. Consider these examples of assessment tools that have low validity:

- a test that includes content not covered in the course
- a test that focuses on only the easiest parts of the course
- a multiple-choice test with poorly worded questions and answers
- any assignment that includes busywork but does not measure the degree to which the objectives of the course have been met

The problems here are obvious: the first test will likely result in lower scores even for students who know the course content well; the second test will likely result in relatively high scores even for students who do not know the course content well; the third test will likely confuse students, so once again even those who know the content well will likely not do well on the test; and the busywork assignment will simply frustrate everyone who realizes that it is a waste of time.

A second consideration when planning assessment is **reliability**—the degree to which the assessment produces the same results consistently. A multiple-choice test, for example, is likely to produce the same results regardless of who grades it, while an essay without clear criteria may earn very different grades from different teachers. Other factors can also affect reliability: for example, a listening test given in a quiet room will likely yield better results than the same test given in a room with significant background noise, and a test given mid-morning will likely yield better results than the same test given at the end of a long day.

We must also consider **fairness**, which is the degree to which the assessment is free from bias so that no student is disadvantaged because of their age, race, gender, religion, or any other factor that should not affect their performance. A test with very small print, for example, may disadvantage a student with poor eyesight or even a student who is prone to headaches, and a test that assumes certain cultural knowledge may disadvantage students who come from cultures that differ significantly.

Finally, when developing assessment tools, it is worth considering their **practicality**. Individual interviews, for example, might be practical in small classes but not in larger classes. Overall, both the number of assignments and the nature of those assignments may vary depending on the number of students in the class and the amount of time the teacher has for grading.

With these issues in mind, we should consider a few basic guidelines to help us develop effective assessment tools:

- Use the course goals and lesson objectives to establish what should be measured.
- Use clear, simple language in the instructions, and give an example (if appropriate).
- Double-check the details to ensure they accurately reflect what was taught in class.
- Write the test answers or the assignment in advance, or (even better) have a colleague do it, to check for possible problems.
- Establish clear criteria for subjective tests (such as writing and speaking tests) and, if possible, have those tests graded twice (by two qualified individuals using those criteria).

Assessing Language Skills and Subskills

Knowing that assessment tools are often the same as or variations of the activities we normally use in class, we can choose common but effective activities to assess students' language skills and subskills:

- *Speaking skills and pronunciation*: Use interviews, presentations, discussions, debates, or any other form of speaking activity that is appropriate for the level of the class and allows us to observe the students speaking. (See chapter 8 for more information about speaking activities.)
- *Listening skills*: Use dictation, dialogue, comprehension questions, or any other activity that is appropriate for the level of the class and requires students to demonstrate their comprehension of the listening material. (See chapter 9 for more information about listening activities.)
- *Reading skills*: Use comprehension questions, critical reading questions, or any activity that is appropriate for the level of the class and requires students to demonstrate their comprehension of the reading material. (See chapter 10 for more information about reading activities.)
- *Writing skills*: Have students write sentences, paragraphs, or longer works, depending on their level. Lower level students, for example, might write only a few sentences in response to oral or written prompts; high level students might write descriptive paragraphs or short essays. (See chapter 11 for more information about writing activities.)

- *Vocabulary*: Use matching exercises (matching each word with its definition, synonym, or antonym), true-or-false questions, or multiple-choice questions; at a more demanding level, have students write a definition for each item and use it in a sentence. (See chapter 12 for more information about vocabulary activities.)
- *Grammar*: Use fill-in-the-blank activities (where students supply the correct form of the verb, for example, or the correct article), error correction activities, sentence transformation activities (such as affirmative to negative, or present to past), or any other activities that target knowledge of specific grammar forms. At a more demanding level, require students to write their own sentences or paragraphs using a specific grammar form. (See chapters 3 and 14 for more information about grammar activities.)

Note that when assessing skills, the activity must be carefully designed to focus on the skill being assessed and avoid relying excessively on other skills. For example, a listening activity that requires students to read possible answers or write their own answers may in fact challenge (and test) the students' reading skills, writing skills, or ability to multi-task rather than their listening skills.

In addition, during the assessment, the instructor must have a way to accurately observe and record the students' performance, especially if there is no written record of the students' work (as in the case of speaking activities). The best methods involve the use of a rubric. (See "Using a Rubric" later in this chapter.)

Assessing Content

Note that when requiring students to demonstrate knowledge (or application of knowledge), we can choose to have students *identify* the answer (by choosing the right answer in matching, true-or-false, or multiple-choice activities) or *supply* the answer (by writing it), which is often more demanding. In either case, there are certain best practices worth noting, as well as potential issues to be aware of:

- *Matching*: Use this format for matching key terms or concepts with their definitions, synonyms, antonyms, examples, pictures, and so on. Each term should be a possible match (i.e., consistent in style and grammar) for each response to avoid giveaways, yet should have only one correct match.
    Note that when the terms are very different, the answers tend to be very obvious, so matching works best with terms that are similar

and easily confused; even then, though, matching a term with its response may indicate an association of ideas more than an understanding of them.

- *True or false*: Begin by writing all true statements. Each statement should contain only one key idea, and the language should be very clear. Then convert roughly half the statements to false by changing a key detail. The false detail in a statement should be obvious to anyone who knows the material, but it should sound plausible to anyone who does not.

    The problem with a true-or-false exercise is that anyone—even a person who knows nothing about the content—has a 50 percent chance of getting a question right, so its usefulness as a measure of knowledge remains questionable.

- *Fill in the blank*: When using this format for testing content, begin by writing clear statements, each of which focuses on one key detail; then replace the key detail with a blank. (Be sure the detail is indeed a key one that students are expected to know, not a random, trivial one.) Double-check to ensure that the statement provides sufficient context to elicit the answer and that only one answer correctly completes the statement.

    Note that while fill-in-the-blank exercises are useful to test students' recall of specific terms or details, they do not measure overall understanding of the content.

- *Multiple choice*: As much as possible, begin with questions, not incomplete statements. Then write one correct answer and three or four incorrect answers, known as distractors. The correct answer should be obvious to anyone who knows the material; the distractors should be plausible to anyone who does not. Also, to minimize strategic guessing, try to make all answers similar in length and style, and be sure to randomize the order of the answers.

    Multiple-choice questions, when carefully designed, can measure not only recall of information but also application—that is, they can require the student to use the information to discover the correct answers. However, guessing is still a factor, and good readers tend to be good guessers.

- *Short answer*: These questions require a short, factual, written response, and the answers should demonstrate the students' knowledge and writing skills. The questions must be very clear and specific to ensure the student knows what is expected, and the teacher should consider using a rubric to ensure consistency in grading.

Short-answer questions may seem to be a more accurate measure of understanding because guessing is minimized, but because they often test basic knowledge, students may simply memorize specific answers without fully understanding them. Questions that require application of knowledge, then, are superior to those that require only the knowledge itself.

When designing any type of question, the wording is key. On the one hand, the language used in the questions (and possible answers, if applicable) should be familiar to the students, and never confusing. On the other hand, it should not be too close to the wording in their readings lest the students answer by simply associating key phrases in the questions with similar phrases in the reading, without actually understanding the content.

USING A RUBRIC

Any form of assessment, no matter how well designed, is fair and reasonable only if the expectations are made clear to the students and if the instructor assesses the students' work according to criteria that support those expectations. For this reason, many instructors develop rubrics for their class assignments, presentations, or other activities that serve as a form of assessment.

A rubric is a tool that lists the criteria that will be used in assessing the students' work. It serves a variety of purposes:

- When given to students in advance of an activity or assignment, a rubric communicates the instructor's expectations, thereby increasing the students' chances of success.
- When used to provide feedback as part of the instructor's assessment, a rubric saves time, as the instructor does not have to rewrite frequently used comments each time.
- If a grade is required, a rubric helps determine what grade is appropriate.

A typical rubric is a chart. The header of the chart lists the quality ratings, such as *Excellent, Good, Satisfactory, Poor*; or *A, B, C, D/F*; or some other descriptors. The left column identifies the criteria used to assess the students' work. The rest of the chart, then, provides descriptors of each criteria at each level of quality (see table 7.1).

Table 7.1: Rubric for an Expository Essay (High-Intermediate Level)

	EXCELLENT	GOOD	SATISFACTORY	POOR
Thesis and Outline	The essay has a clear, focused thesis that answers the question and a strong outline to support it. It is logically organized and easy to follow.	The essay has a thesis that addresses the question reasonably well, but both the thesis and the essay outline could be better focused to address the question.	The essay addresses the question in a general way but is not sufficiently focused. The thesis and/or the outline are in need of revision.	The essay is related to the topic but does not address it directly and wanders in various directions. Overall, it does not really answer the question.
Development	Shows a strong understanding of the topic and thoroughly addresses the details of the question.	Addresses the topic well and answers the question, but at times the focus is too broad and lacks sufficient detail.	Broadly relevant but often unfocused. Argument is generally correct but not clearly or sufficiently explained.	Poor understanding or limited engagement of the topic. Lacks a cohesive explanation.
Closing	Closes with a succinct, thoughtful reflection and does not merely repeat the details of the introduction.	Closes with a clear summary in fresh wording, but ends on a bit of a dry note.	Gives a sense of closure but largely repeats the details of the introduction.	Ends abruptly. Feels incomplete.
Writing	A pleasure to read. Paragraphs are unified, coherent, well developed. Sentences are clear, logical, and free from errors.	Paragraphs are well developed but at times lack focus. Sentences are generally clear, though with some errors.	Some paragraphs lack focus or development. Sentences contain some errors in grammar or logic. Meaning is at times unclear.	Paragraphs lack focus or development. Sentences contain numerous errors in grammar or logic. Meaning is often unclear.

The steps involved in creating a rubric are straightforward:

1. Identify the objectives that are being measured, and use them to determine the specific criteria.
2. Create the chart using the criteria and the quality ratings as side and top headers, respectively.
3. Write a descriptor for each criteria at each level of quality. (Note that the levels are relative in most cases; excellent work in a beginner class, for example, looks very different from excellent work in an intermediate class. In every case, we must determine what "excellent" looks like for that particular level.)
4. Reconsider and, as necessary, revise the descriptors after using the rubric, always aiming to make it better.

Note that the rubric in table 7.1 uses only broad categories as criteria. It could be further developed to give more specific feedback: writing, for example, could be broken down into a number of more specific criteria such as paragraph structure, sentence structure, fluency, spelling, voice, and so on.

There are also times when a much simpler rubric will suffice, such as when assessing a student's overall speaking ability (see table 7.2).

Table 7.2: A Simple Rubric for Speaking

OVERALL SPEAKING LEVEL	
5	Uses natural language; few errors; communicates clearly; minimal hesitation.
4	Uses longer sentences; engages in conversation, though with hesitancy; some errors.
3	Uses short sentences with frequent errors; communicates basic meaning.
2	Uses short phrases to answer basic questions; often difficult to understand.
1	Uses yes/no, single words, occasional phrases; minimal communication.

REMEMBERING THE PURPOSE

And Monty? After six months of providing entertainment in his classes and one very serious conversation with his employer, he finally realized that there is much more to teaching language and that his students deserved better. He began to learn about assessment and to meet regularly with two of his senior colleagues to discuss what worked best for them.

Over time, learning about assessment caused Monty to reconsider his teaching methods. With guidance from his colleagues, he assessed his students' needs, set clear goals based on those needs, and redesigned his courses to ensure there was clear progression toward the overall goals; and, of course, he also added various forms of assessment to measure that progress—as well as his own.

☞ *Consider: How might thinking about assessment make us not only better assessors but better teachers overall?*

QUESTIONS FOR REVIEW

1. In what ways can assessment provide more than just a measure of student achievement?
2. How does formative assessment differ from summative assessment? What advantages does formative assessment offer the student?
3. In what situations might standardized test scores be required?
4. How might assessment be both formative and informal? When might such assessment be appropriate?
5. What are the advantages of portfolio assessment? What might make it challenging?
6. How can forms of formative assessment and summative assessment both contribute to portfolio assessment?
7. Why are clear, measurable objectives (for the course, the lesson, and the activity) essential to keep in mind when planning any type of assessment?
8. Explain how well-made activities have their own built-in assessment.
9. What does it mean to say that an assessment tool is valid, reliable, fair, and practical?
10. What are the advantages (for students and teachers) of using a rubric?

FURTHER READING

Lyle Bachman and Barbara Damböck's *Language Assessment for Classroom Teachers* (Oxford, 2018) is a guide to developing and using language assessment tools.

Margo Gottlieb's *Assessing English Language Learners: Bridges to Educational Equity* (Corwin, 2016) is a thorough overview of assessment in the language classroom.

Tricia Hedge's *Teaching and Learning in the Language Classroom* (Oxford, 2000) includes a helpful chapter on "Classroom Assessment" by Pauline Rea-Dickins.

Arthur Hughes's *Testing for Language Teachers* (Cambridge, 2002) is a practical guide to testing in the language classroom.

PART II
TEACHING LANGUAGE SKILLS AND SUBSKILLS

CHAPTER 8
Teaching Speaking

When Jane first began teaching English overseas, she was excited to learn that her young adult students had already studied English for six to eight years in school, and she looked forward to having many conversations with them and learning about them. After her first few classes, however, Jane mentioned to her colleagues that she was surprised how little her students could say; they had an extensive vocabulary, a good grasp of grammar, and decent reading skills—but they were hesitant to speak at all, and when they did, it was in a low voice and halting English.

Jane had discovered what many new language teachers discover: students often have the vocabulary and grammar necessary for basic conversation in English, but they lack the fluency and confidence needed to speak effectively. Simply put, they have a strong knowledge of the language, but they've had very little practice speaking it.

"CONVERSATIONAL" ENGLISH?

Many private language schools and volunteer organizations offer classes in "conversational English" for students who wish to improve their speaking and listening. These classes are usually smaller (5 to 12 students) and loosely structured, often following a theme-based textbook or simply discussing a variety of topics suggested by either the teacher or the students themselves. The classes may include written work and even a bit of grammar, but the focus is on authentic oral practice—in other words, conversation.

Conversational English classes often use a variation of communicative teaching methods (those that emphasize language functions and authentic communication—see chapter 3). Ads for foreign-language teachers often emphasize the apparent "ease" of teaching such classes. After all, what could be so difficult about having a conversation with students?

Experienced teachers, however, know that if we wish to empower students to communicate effectively in a variety of unrehearsed situations, we need a carefully planned approach to speaking classes, resulting in a more enjoyable, successful experience for both teachers and students.

THE TEACHER AS LANGUAGE COUNSELLOR

One of the challenges of speaking classes is getting students to actually speak. Many students have previously studied English in schools where they were expected to listen and study, not speak, so they may not be accustomed to speaking up in class. They may lack confidence in their ability to speak English and may even be embarrassed by what they perceive as their poor pronunciation or poor overall English. A large part of the teacher's job, then, is providing comfortable, meaningful opportunities for students to speak, and helping students overcome their reluctance to speak.

Like most people, students are more likely to speak freely with people they know and are comfortable with. For this reason, it is important to get to know our students and to encourage them to get to know one another. In new classes, get-to-know-you activities can help break the proverbial ice; in later classes, encouraging meaningful conversations in small groups will help further develop the students' confidence. (Note that speaking in small groups is less threatening than speaking to the larger class and also allows each student more opportunities to speak.)

The teacher's role in creating an encouraging atmosphere is particularly important. A teacher seen as a strict authoritarian is likely to stifle conversation, whereas a teacher seen more as a language counsellor—a positive, supportive mentor guiding students through the process of language acquisition—will help create what students see as a safe environment for speaking up. The teacher's authority, then, generally remains in the background as they earn the students' respect by demonstrating an authentic desire to see students succeed. This last point is key: if students understand that the teacher's priority is to help them improve their English, and if they realize that they might even enjoy doing it, then they are much more likely to do what is required of them, and their anxiety about speaking in class will begin to fade. In this way, teachers help build not only the students' *fluency* but also their *confidence* in their ability to speak.

Students' hesitancy to speak can itself be a topic of conversation. In a particularly quiet class, have students work in small groups to list reasons why language learners don't like to speak in class, and then address each reason and encourage students to take small steps toward speaking regularly in class.

Finally, in classes where students are particularly timid about using their voices and perhaps embarrassed by their pronunciation, we can use oral reading activities to build their confidence. When reading aloud, students do not have to make choices about grammar and vocabulary, so they can focus on their speaking (i.e., their performance), and as teachers we can focus our feedback on pronunciation and fluency. Over time, students not only improve but also get used to hearing their own voices speaking English in front of others, and they become more willing to speak up.

✓ Teachers help students develop not only fluency but also confidence.

TOPICS AND TASKS

Some students will speak at least briefly on almost any topic, but most students are much more likely to speak up when the topic interests them and is framed in a way that captures their attention. A topic that is too broad, too obscure, or not relevant is likely to produce a brief response or two and a lot of silence.

The range of topics for a speaking class is almost limitless, so there is no need to force unpopular topics on our students. Everyone has something they like to talk about, whether it is news, sports, hobbies, families, community events, ongoing public issues or debates, or anything else that comes to mind. In fact, there are just four guidelines to remember when developing effective topics:

- *Keep it interesting*: Discovering what our students are interested in might take a bit of detective work. Simply asking them *What's new?* might be a place to start, but asking specific questions might reveal more: *What is your opinion of … What do you think of … Do you agree that …* As we get to know our students, we will have a better idea of what interests them, and if we understand our students' first language, we might consider eavesdropping on their conversations as they enter the classroom to discover what they normally talk about. Finally, we must also keep in mind that what interests us may not interest them—and in this case, it is their opinion that counts.
- *Keep it relevant*: Talking about apartment hunting might be relevant to recent immigrants who are searching for better accommodation, but it

is largely pointless for immigrants who have long settled into their own houses. We must ask ourselves, then, what topics are relevant to our students, and we should choose topics that all students can relate to. Once again, to do this effectively, we must get to know our students, perhaps through general conversations about their day, their lives, and so on. Such conversations are a great way to begin class.

- *Keep it familiar*: The topic should be reasonably familiar to the students, or at least easy to talk about. New teachers often fall into the trap of introducing topics that are new and particularly challenging for students. Such topics are fine for a content-based class, but in a speaking class, the topic should be one that students can easily talk about without getting bogged down in content. After all, the objective of a speaking activity is to build students' confidence and fluency, not to introduce new content.
- *Keep it appropriate*: Every teacher occasionally has at least one student who wishes to stretch the boundaries of what is appropriate, whether it is the eight-year-old boy who brings up certain body functions, the middle-aged man who likes to talk about young ladies he has encountered, or the woman who speaks negatively about "the lower classes" or other ethnic groups. In such cases, it is best to deliberately steer the conversation in another direction before it goes too far, and if necessary, to speak individually to the student about what is appropriate and what is not. Thankfully, most students, regardless of age or background, have enough sense to know and respect such boundaries, and they will appreciate our delicate handling of those students whose poor judgment and questionable social skills require a little extra grace. That said, it is possible for a topic to be appropriate and yet controversial, and such topics often lead to the liveliest, most interesting classroom conversations.

Beyond choosing a topic, it is important to limit the topic by giving it a particular focus, either as a specific question or as a clear task. Climate change might be a significant concern to a group of environmentally conscious students, for example, but students are more likely to be engaged by a specific question or series of questions: *What can we do to limit our impact on the environment?* or *Do you think climate change is caused by human activity, or is it just a natural phenomenon?*

Even better, consider framing the topic as a task in order to generate better discussion among students. Simply asking general questions about climate change, for example, will likely produce a few short answers and little else, but

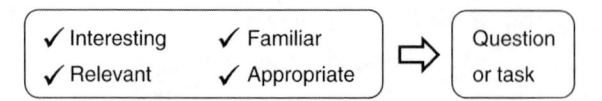

Figure 8.1: Topics and Tasks

asking students to work in small groups to produce a list of five ways they can reduce their own carbon footprint will likely lead to much more discussion.

COMMON SPEAKING ACTIVITIES

There are two general types of speaking activities: controlled and authentic. Controlled speaking activities are essentially oral drills that require students to practice grammar or pronunciation. These drills are repetitive and require instant correction, and their aim is to improve the students' accurate use of particular grammatical forms or particular sounds or sound patterns. (For more information on controlled activities, review "Drilling It In: The Audio-Lingual Method" in chapter 3.)

Because controlled speaking activities have more to do with grammar or pronunciation than actual communication, we will focus in this chapter on authentic speaking activities—those that develop the students' ability to communicate naturally and effectively in a variety of situations.

Authentic speaking activities involve real communication: students decide what to say and how to say it, and the conversation is not preplanned or contrived. Most authentic speaking activities are variations of conversation and discussion, but because we all like variety, and because what appeals to one class may not appeal to another, it is good to have a collection of suitable activities to draw from. Here are a few of the more commonly used ones:

- *General discussion*: When properly facilitated, class discussion serves well as a speaking activity. The activity should be framed with a lead-in that generates interest and gets students thinking about the topic and with a closing that doesn't leave students hanging. It may include preparation time to allow students to look up needed vocabulary or to build confidence by comparing ideas in pairs before speaking to the larger group; if the topic is not familiar to everyone, it may be necessary to have one or more students summarize the issue for the class in order to bring everyone up to speed.

A good discussion activity also provides "talk time" for everyone, not just for the stronger students, and it is often the teacher's role to ensure this by indirectly managing the conversation—that is, to subtly steer and assist the conversation without interrupting the flow. The teacher may also take an opposing position in the discussion just to ensure the interaction remains lively, though the vast majority of the speaking should come from the students themselves, and the teacher may need to learn how to keep quiet.

- *Pyramid discussions*: Consensus is often reached through discussion, or in this case, multiple discussions. For example, students may work in pairs to list the five best restaurants in their city: first they define their criteria, then they discuss their choices, and then they make their list along with the reasons for their choices. Each pair will then join another and discuss their lists (and reasons) until they agree on the top five. Each group of four will then join with another, and so on, until eventually the whole class comes to a consensus. (Note that at each step they must be able to explain their choices, not simply list them.)

- *Debate*: Sometimes students prefer a more formal, structured form of discussion in which they take opposing views on an issue. The topic is chosen and phrased by the teacher (though possibly with student input) as a clear statement of opinion with which one side agrees and the other disagrees. (The sides are usually assigned more or less arbitrarily, regardless of students' actual beliefs about the topic.)

    Debates often generate better discussion than free conversation because each student is required to speak and is given an allotment of uninterrupted time, and all students have the added incentive of wanting to do well in the debate. It is often the case that students who are quiet in class are surprisingly effective debaters.

    Note, however, that debates can be stressful for some students. Having students work in teams and giving them adequate time to prepare tends to help, especially if the topic is difficult. That said, some classes may not be ready for a debate.

- *Anecdotes and stories*: Almost everyone loves telling stories to a captive audience. Sometimes stories arise spontaneously as part of a conversation, but often they must be elicited with questions such as *What is the most embarrassing situation you have been in?* or *What is the most dangerous situation you have been in?* Such questions will often arise from a related activity, though at the lower levels, students will generally need time to decide which story to tell and how to tell it, so give the question well in advance (preferably in an earlier class for students who prefer lots of time to prepare) whenever possible.

- *Retelling the story*: Students are asked to retell a story in their own words. Such stories may come from newspaper articles, websites, or other sources of interest to the students.
- *Simulation*: Sometimes speaking practice can take the form of rehearsal for real-life situations, such as a job interview, a doctor's appointment, or checking in at a hotel. The process begins by preparing students for what to expect, including key vocabulary and phrases that they are likely to encounter or need, and possibly a model dialogue or demonstration. Students then act out the scenario while the teacher takes notes on what was done well and on what they might improve or add. The objective, of course, is for students to be able to successfully navigate the same situation in real life.
- *Role play*: A related but more creative activity, role-playing gives students the chance to take on a new character (role) in a particular situation and act accordingly. The use of roles often helps students overcome some of the shyness and general reluctance that hold them back from speaking in class.

  A good role play activity begins with specific roles prepared in advance and distributed to students on handouts or role cards. A role card may contain only basic roles and tasks, or it may include detailed descriptions (name, job, gender, age, appearance, character, interests, and so on). The best roles often include personality traits that the students must adopt, and the best role plays include conflict, ensuring that the resulting drama will be lively and entertaining.

  When running a role play, be sure students understand the concept (if it is their first time), possibly by demonstrating one. Then, when distributing roles, be sure the situation is clear, and give students ample time to digest their roles and prepare their lines, assisting them as necessary. Remind them that when they get up to perform, they must do so without notes—after all, they are practicing authentic interaction (even if in imaginary scenes), not reading.

  When students become comfortable with role plays, consider adding a surprise character midway through the performance of a role play, just to stir things up a bit.
- *Small-group planning activities*: Students often like to work in small groups to complete certain tasks such as planning a holiday or a party.

The particular task should be one that requires a lot of discussion in order to make choices. Materials and information needed for the task can be provided in class or assigned in advance as homework.
- *Surveys/interviews*: Students develop a list of questions (as a survey, questionnaire, or interview, usually on a specific topic) to ask other students and then report their results in groups or to the class.
- *Describing and drawing*: Students work in pairs. One student describes (but does not show) a picture to another student who draws the picture as it is described.
- *Finding the differences*: Students work in pairs. Each student has a picture that differs slightly from their partner's picture. They take turns describing (but not showing) the pictures to one another until they have noted all the differences.
- *Games, board games, puzzles, and similar activities*: Various other activities may also be suitable for a speaking class provided they require fairly constant verbal interaction from the students.

☞ Try: Choose three conversation topics and frame them as open-ended discussion questions; choose three debate topics and frame them as one-sided statements that students would argue for or against; and choose a topic for role play and develop the scenario and roles (using the role play in appendix 8B as an example).

NECESSARY SUBSKILLS

Earlier in this chapter, we noted the importance of fluency and confidence, but certain subskills are also necessary for successful speaking:

- *Accuracy*: Speakers need reasonably accurate vocabulary, grammar, and pronunciation in order to make themselves understood. (See chapters 12, 14, and 16, respectively.)
- *Levels of formality*: Students should be made aware of the differences between formal and informal language. For example, formal language generally uses standard vocabulary (not slang or texting-style language), indirect requests (not commands), and particular forms. These are best taught by giving examples that use different levels of formality for a particular language function. Consider, for example, various ways of greeting someone and how they would be appropriate (or not) in different contexts: *Wassup? Hi, how are you? Nice to meet you. It is a pleasure to meet*

you. (For more on language functions, see "CLT Lessons" in chapter 3 and "Language Functions" in chapter 18.)
- *Politeness*: Closely related to levels of formality is the concept of politeness, which can differ widely from one culture to another and often determines the way we speak. (See "Politeness" under "Cultural Norms: Social Interaction" in chapter 18.)
- *Discourse markers*: Students need to know conventions, including particular words or phrases, that are used to indicate the speaker's attitude or intention. (See appendix 8A.)
- *Cultural awareness*: In addition to understanding the **cultural norms** of formality, politeness, and the use of discourse markers, students need to know the cultural rules of conversation, such as those for turn taking and interrupting, and other aspects of culture that help determine how people interact. (See chapter 18.)

These subskills are necessary to produce spoken language that sounds natural, but they are often particularly complex and difficult to master. The first step is becoming aware of them, generally through class activities that provide both explanation and practice. We can then draw attention to them in regular class activities that involve speaking.

To really master speaking subskills, however, students often need extensive exposure to them, particularly through extensive listening. Movies, television, videos, and audio programs that authentically model specific subskills are particularly helpful, especially if students already understand and have practiced them. (See chapter 9 for more information on extensive listening.)

THE TEACHER'S ROLE

The teacher's job is to set up and facilitate the activity—and to avoid talking too much. In fact, the main purpose of the teacher's voice in a speaking lesson is to encourage others to speak. Beyond that, the teacher serves in a supporting role.

Setting Up

Launching an activity may be as simple as asking an open-ended question to begin a discussion, but students tend to respond better to something that grabs their attention. A discussion on a current controversy, for example, might begin with a provocative question as well as a picture or headline from a newspaper. Be creative—the stronger the start, the sooner the conversation will take off.

Setting up a debate or role play requires preparation before class. Debate topics must be chosen and worded carefully to ensure they are appropriate to the level and interests of the class, and the details of role plays (characters, situation) should be carefully developed and prepared on role cards. Similarly, small-group planning activities may require substantial set-up, particularly if we need to gather information and prepare handouts in advance.

Set-up also includes making decisions about grouping. In a discussion, do we have students talk in small groups in order to give everyone more chances to speak? For a role play, do we have each group perform for the whole class, or just for certain other groups? Such decisions are often based on the size of the class and our objective for the activity, but we should always keep in mind that having multiple small groups work simultaneously can give each student more opportunities to speak.

Managing and Facilitating

Part of the teacher's job is to keep the activity flowing smoothly. If the conversation is dull, the teacher may need to stir things up in order to get students speaking, or if students are struggling to express themselves, the teacher may need to provide assistance with vocabulary, pronunciation, or phrasing. However, if students are simply shy, the teacher may need to prompt them and then keep quiet until the students speak. (Again, always keep in mind that the teacher's voice should be used primarily to encourage or lead others to speak, not to fill in all the gaps in the conversation.)

Some students may simply need encouragement, whether an affirming nod with an "uh huh" or a brief word of agreement. Other students may say very little until they are asked specific questions that draw out their opinions or encourage them to elaborate on a previous response.

Timing is also an issue that teachers must be concerned with. If a conversation planned for 20 minutes has really taken off and shows no sign of abating after 30 minutes, the teacher must decide whether to let it continue or signal the approaching end with an interjection such as "Two more minutes!" In contrast, an activity that is slowly dying long before its suggested expiration date may need to be put out of its misery with a quick comment such as "Okay, let's move on."

Giving Feedback and Correction

As we discussed in chapter 6, effective feedback, including correction, is necessary if our students are to improve, and we may have to explain to students that errors are okay and corrections should be seen as helpful—even during a conversation.

Whenever possible, help students correct their own errors during conversation, and use correction to empower them to speak correctly, not to have them feel bad about errors. At other times, such as during debates or role plays, do not interrupt the activity; instead, make a list of errors that need to be corrected and address them at the next natural pause or at the end of the activity. (For more information on what to correct, when to correct, and how to correct, see "Dealing with Errors" in chapter 6.)

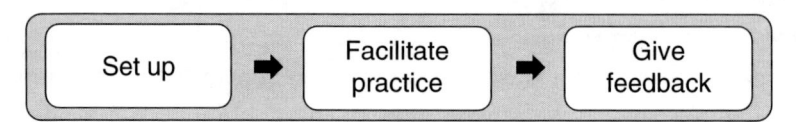

Set up → Facilitate practice → Give feedback

Figure 8.2: The Teacher's Role

INTEGRATING SKILLS: SPEAKING IN VARIOUS CONTEXTS

Jane began building her students' fluency and confidence by providing them with opportunities to speak in a variety of activities, particularly in small groups. She soon realized, however, that her class should not become just "conversation practice," using what students already know; rather, she would need to develop a long-term strategy for overall improvement, integrating all areas of language learning—speaking, listening, reading, writing, pronunciation, vocabulary, and grammar—even while focusing on speaking more than the other areas until students became more comfortable with it.

Jane also realized that students got much-needed practice in speaking not only from designated activities but during other types of activities as well. Students could answer questions as part of a lead-in to another activity, or they could explain instructions to one another. In fact, over time Jane learned to use her voice primarily to encourage others to speak, regardless of the activity, so that her students had regular interaction throughout the class.

THE REWARD

Overall, speaking classes can be particularly rewarding because they give us a chance to get to know our students on a more personal level. Moreover, students themselves tend to enjoy speaking classes because developing self-expression feels good—we are, after all, social creatures by nature, and learning a new language broadens our ability to experience the lives and dreams of those around us.

QUESTIONS FOR REVIEW

1. Why do many language learners lack the fluency and confidence necessary to speak effectively?
2. What do we mean when we say that a language teacher often acts as a language counsellor?
3. What are the key criteria when choosing a topic for a speaking class?
4. What makes a speaking activity "authentic"? Why is this important?
5. What is a pyramid discussion?
6. How does simulation differ from role play?
7. What kind of preparation might be necessary for various types of speaking activities?
8. How do classroom set-up and student grouping affect a speaking activity? Give examples.
9. Why are feedback and correction important during/after speaking activities?
10. How can speaking practice be integrated into every lesson, even when other skills are the focus?

FURTHER READING

Nick Bilbrough's *Dialogue Activities: Exploring Spoken Interaction in the Language Class* (Cambridge, 2007) provides more than one hundred speaking-related activities for the classroom.

Keith Folse's *The Art of Teaching Speaking: Research and Pedagogy for the ESL/EFL Classroom* (Michigan, 2006) provides a collection of common but useful tips and ideas.

Alan Maley and Alan Duff's *Drama Techniques: A Resource Book of Communication Activities for Language Teachers* (Cambridge, 2005) provides ideas and activities for oral fluency practice.

Paul Seligson's *Helping Students to Speak* (Richmond, 2007) provides practical advice on getting students to speak up in the classroom.

Scott Thornbury's *How to Teach Speaking* (Pearson, 2005) gives very practical advice.

Penny Ur's *Discussions and More: Oral Fluency Practice in the Classroom* (Cambridge, 2014) includes both theory and a wide variety of classroom activities.

CHAPTER 9
Teaching Listening Comprehension

Eryk was frustrated. He had studied English for more than ten years, he had always earned top grades, and his teachers told him his English was excellent; yet on his first visit to Canada and the United States, he often couldn't understand what people around him were saying. Sometimes he caught key words and could guess the meaning, but even then he was unsure; at other times he heard expressions that simply made no sense to him. What frustrated him most, however, was that much of the English spoken around him should have been familiar to him—in fact, if it were spoken slowly or written down, he could understand it perfectly—but when spoken naturally, it sounded completely foreign to him.

LISTENING GAPS

Having difficulty understanding spoken language is not unusual for language learners, particularly if they have had little exposure to it. Students in many countries, for example, study English in school, but they spend much of their effort on grammar, reading, and writing, and very little time listening to English spoken fluently. As a result, their listening skills lag behind their other language skills.

Consider that when listening to someone speak in a language we know well, such as our native language, we can often guess the end of a sentence before it is spoken. Moreover, if certain words are spoken softly and we don't quite catch them, we can often guess them from the context. In fact, we tend to focus on the more important words (especially nouns and verbs), and we can often understand the meaning of the sentence even if some of the less important words are missing.

Filling in these gaps is a natural part of using language, but it is a skill developed over time as a language is mastered. For language learners, this skill is largely undeveloped in their adopted language, so they are unable to fill in many of the gaps and much less likely to be able to guess the meaning of what is spoken.

These gaps in a learner's comprehension are usually caused by one or more of the following common problems:

- *Lack of vocabulary*: If a language learner does not know one or more of the words spoken, the entire utterance may be incomprehensible. In fact, even if the word is not particularly important to the meaning of the sentence, the learner may miss the overall meaning of the utterance because of a fixation on the unknown word.
- *Unfamiliar pronunciation, stress, or intonation*: Students are often surprised to discover that native speakers generally do not pronounce words the way they are taught in school. In many cases, the difference may be one of accent, particularly if the students have not been exposed to the wide variety of accents for spoken English. The difference may also lie in the fact that a word's pronunciation may change depending on the words surrounding it. In particular, unstressed words or syllables are often devoiced or minimized in a sentence; consider, for example, the word *to* in a typical sentence: *I went to the park yesterday.* In still other cases, the student may not be familiar with the proper word **stress** or sentence stress, or may find that the words seem to blend together when spoken quickly; and even if the literal meaning is obvious, the intended meaning (such as in the case of sarcasm) may be missed.
- *Inaccurate focus*: Language learners often strive to catch every sound and every word in order to construct the meaning of what is being said, but their intense focus on the details actually causes them to miss the overall meaning. This type of focus is known as **bottom-up listening**, and it needs to be combined with **top-down listening**, which draws from prior knowledge and available context in order to understand the overall idea of what is being said, even when not every detail is understood.
- *Listener fatigue*: Those who have spent more than a few minutes conversing in a language they are not strong in know that it requires intense concentration. As mental exhaustion begins to set in, their overall understanding begins to decline.

Filling in the Gaps

Helping language learners fill in the gaps in their listening takes time, patience, and practice, but we can begin by giving them a few helpful hints:

- *Listening is improved along with other skills*: Given the importance of vocabulary, grammar, and pronunciation when listening for meaning, students may need to be reminded that these skills should all be developed.
- *Make use of the available context for clues*: Just as we do in real life, students should use whatever clues are available to predict what the conversation will be about. (Teachers, then, should provide such context in a way that mimics real-life listening. See "Adding Authenticity to Listening Materials and Tasks" later in this chapter.)
- *Successful comprehension does not require total comprehension*: In everyday listening in our first language, we often guess the meaning of the whole using the parts we hear and understand; students should strive to do the same.

Then comes practice, and lots of it. In fact, a big part of the teacher's job is to provide meaningful opportunities for students to listen to the spoken language and respond to it in a way that demonstrates successful comprehension. Over time and with sufficient practice, students will learn to focus on the important words in a sentence and improve their comprehension, and they will become less fatigued when listening for longer periods.

INTENSIVE LISTENING PRACTICE

In everyday life, we listen in order to understand something. Such listening is replicated in language classes through intensive listening practice, also known as *listening comprehension practice*. This type of practice often targets weaknesses common among language learners in order to prepare them for real-life listening.

Intensive listening activities consist of listening material that the students must listen to and a task that the students must complete in response to what they have heard. It is essential that both the listening material and the task are chosen or designed carefully in order to provide the kind of practice that students need.

Listening Materials

There are a number of considerations when choosing or designing listening materials:

- *Topic*: As with topics for any kind of lesson, choose one that is interesting and relevant to the students.
- *Live or recorded*: "Live" listening material is spoken by the teacher, a student, or a guest, and it provides listening practice that is interactive, authentic, and natural. It can also be adjusted on the fly to increase or decrease the level of challenge. However, live performances are limited by the class situation, including the number of available speakers.

    Recorded listening material may be authentic (a podcast, online video, or radio program, for example), pre-made (often packaged with a text), or custom made (by the teacher). Recordings have the advantage of offering a variety of speakers and a variety of accents, and they are available for reuse without additional preparation or rehearsal. They are also easily replayed multiple times, which is essential in many listening activities. However, they lack facial expressions and gestures, which are an important part of authentic communication—though recorded video can largely overcome this problem.
- *Language level*: In most language activities, we aim for a level just above where the student is proficient. The same is often true in listening activities, but we can also use material at a significantly higher level as long as the task level is realistic. An authentic radio or television program, for example, is challenging for even higher-level students, but if our task requires only partial understanding, then it is both reasonable and realistic—in fact, it is not unlike everyday listening situations for a language learner.
- *Length*: Keep recordings short. Even 30 seconds can contain a lot of information to absorb, and two minutes should be considered an absolute maximum. Anything longer should be broken up and spread over multiple activities (and possibly multiple classes).

Listening Tasks

A listening task is something the student does while listening, and a good task demonstrates successful comprehension. In other words, the students should not be able to complete the task without successfully comprehending the listening material. Common listening tasks include the following:

- *Listen to a conversation between Jack and Tina. What are they talking about?*
- *Listen to the conversation and answer the questions.*

- *Listen to the conversation and complete the chart/lists/diagram/map/picture.*
- *Listen to the conversation and mark the statements true (T) or false (F). Be ready to explain why they are true or false.*
- *Listen to the conversation and correct the statements.*
- *Listen to the conversation and fill in the blanks in the sentences.*
- *Listen to the conversation and number the statements/pictures from 1 to 5.*
- *Listen to the conversation and check off items chosen/ordered/selected by the speakers.*
- *Listen to the instructions and rearrange the objects according to what you hear.*

Note that some tasks require more effort than others and may distract students from listening. Having students answer five lengthy multiple choice questions while listening to a 40-second recording, for example, would require a significant amount of reading while listening. Even if the questions were read in advance, the activity would challenge the students' memory (or reading speed, or multi-tasking abilities) as much as their listening.

The same problem may occur with many of the tasks listed above. Reading, writing, or other tasks that require time and mental effort can easily distract students as they try to listen, so such tasks must be kept reasonably short and specific. Remember, the task itself should be easy to complete as long as the listening material is clearly understood; the level of difficulty comes from the listening material, not from the task.

A better option is to have each student complete a chart, either by checking off specific details or by adding very brief details supplied in the listening material. Even then, though, note the difference:

- *Listen to Jack and Tina order food in a restaurant, and write down the items you hear.*
- *Listen to Jack and Tina order food in a restaurant, and check off the items you hear.*

The first example sounds reasonable, but if we try it in class, we'll soon discover that many students will be focused on writing (and correctly spelling) the items in the answer and will therefore be distracted from listening as the conversation continues. In contrast, the second example allows students to remain focused on listening while quickly checking off the answers on the provided chart.

This task can be further improved, however, by adding a bit more challenge. Again, compare the following tasks:

- *Listen to Jack and Tina order food in a restaurant, and check off the items you hear.*
- *Listen to Jack and Tina order food in a restaurant, and check off the items they order.*

The first example makes the task too easy, as students would be able to complete the task simply by recognizing individual words, even without comprehending the conversation. The second example, however, could be paired with a conversation in which Jack and Tina discuss their options while making their choices, so students would be required to understand what is ordered (and not simply discussed) in order to complete the task.

Once a task has been designed, always check (again) that it cannot be completed without successfully understanding the listening material. If it can be, then the task is essentially useless since it demonstrates thinking, not listening. If, however, the task can be completed only after successfully understanding the listening material, then successful completion of the task demonstrates successful comprehension. In this sense, a good listening activity has its own built-in form of assessment.

Gist versus Details

Finally, when using multiple tasks, be sure to put them in a logical order and use separate playbacks for each. Begin with a fairly simple "gist listening" task, which requires a general understanding of the listening material and encourages top-down listening. Such a task may consist of a general question or two, such as *Who is speaking?* or *What is the conversation about?* Then follow with progressively more difficult tasks that require students to listen for particular details.

Adding Authenticity to Listening Materials and Tasks

If we wish to make our listening activities as authentic as possible, we must consider what is normally part of "real" listening and attempt to replicate those aspects in the classroom. Consider the following:

- In real life, listeners often know something about a conversation before it begins, such as the social context or the relationship between the speakers, and they use that information to help construct the meaning of what is said. It is therefore reasonable to state certain contextual details at the beginning of an activity.

- Real listening includes visual clues about the speakers and the context, so it is appropriate to include pictures, sketches, diagrams, or other visual materials in the activity. Even better, use video instead of audio alone so the students can "see" the conversation as they listen to it.
- Real listening is interactive, so tasks should be completed as the recording is played (and perhaps paused), not simply at the end of the recording.
- English is spoken in many countries around the world, both as a native language and as a second or even third language, so including a variety of accents in listening material is both realistic and helpful.
- Everyday speech is often informal and includes colloquialisms, rephrasing, elaborations, self-corrections, pauses, and interruptions, as well as variations of pace, volume, and **pitch**, so it makes sense to include these in our recordings.
- Everyday speech also includes polite conversations and requests, so we should include these too, though the focus should remain primarily on the language that the students will encounter most.

> ✓ Students cannot complete the task without comprehending the listening material.
> ✓ The level of difficulty comes from the listening material, not from the task.
> ✓ Authenticity is added: context, visuals, interaction, variety.

☞ Try: Using appendix 9A (parts I and II) as examples, write a short dialogue and create corresponding listening activities that include effective tasks for both the gist and details.

RUNNING A LISTENING ACTIVITY

Simply giving students a handout and playing a recording might work in a few cases, but most students will appreciate a little more guidance. The following steps simplify and clarify a listening task and increase the chances of its success:

1. *Introduction*: Use a lead-in to activate students' prior knowledge about the general topic.
2. *Pre-teach key elements*: As necessary, pre-teach any vocabulary or content that is unknown to the students yet necessary to understand what is being said.

3. *Introduce the context*: Use a few short sentences to provide certain background details (such as the social context) and set up the "gist listening" task. For example: *Listen to Tommy and Sally discuss their plans for the weekend. What problem do they have?* Then play the recording once for gist listening and have students answer the question before moving on to the next task.
4. *Set the main task(s)*: Distribute any necessary worksheets and give the students time to read them; then clarify the students' task before they begin listening and double-check to ensure they understand. (Best method: Have them explain the instructions back to you in their own words.) When using multiple tasks for a single recording, don't explain them all at the beginning. Instead, clarify the details of each task just before it is done, and be sure to use separate playbacks for each task.
5. *First playback*: Play the recording, pausing occasionally (if necessary) so students can complete the task.
6. *Check and replay*: If students have not yet found the answers, replay the recording as many times as necessary. If students struggle, let them work for the correct answer—don't give hints unless it is obviously impossible for them to complete the task even after multiple tries.
7. *Confirm and review*: If some answers were missed by more than a few students, replay the relevant parts of the recording to show where the answers were found.
8. *Repeat*: Move on to the next task and repeat the procedure until all listening tasks are complete.
9. *Total replay*: When all students have completed the task(s), consider replaying the recording in its entirety while students follow along and double-check their answers. (Students will likely ask for this.)
10. *Close*: Wrap up by congratulating students on their progress.

INTEGRATING SKILLS: LISTENING IN VARIOUS CONTEXTS

Listening is naturally included in many types of lessons. A content-based lesson, for example, may include a mini-lecture or oral reading that students listen to while taking notes, or a task-based lesson may include live or pre-recorded instructions that students must follow in order to complete the task.

In fact, almost every class includes listening comprehension. Every time we as teachers verbally explain something or give instructions, students must listen and try to comprehend what we are saying. In a sense, the situation is ideal: the teacher provides a "live," interactive model of spoken English, the context is authentic, and we can check students' comprehension as we normally do in class.

However, because students frequently have trouble understanding English that is spoken at normal speed, especially when the pronunciation is unfamiliar to them, teachers tend to slow down their speech and enunciate words very carefully, often to the point of sounding unnatural. This practice has the advantage of improving students' immediate comprehension, but it does little to improve their overall comprehension of "natural" English.

One compromise is to speak at a speed that is slightly challenging for students but still below what we would normally use, and to gradually increase the speed over time. However, there are two further ways to improve students' immediate comprehension without sacrificing long-term progress:

- *Pause between statements*: By giving students time to digest one statement before we make another, we can speak at closer-to-natural speeds while still improving students' chances of comprehending what we say.
- *Vary tone to emphasize key words*: We do this naturally anyway, but it might be helpful to point it out to students so they will learn to focus on stressed words instead of all words. Again, this practice may allow us to speak more naturally without sacrificing students' comprehension.

EXTENSIVE LISTENING

Outside of class, students can improve their listening skills (and overall language skills) through extensive listening—that is, listening for longer periods of time at a level that is comfortable for them. The method is simple: have students find something enjoyable (and not too challenging) to listen to, such as a television show, a movie, a radio program, an audio book, a podcast, or an Internet video. Then have them listen to it in their free time.

Note that there is no task associated with extensive listening; nonetheless, it is important that students understand what they are listening to, so choosing audio material at the right level is key. A popular option is to have students listen to the audio CDs that come with **graded readers**. These CDs and texts are made for language learners at a specific level, so learners can choose titles that are suited to their level and interests. (The readers and accompanying CDs—or, in some cases, online digital audio files—are available from many ESL publishers.)

Alternatively, some students choose audio or video that is more difficult, but they mitigate the extra challenge by using subtitles or a transcript to help them follow along as they listen to it for the first time, and they may reduce playback speed (using a smartphone app or computer program) to 80 or 90 percent. Later, they can listen again without subtitles and at normal speed, and because they already understand the gist of what they are listening to, they are less likely to get "lost" while listening.

In either case, while the goal of extensive listening is general comprehension (not 100 percent comprehension), students often choose to listen to the same material multiple times (though not all at one sitting), each time trying to comprehend more than they did the previous time.

Overall, extensive listening vastly increases the amount of listening practice available to students, and it exposes them to more voices, more vocabulary, and more everyday language than we could ever hope to provide in a classroom. Over the long term, it has significant effects on students' listening abilities and vocabulary, as well as their ability to recognize common language structures. Keep in mind, however, that extensive listening produces the best results when combined with intensive listening and with other types of language instruction and practice.

FEEDBACK AND ENCOURAGEMENT

Many students find listening practice more frustrating than other types of language practice, particularly if the listening material offers sufficient challenge. They may need to be reminded that total comprehension is not necessary or expected, and that their rate of progress (which they find slow) is normal. As with other activities, try to keep the mood light and encourage students by emphasizing their success and keeping the focus on long-term goals.

QUESTIONS FOR REVIEW

1. What are listening gaps? What causes them, and how might they be addressed? Give examples.
2. What are the advantages and disadvantages of "live" listening material and recorded material?

3. "Listening tasks should be easy to complete if the listening material is understood, and impossible to do if the listening material is not understood; the difficulty of the activity should come from the listening material, not the task." Explain with an example.
4. What is the difference between gist listening and listening for details?
5. Why might we add pauses, interruptions, accents, and rephrasing to listening materials?
6. In what sense does every class include a certain amount of listening comprehension? How can we adjust the way we speak in order to improve students' immediate comprehension without reducing the effectiveness of these natural opportunities to practice authentic listening?
7. What is extensive listening? What are its advantages?
8. Why and how should we encourage students during listening activities?
9. Read through the sample listening activities (appendix 9A) in light of the instructions and explanations provided in this chapter. Then develop a few of your own on a topic of your choice.

FURTHER READING

John Field's *Listening in the Language Classroom* (Cambridge, 2009) provides insightful guidance for designing listening activities.

John Flowerdew and Lindsay Miller's *Second Language Listening: Theory and Practice* (Cambridge, 2005) includes theory, case studies, and activities.

Tony Lynch's *Teaching Second Language Listening* (Oxford, 2009) is a handbook of theory and activities.

Jack Richards and Anne Burns's *Tips for Teaching Listening* (Pearson, 2018) gives practical advice for listening practice in the classroom.

Penny Ur's *Teaching Listening Comprehension* (Cambridge, 1984) is a classic that includes both theory and activities.

J. J. Wilson's *How to Teach Listening* (Longman, 2008) gives practical advice and sample activities.

CHAPTER 10
Teaching Reading

Jane's class of young adults was struggling. Each of her students had studied English for at least six years in the public school system, but they still found that their reading skills were inadequate. Some complained that reading in English simply took too long; others found that they could read almost every word of a text but could not understand the overall meaning. Still others seemed to understand the literal meaning of a given text but had trouble discovering the author's "real" message.

Although frustrated by their attempts to read, the students pressed on with their reading improvement class—though somewhat reluctantly at times. Jane, as a seasoned English teacher, knew that students had problems with both motivation and reading skills—but she also knew ways to address both.

ADDRESSING READING PROBLEMS

Many language learners who have had previous training will already have good basic reading skills but may be unsatisfied with their overall ability to read. Problems they cite might include lack of vocabulary, slow reading speed, poor overall comprehension (even if individual words are understood), or insufficient knowledge of the context.

The importance of vocabulary and reading speed, in particular, is often underestimated. Consider that a student who knows 90 percent of the vocabulary in a given text will encounter 20 to 30 new words per typed double-spaced page, while a student who knows 98 percent of the vocabulary in the text will encounter only 4 to 6 new words per page. The former student will quickly become overwhelmed, while the latter will feel reasonably comfortable with the text. Likewise, a student who reads 80 words per minute likely comprehends very little and will soon tire of reading, while a student who reads 150 words per minute will feel a greater sense of progress and is more likely to enjoy reading.

In order to help students read more successfully, we must address such issues by developing their vocabulary, teaching common prose structures, teaching reading strategies, and facilitating frequent reading practice.

Help Build Vocabulary

Vocabulary presents us with a bit of a chicken-and-egg conundrum: students need significantly more vocabulary in order to read better, yet reading is a great way to learn and internalize new vocabulary. To address these issues, we can help students tackle vocabulary in a variety of ways:

- Students should continue to develop their vocabulary in the usual ways, whether through daily interaction with English speakers or through vocabulary-building textbooks and classes. They may find it useful to keep a vocabulary journal or use some other method to review and reuse new words until they become internalized. (See chapter 12 for more information on teaching vocabulary.)
- When reading about a specific topic that is not familiar, students should consider looking up the meaning of key words before they begin.
- Remind students that not all new words are necessary to the general meaning of the text, so while it might be important to look up key words in an academic text, it is not necessary to understand the precise meaning of every word in everyday reading. In many cases, students can guess the approximate meaning of a new word from the context.
- Students should learn to view reading itself as an excellent way to build vocabulary. The more they encounter a new word in a text, the more likely they are to internalize it. However, to avoid being distracted by countless new words, they should try to choose texts that introduce only a few new words per page. (See the discussion of extensive reading in "Other Types of Reading Practice" later in this chapter.)

Teach Common Structures

Understanding the overall structure of a text helps readers quickly make sense of what they are reading. It also helps them know where to look for key information. While some of these details about structure may seem obvious, we must keep in mind that paragraph structure and overall text structure are largely cultural—Western writing, for example, is generally direct and linear, while writing in some Eastern cultures is indirect and circular. Standards that seem "normal" in one language, then, might not be normal at all in another, so they must be taught to students.

There are numerous possible paragraph structures and text structures, but they tend to have certain features in common. Understanding how these features work will help students understand a given paragraph or text more quickly. The more common features in English writing are as follows:

- *Topic sentence*: Most paragraphs have one sentence that contains the main idea, and all other sentences in the paragraph support it by adding additional information. Although the **topic sentence** may be found anywhere in the paragraph, or even implied but not stated, it is most often at or near the beginning of the paragraph.
- *Supporting sentences*: Other sentences in the paragraph develop the main idea by adding information about it. For example, they may compare the idea to something else, give examples of it, give further details, analyze the idea (i.e., break it into its parts), or define the idea (i.e., explain exactly what it means). Each supporting sentence may link back to the topic sentence or link to the sentence that precedes it. (These are the two most common ways to create "flow" in a paragraph.)
- *Organization of ideas*: The order of the key ideas in a text is usually determined by the type of writing. A written argument, for example, will often list its evidence in order of importance, beginning with the strongest point—or, for dramatic effect, ending with the strongest. A **narrative**, however, will likely tell events in chronological order, though it may play with the order for effect. An expository essay will likely explain details in the order in which they are most easily understood, while a descriptive essay commonly describes a scene from top to bottom or left to right.

Teach Reading Strategies

Some readers quickly adapt to whatever type of reading is required, but many do not. For those who do not, we can introduce strategies that help them read more effectively and efficiently. A few of the more common reading strategies that we can recommend are as follows:

- *Consider purpose*: Before reading something, we should ask ourselves why we are reading it. Our reasons for reading will help determine our reading strategies.

- When reading to find a specific detail, we can **scan** the text by looking it over quickly while watching for that specific detail; the rest can be ignored.
- To find the gist of the material, we can **skim** the content by looking over the text quickly while focusing on key words and topic sentences.
- When reading for detailed information on a topic, we read at a slower pace and with more concentration, and then reflect on the material so we can draw our own inferences and conclusions. This is called *intensive reading*. It generally makes use of texts that are challenging and is often done in class or as homework, in conjunction with reading strategies and activities that promote comprehension and critical thinking. (Many of the reading strategies and activities in this chapter are particularly helpful for this type of reading.)
- When reading for pleasure, we can read quickly and with little thought about how the text is written. This is called *extensive reading*. (See "Other Types of Reading Practice" near the end of this chapter.)

- *Consider relevance and prior knowledge*: Before reading, we should consider what we already know about the topic and what we hope to learn. The more thoughtful we are about the topic, the more engaged we will be when reading.
- *Predict content and structure*: After reading the title and the first few sentences, we can try to guess what the text is about and how the information is organized. Then, by keeping these predictions in mind as we read and modifying them as we discover the answers, we are more likely to be engaged by the text and to comprehend it.
- *Preview the material*: Our reading comprehension will be much better if we have a general idea of the material's content and organization before we begin. Consider these tips:
  - Read the title and skim the introduction for key words and phrases; then do the same for a few more paragraphs. Are there any unknown words that might be important to our understanding? Consider looking them up in a dictionary.
  - Read the introduction; then read the first line of each body paragraph. What is the text about? How is it organized? (How does each paragraph relate to the main idea?)

- *Make note of rhetorical markers*: Texts frequently use certain words or phrases to guide readers, and underlining them can help us see the relationships between parts of the text.
  - Comparisons: *as, both, in the same way, like, likewise, same, similar...*
  - Contrasts: *although, however, in contrast, nonetheless, on the other hand, whereas...*
  - Cause and effect: *accordingly, as a result, because, consequently, that is why, therefore...*
  - Time and chronology: *after, at last, before, earlier, from then on, in the end, meanwhile, next, previously, soon, then, while...*
- *Make notes*: When reading intensively, we can make brief notes about what we read, or at least underline key points so we can go back and review them later.
- *Review*: After reading a text, we can go back and skim the introduction, the topic sentence of each body paragraph, and the conclusion in order to help improve our overall understanding.
- *Summarize*: Writing a summary or an outline of what we've just read can help us get a better grasp of the overall meaning and sort out important points from secondary ones.

Of course it is not necessary (or even recommended) to use all of these strategies for every text. Rather, it is important to use selected strategies that are best suited to the text and the reader. Writing a summary of the classifieds, for example, makes little sense, but scanning the classifieds for a particular item makes perfect sense, as does taking notes while reading an academic textbook so the content can be quickly reviewed later.

☞ *Try: Choose an interesting news or magazine article. Skim through it and underline the key points while making note of any rhetorical markers.*

CHOOSING AND ADAPTING READING MATERIAL

Reading material for language classes can be found almost everywhere: in language textbooks, in newspapers and magazines, on the Internet, and even on everyday items such as menus and labels. While the choices may seem endless, the best options are those that are interesting to our students and relevant to their needs; and whether they want to read for pleasure, for work, for school, or for everyday information, the best reading materials are authentic:

- Well-chosen magazine articles, newspaper articles, and short fiction can be enjoyable and interesting and can help improve student motivation.
- Editorials and opinion pieces are ideal for teaching students about bias in writing and often lead to interesting (and perhaps animated) discussion.
- Academic texts, journal articles, and other types of expository prose are ideal for students preparing to study or to do research, particularly if they also learn the common structures of expository writing.
- Pamphlets, schedules, menus, labels, ads, and other types of everyday reading can be very practical for students living in a culture that is new to them.

Although authentic reading material is often written for readers fluent in the language and may be difficult for language learners, it can easily be adapted for both length and difficulty. To create a good adaptation, consider the following steps:

1. Eliminate non-essential details that make the article longer than we want it to be.
2. Reword particularly difficult phrases.
3. Shorten sentences that are long and difficult to follow.
4. Restructure paragraphs to make them shorter, each with a clear topic sentence.

The result should be an article of appropriate length and at a level that provides a bit of challenge for our students without overwhelming them.

☞ *Try: Choose an interesting news or magazine article, and rewrite it to make it easier to read for lower-level students.*

ACTIVITIES THAT PROMOTE INTENSIVE READING

As noted, intensive reading is usually accompanied by activities that promote deeper comprehension and critical thinking, and whether the reading material is academic, work related, or something more general, students will become more familiar with it (and more satisfied with their understanding of it) if we use a variety of activities for a single text. The choices are numerous, but the activities described here are among the most effective.

Introductory Activities

Consider using one or more of the following to help students become familiar and comfortable with a text before they attempt to read it on their own:

- Have students skim five short newspaper or magazine articles to decide which one they want to read. (This step provides realistic practice of skimming to choose reading material.)
- Have students predict the content based on the title and key words from the first paragraph.
- Give students a randomized list of the main ideas from the text; then have them skim the text and put the ideas in order.
- Read the text aloud while students follow along and underline unknown words and difficult passages. Pause after each paragraph to clarify new vocabulary or difficult passages.

Overview-Oriented Activities

Consider having students complete one or more of the following activities to help them understand the overall structure and direction of a text:

- read the text and retell the main idea in their own words
- underline or paraphrase the topic sentence in each paragraph
- provide a title for each paragraph
- write the missing final paragraph

Comprehension Activities

Consider having students complete one or more of the following activities to help them understand the details of the text as they relate to the larger context and overall structure:

- answer questions about the content of the reading
- label statements about the text as true or false, and give reasons for their answers
- complete a cloze activity based on the information in the text
- complete a multiple-choice activity on the content of the text
- find mistakes in a corresponding picture
- make notes under given headings
- write a summary

When writing short-answer questions, true-or-false statements, a cloze activity, or multiple choice questions, be sure the wording in the activities varies from the original but carries the same meaning—otherwise students will find the answers by matching phrases instead of actually comprehending the text. Also note that summaries can be difficult at the lower levels and may reflect writing skills as much as reading skills; other types of activities in the above list give more support and structure.

Critical Thinking Activities

Consider having students complete one or more of the following activities to help them read a text carefully and critically while asking questions about purpose, bias, and truth:

- consider the author's purpose—to educate? to argue a point? to entertain?
- label selected sentences in an editorial as fact or opinion
- examine the reading to determine whether the author supports claims with details and evidence, or merely speaks in generalities
- discuss whether the author has considered all sides of the issue and all available evidence
- write a response to an editorial, challenging its argument, or a review of an article, questioning its assumptions

☞ *Try: Choose an interesting opinion article and write five comprehension questions and five critical thinking questions that can be answered only after reading the article very carefully.*

READING LESSONS

While reading activities can be integrated into a variety of lesson types, there are times when we may wish to develop an entire lesson that is devoted to reading and understanding a particular text.

A typical reading lesson is a series of related activities that are logically ordered and help students explore and interact with a text by using more than one relevant reading technique. A class focused on reading comprehension, for example, might begin with skimming activities to help students get the gist of the reading and predict what it is about, and it might end with scanning activities used to confirm specific details. In between, the bulk of the lesson is likely to consist of comprehension-related activities and critical thinking activities.

These activities, of course, are normally set in a larger context that makes up the whole lesson. A lesson focusing on comprehension of an expository text, for example, might look like the following:

1. *The introduction or lead-in* helps generate students' interest by activating their prior knowledge and connecting the topic with their lives.
2. *Pre-reading tasks* (such as previewing new vocabulary or predicting content) help prepare students for what they are about to read.
3. *The first reading and related tasks* help students form a basic understanding of the text (in particular its overall structure and main ideas).
4. *Subsequent reading(s) and related tasks* lead students to a deeper comprehension and (ideally, depending on their level) to a more critical, evaluative understanding of the text.
5. *Post-text activities* include discussion, debates, written response, or other ways to further explore the topics introduced by the text.
6. *The closing* includes any form of conclusion, final comments, review, or other means of wrapping up the topic and winding down the class—and yes, this is also the time to assign homework, such as a text to be read purely for pleasure.

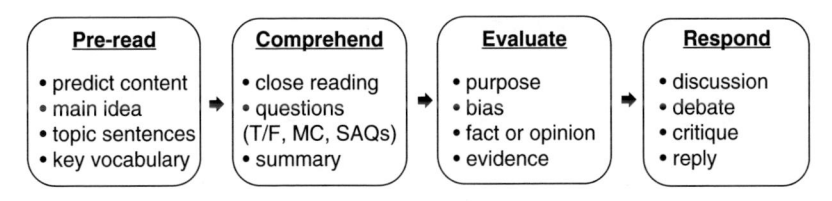

Pre-read	Comprehend	Evaluate	Respond
• predict content • main idea • topic sentences • key vocabulary	• close reading • questions (T/F, MC, SAQs) • summary	• purpose • bias • fact or opinion • evidence	• discussion • debate • critique • reply

Figure 10.1: A Typical Reading Progression

Of course, this outline is just an example, and for any particular class, the activities should be chosen and ordered according to the needs of the students.

Facilitating a Reading Lesson

While planning a class may seem intense and laborious (though it gets much easier with practice), running the class is generally enjoyable, particularly if the class has been well planned. The teacher's role is threefold:

- *Facilitator*: The teacher sets up and organizes reading activities, and makes decisions as needed.

- *Reading counsellor*: The teacher introduces students to reading strategies, encourages them to develop and practice those strategies, and reminds them of the long-term outcomes (better reading speed, better comprehension) of the activities done in class.
- *Helper*: The teacher explains (or pre-teaches) new vocabulary or new grammar forms, breaks down challenging sentences into manageable chunks, and explains concepts from the text.

☞ *Consider: Why is the progression of activities (i.e., the choice of activities and the order in which they occur) in a reading lesson particularly important to the lesson's potential for success?*

OTHER TYPES OF READING PRACTICE

Building vocabulary, learning common structures, and using reading strategies are all helpful in addressing reading problems, but such efforts are most effective only when combined with reading practice—and lots of it. Practice needn't be difficult, nor academic, and it need not take place in the classroom. In fact, because class time is limited, reading at home (or on the bus, or in the park) is essential if students are to become better readers, and both reading material and style can vary:

- *Oral reading* can be helpful when teaching pronunciation or helping shy students find their voices in class, but it is generally not helpful as reading practice, largely because students tend to be nervous when reading aloud and focus on their performance rather than on the content of the text.
- *Extensive reading*, mentioned earlier in this chapter, is particularly valuable. It requires less effort on the part of the teacher and the students, but the benefits are not to be underestimated. It has a significant effect on the students' vocabulary, comprehension, reading speed, and overall confidence in reading.

    Extensive reading makes use of texts that are relatively or at least moderately easy for students, such as graded stories or novels (available from many ESL publishers) that use a limited vocabulary and an overall writing style appropriate to a given level. Teachers can help students choose texts that interest them and that are written at an appropriate level, and students can simply enjoy reading them. Such reading makes excellent homework—though perhaps we needn't call it that.

- *Paced reading* is used to help reasonably strong readers increase their reading speed by requiring them to read at a speed just beyond their usual level. Consider, for example, giving students a short reading (appropriate to their level) with a mark in the margin at every 50 words. We then have the students begin reading, and we tap the desk every 20 seconds to indicate when students should be at the next mark (in this case, assuming a reading speed of 150 words per minute [wpm] at the start). Once the students become comfortable with the process, we repeat it with a different text marked at every 60 words, thereby requiring students to read 180 wpm in order to keep up. We repeat this process with new texts until students become comfortable reading at this speed, and then we move on to higher speeds. There are a few points to keep in mind when using **paced reading**:
    - We must first discover the students' initial reading speed by timing them. A student who takes 10 minutes to read a 1,000-word reading, for example, reads at 100 wpm, so we begin at that speed.
    - Students in the same class do not necessarily read at the same speed, but we can have them participate in the same paced reading activity by providing readings marked every 40 words (for readers at 120 wpm), 50 words (for readers at 150 wpm), 60 words (for readings at 180 wpm), and so on.
    - We should prepare questions to check whether students sufficiently comprehend what they are reading; if they do not, we must ask whether the reading is too difficult or the pace is too fast.
    - This entire process takes place over a period of time. Students may practice one or two readings per class and move to another level only after multiple classes of practice. Overall, the pace should be comfortable yet still a bit challenging for the students.

INTEGRATING SKILLS: READING IN VARIOUS CONTEXTS

As noted above, reading activities are found in many types of lessons and assignments, not just reading lessons. Speaking and writing lessons may begin with a short reading to inspire the students' creativity; content-based lessons often include significant reading and related activities to help students discover and learn the target content; task-based lessons may include written information to be used in the task; and homework assignments may include extensive reading to help build the students' reading fluency. Overall, there are numerous opportunities to provide students with reading practice that is appropriate for their level and their needs.

FINDING SOLUTIONS

The ability to read well opens up a world of knowledge and adventure; if we keep this in mind (and mention it to our students from time to time), then a reading class becomes a way of finding solutions to problems that might otherwise bar the path to such adventure. Indeed, it becomes part of a journey that can be adventurous (and fun) itself.

Remember Jane's struggling class? After analyzing the students' needs, Jane planned and implemented a three-month program (in a class that met twice a week) that taught students specific reading strategies and provided meaningful opportunities to practice them. She always chose texts that were interesting and relevant to her students, along with activities that were well-suited to their needs and level. She also had students read extensively on their own while keeping a reading journal in which they recorded their own reading experiences and difficulties, as well as their successes.

At the end of three months, the students' reading skills had improved remarkably. Of course, they still had lots of room to improve even further, but they were now taking more responsibility for their own learning and were eager to continue.

QUESTIONS FOR REVIEW

1. What factors might discourage students from reading in their new language?
2. What is a topic sentence?
3. Why is it important for students to consider their purpose when reading a particular text?
4. In what ways can students preview material before reading it? How might this be helpful?
5. What are rhetorical markers? How do they help readers?
6. Why and how might a text need to be adapted?
7. How are comprehension activities different from critical thinking activities?

8. Read the sample lesson plan (appendix 10A). In what kind of class might you use it? Which parts are well designed? What improvements might be made?
9. What do content-based activities (see chapter 3) and reading activities have in common? Can a single lesson achieve objectives related to both content and reading skills?
10. Why is oral reading generally not helpful in promoting reading comprehension?
11. What is the difference between intensive reading and extensive reading? What is the purpose of each? What are the benefits?
12. What is paced reading? Why might we use it in class?

FURTHER READING

Julian Bamford and Richard R. Day's *Extensive Reading Activities for Teaching Language* (Cambridge, 2004) describes more than one hundred activities related to extensive reading.

William Grabe's *Reading in a Second Language: Moving from Theory to Practice* (Cambridge, 2008) applies recent research to develop ideas for reading instruction.

I. S. P. Nation's *Teaching ESL/EFL Reading and Writing* (Routledge, 2008) provides helpful advice for classes at all levels.

Peter Watkins's *Teaching and Developing Reading Skills* (Cambridge, 2018) includes both theory and practical activities to help improve learners' reading skills and strategies.

CHAPTER 11
Teaching Writing

Writing class—for many of us, the phrase itself conjures up images of painful classes where we sat at our school desks feeling frustrated. We didn't know what to write, the teacher didn't know why we wouldn't or couldn't write, and most of what we wrote (in class, at least) wasn't at all inspired. It's not that we disliked writing—it's just that we didn't know what to write about or how to write it.

Writing, though, is so much more than this. We write letters or emails to friends to let them know how we're doing. We write letters to companies to complain about poor service or a faulty product (in hopes of getting a refund, perhaps). We write letters to the editor of the newspaper to suggest changes in our community or society. We write shopping lists so we won't forget what we need to pick up on the way home. And yes, we even write notes in classes because writing helps us remember what we've heard and feel that we are in control of the material.

Given that we all need to write from time to time, and that our writing generally gets better with practice, isn't there a better way to teach writing (or to learn how to write)?

TYPES OF WRITING ACTIVITIES

The word *writing* brings to mind different ideas for different people because there are many different types of writing that we regularly encounter. Likewise, there are many different types of writing activities, though they can be categorized generally as controlled, free, or assisted.

Controlled Writing

Controlled writing is a form of practice that requires students to complete specific tasks with a given text. Its focus is not fluency or content but grammar and style. It is best used as preparation for a more difficult writing task or as practice in noted problem areas, and correction should be specific and immediate (though still kind, of course). The following examples are listed from most controlled to least controlled:

- *Guided writing* (or *text manipulation*) provides a limited amount of text and has students make specific changes, such as changing the tense, the number (singular to plural), the voice (passive to active), or almost any other grammar form. It is best used to teach or review areas of grammar.
- *Sentence combining activities* provide short sentences that the students must combine using a variety of techniques. Sentences can be given in lists of two or three at a time (each list becomes a sentence) or as longer lists (students decide how many to combine into each new sentence). Such activities help improve sentence length and variety and can help introduce new sentence structures.
- *Model writing* provides a model for students to imitate. A paragraph on a favourite cat, for example, may provide much of the vocabulary, structure, and style needed for students to write about their own pets. Higher-level classes might also analyze the structure of the paragraph before imitating it.
- *Question and short-answer exercises* provide specific questions to guide students' writing. They are most often used with short anecdotes, stories, or articles, but they can also be used with pictures, diagrams, and so on. Such exercises give students more freedom in how to write but keep them on a common topic. They are particularly well-suited as preparation for more extensive writing on the same topic.

Free Writing

Free writing is in many ways the opposite of controlled writing. It focuses on content (getting relevant ideas down on paper), audience (knowing who you're writing for), and fluency (writing quickly, with minimal hesitation). Students write as much as they can within a given time, without worrying about accuracy. The teacher encourages the students to "keep writing," and feedback is limited to positive comments about the content and quantity of writing.

Free writing is often used as a type of brainstorming to help students come up with ideas on a given topic for a more formal writing exercise that will follow.

In this sense, free writing helps provide "raw material" that will later be refined into something more significant.

Free writing may also be used on its own to help students overcome perfectionism or other hang-ups about writing, including a seeming inability to get started. In this case, students are encouraged to keep writing without any pauses, just to get them accustomed to writing. The result may be an aimless, almost impossible-to-follow piece of work not fit for much of anything, but that's okay—free writing used in this way has more to do with the psychology of writing than with producing a product.

Assisted Writing

Assisted writing covers the broad middle ground between controlled writing and free writing, and it is commonly used in writing classes. In this approach, the student has a lot of freedom in how to write, but the teacher assists in various ways, including any of the following:

- content ideas, ranging from a simple topic to a brainstorming session or writing sample
- structural help, ranging from sentence grammar to paragraph organization to essay outlines
- feedback on content, grammar, style, or any other aspect of writing

Note that various types of assistance are often combined into what is called a "process approach" to writing, which focuses not simply on producing a finished piece of writing but on the various steps that lead to successful writing. (We will consider a variation of this approach below.)

Communicative Writing

Communicative writing is a type of assisted writing that attempts to improve student motivation and classroom relevance by replacing what might be considered "pointless" writing tasks with authentic ones, specifying a real purpose in writing to a real audience. Consider how the following tasks differ:

- *Change the following paragraph about Sam the cat from present tense to past tense.*
- *Read the following paragraph about Sam the cat. Then write a paragraph about your pet.*
- *Using the following paragraph as a model, write a letter to your pen pal about a funny thing that happened to your own pet.*

The first task is essentially a grammar exercise—possibly helpful but probably not inspiring. The second task gives the student more freedom in writing, but it still feels like "just an exercise" in writing. The third task, however, gives the student a purpose and an audience, and it is likely to inspire better writing.

Topics for communicative writing may be chosen by the teacher or by the students themselves, but in either case, they should be appropriate for and relevant to the students' needs and interests.

ONE TOPIC, MANY TASKS

A writing class (or a series of classes) may include numerous writing tasks, but that does not mean we need numerous topics. Rather, we often need just one topic with numerous tasks. In fact, the more students work with a particular topic, the more they will grasp the nuances of that topic, including the vocabulary and language commonly used with it.

Consider a simple topic such as *jobs*. Students could write an email to a pen pal describing the best job they ever had (or a job they would like to have), a blog or newsletter about how to choose a good job, a job application letter, a questionnaire to discover their classmates' opinions on certain job-related issues, an essay on the job market today, a personal anecdote about something zany that happened at a job they once had, a personal journal about what they are learning at their current job, and so on.

Keep in mind that just as we choose topics that are interesting and relevant to our students, we should also choose tasks that our students will enjoy and might actually use—relevance, after all, is directly linked to student motivation.

☞ *Try: Choose one topic and develop at least three different writing tasks related to it. Be sure to specify a purpose and audience.*

PROCESS WRITING

While writing activities can be used in any class, there are also classes that focus exclusively on writing, and particularly on a process that leads to a finished product. **Process writing** generally has three parts: pre-writing (preparation), writing (first draft), and post-writing (revision and editing). The amount of time allotted to each varies depending on the needs of the class, but as a rule of thumb, begin by allotting one-third of available time for each, and then adjust as necessary.

Pre-Writing

1. *Introduce the topic*: For a class in which all students are writing on the same general topic, consider introducing the topic with a strong lead-in that generates interest and activates the students' prior knowledge on the topic. The lead-in may be similar to those of other types of lessons (a question, an anecdote, a controversial statement), or it may focus particularly on writing, such as asking students to write a "top five" list on some aspect of the topic.

2. *Set the writing task, including the audience and communicative purpose*: To increase student motivation along every step of the writing process, emphasize the main task (i.e., final product), the audience, and the purpose. Make it clear that the process is moving toward a finished product that is designed to accomplish something. For example, *Today we will write a letter to the city to request that Central Park not be turned into a parking garage.* Consider showing the students a sample of the finished product.

3. *Help students gather and develop ideas*: Moving from a general topic to specific ideas can be a difficult struggle, often resulting in long stares at a blank page. To help students get some ideas down on paper, consider one or more of the following:
    - *Idea map*: Write the topic or title in the centre of the board and have students call out anything that comes to mind. Write their suggestions on the board, arranging them around the topic while grouping similar ideas. (Save any discussion, comments, and selection for later.)
    - *Fast writing*: Essentially a form of individual brainstorming on paper, fast writing is a variation of free writing that requires students to write without stopping for a specified period of time (perhaps five minutes). During this time, students must not look back or revise. They are simply producing raw material to draw from at a later stage.
    - *Guided discussion*: Some students may find brainstorming too "scattered" and fast writing too difficult; they may prefer a discussion on the topic, discovering their own ideas as they respond to those of others.
    - *Interviews*: Students may wish to discover others' ideas on the topic by conducting interviews. Students who have difficulty keeping up with class discussions (especially while taking notes) may find this approach more suitable, as they can set the pace.
    - *Text starts*: Consider using a short reading activity to get students thinking about their topic. After all, real-life writing is often in response to something we've read, and the reading may serve as a model for the

students' own work, providing natural support in areas such as vocabulary and organization. Text starts are particularly relevant when writing letters to the editor, answering a personal letter, summarizing a text, or writing a how-to guide based on given information.
- *Image starts*: Pictures, graphs, charts, or other types of images can also give students something to focus on as they begin to write and may help inspire their thoughts.
- *Vocabulary and grammar*: If the activity requires unfamiliar vocabulary or grammar that needs to be reviewed, this is a good time to cover it.

4. *Help students select and organize ideas*: Obviously, not every idea that is generated through brainstorming or discussion will be a winner, so have students make a list of the main points they wish to include in their writing. The rest can be set aside. Then have students organize their main points into a general outline or a diagram, writing one full sentence for each main point. Provide examples as necessary, and remind students that an outline is only a guide and may be changed later.

If the final work requires a specific format (such as that of a business letter or an expository essay), explain it here, and consider providing a sample to show how it is set up.

Finally, provide feedback on the students' outlines, or have them give each other feedback. (*Is it standard format? How might it be improved?*)

Writing

5. *Have students write their first drafts*: Using their detailed outlines as a guide, students can now write a complete first draft.

Post-Writing

6. *Provide feedback*: Reading and providing feedback on each student's work is ideal but can be very time-consuming, particularly if the class is large. Consider having students work in small groups to read each other's work and provide **peer feedback**, particularly in the areas of organization and overall effectiveness. For best results, give them specific questions to consider: *Is the main idea clearly stated in the introduction? Does each paragraph have a main point that supports the overall idea? Are the ideas/paragraphs in a logical order? Is the writing clear and easy to follow?*

7. *Assist with revisions*: Have students revise their work to address any issues raised in the feedback they received. Focus in particular on overall structure,

then paragraph structure. Consider using a post-writing outline to ensure paragraph order is ideal, and if time allows, consider using controlled writing activities for practice in troublesome areas noted in the first draft.

8. *Oversee proofreading and refinement*: Have students read through their own work, and then through each other's work, to check for mistakes in spelling and grammar and to ensure the writing style is smooth and clear.

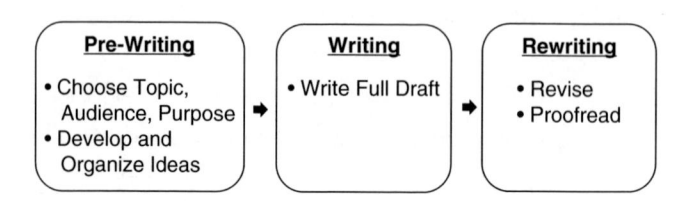

Pre-Writing
- Choose Topic, Audience, Purpose
- Develop and Organize Ideas

➡

Writing
- Write Full Draft

➡

Rewriting
- Revise
- Proofread

Figure 11.1: A Typical Writing Process

GIVING FEEDBACK

Perhaps the most daunting aspect of teaching writing is providing feedback. When do we give feedback, where do we begin, and—perhaps more relevant to language classes—where do we end? After all, except in advanced classes, student writing is likely to have many more errors than we can possibly address.

When Is Feedback Most Effective?

We've all seen students skim over comments on their work and pay little attention to them; after all, the assignment was completed days earlier and the class had already moved on. Feedback is most effective, then, not at the end of the writing process but during the process because students can apply our suggestions to improve their writing before the final version is completed. Such an approach not only results in a better final product but also motivates students to make better use of feedback, which in turn results in a more effective learning process. Besides, spreading feedback throughout the process results in smaller bites that are easier to provide (whether by the teacher or by other students) and easier for students to digest.

How Do We Give Feedback?

Student writing generally has more errors than we can address, so our overall focus should be on giving step-by-step advice on how the work can be made better.

If time allows, this is done best in person with the student on a one-to-one basis. However, if many students have the same types of errors, those errors can be addressed as a class, and those students who no longer make these mistakes may be able to help those still struggling. Written feedback may also be effective, though it doesn't allow the interaction that is often necessary for clarification of either the student's intended meaning or the teacher's feedback.

Errors that impede comprehension, whether structural (essay level or paragraph level) or grammatical (sentence level), should be our main focus. Correcting such errors generally requires the student to rewrite a sentence or a paragraph, or even to move paragraphs, so it is best to address these errors early in the writing process if possible.

Smaller errors (mostly in grammar or word usage) that remain at the end of the process are generally too numerous to deal with, though errors that are common among students at a particular level can be addressed by using a checklist to help students identify specific areas they should improve. (The specific areas for a given class will become evident after reading a few samples of their work.)

In either case, there are a few additional tips that can help us make our feedback more effective:

- Try to identify not only the error but also the source of the error (*Why is the student making this mistake?*) in order to help students avoid such errors in the future.
- Have the students make the corrections according to your advice; don't simply fix the errors for them.
- Collect common errors over a period of time to use as a review in future classes.

INTEGRATING SKILLS: WRITING IN VARIOUS CONTEXTS

Writing tasks are used in many types of classes, not only in writing classes. Grammar classes often include written practice, and speaking classes may include written answers to help students formulate their ideas. Content-based classes and reading classes, in particular, often include writing as a response to reading material or other content. In any of these situations, it is helpful to remind students that strengthening one language skill will help them develop their other skills as well, moving them closer to their overall goals.

QUESTIONS FOR REVIEW

1. What is the purpose of controlled writing? When is it best used?
2. What is the purpose of sentence-combining exercises?
3. How can free writing be used to help students overcome some of the difficulties they have when beginning a new piece of writing?
4. Why is it important to have a clear audience and communicative purpose in mind when writing?
5. Why is it a good idea to choose one topic and numerous tasks instead of numerous tasks on numerous topics?
6. Why is it a good idea to use a variety of types of writing (not only essays)?
7. What is the advantage of the process approach to writing?
8. How can we help students give better peer feedback?
9. In a writing class, when is feedback most effective? What kind of feedback should we give, and how?
10. Review the sample lesson plan (appendix 11A). What kind of students might find this lesson relevant and interesting? Would you use this lesson in a class? How might you change it or improve it?

FURTHER READING

Arthur Brookes and Peter Grundy's *Beginning to Write: Writing Activities for Elementary and Intermediate Learners* (Cambridge, 1999) contains more than one hundred practical activities for lower-level writing classes.

Dana Ferris and John Hedgcock's *Teaching L2 Composition: Purpose, Process, and Practice* (Routledge, 2013) is a thorough and practical guide to teaching writing in the language classroom.

Jeremy Harmer's *How to Teach Writing* (Pearson, 2004) contains numerous practical tips.

I. S. P. Nation's *Teaching ESL/EFL Reading and Writing* (Routledge, 2008) provides helpful advice for classes at all levels.

Ann Raimes's *Techniques in Teaching Writing* (Oxford, 1983) is a classic filled with practical advice.

CHAPTER 12
Understanding and Teaching Vocabulary

Many of us who have taken a language course in school or in university can remember those dreaded lists of vocabulary that had to be memorized. Sometimes we simply pored over the lists, trying to cram them into our heads; at other times we studied with friends, made rhymes or songs with the words, or labelled everything in sight with sticky notes, hoping that constant encounters with the words would make them stick in our brains. These latter techniques underline two assumptions we may hold about learning vocabulary: we need to encounter these words numerous times in order to remember them, and learning new vocabulary can be more fun if we are creative in our methods.

We may also remember that some words were more difficult to use correctly than others. The meaning may have been non-literal, or the word may have been used differently from its nearest equivalent in our own language. In either case, it took repeated use in a variety of contexts before we could use such words in a way that sounded natural.

WHY LEARN VOCABULARY?

When we talk about learning a language, we often refer to speaking, listening, reading, writing, and grammar, but vocabulary tends to be mentioned only as an add-on, as if its supposed lack of complexity somehow makes it inferior to "real" learning. Vocabulary, however, is arguably the most important aspect of any language; without it, we cannot express or understand anything except perhaps with gestures.

Think of it this way: I may not know how to say "I'd like a cup of coffee please," or "Could I have some coffee please," or any other polite, grammatically correct way to ask for coffee, but as long as I know the word *coffee*, I can still express my wish (or need, if you prefer).

Listening comprehension and reading comprehension are also highly dependent on a learner's knowledge of relevant vocabulary. After all, the learner will struggle to form even a basic understanding of a conversation or a reading if key words related to the topic remain a mystery.

Think also of lower-level language classes. They typically begin with names of common items and actions, as well as adjectives, numbers, and other words necessary for even basic communication. Grammar, speaking, listening, reading, and writing are all contingent on first learning at least some basic vocabulary.

Mid-level and upper-level classes continue to demonstrate the importance of vocabulary. In many cases, vocabulary is a component in a speaking, listening, reading, or writing lesson, giving the students the verbal tools necessary to complete a later part of the lesson. A lesson on writing resumés and cover letters, for example, may include a component on vocabulary relevant to job hunting. In addition, sometimes an entire lesson may be developed around vocabulary related to a certain topic for the simple purpose of developing the students' overall vocabulary.

DEFINING VOCABULARY

The word *vocabulary* refers not only to individual words but also to phrases that constitute a single unit of meaning. Consider the phrase *swimming against the tide*, for example. It has four words and yet is a single unit of meaning. (Because the term *vocabulary* is sometimes thought to refer to only individual words, some texts use the term **lexis** to include any word or phrase that acts as a single unit of meaning. In this chapter we use the more familiar term *vocabulary*.)

Vocabulary in a language class, then, includes individual words (such as *table, chair, laugh, green*), multi-word nouns (such as *stock market, swimming pool*), phrasal verbs (such as *run away, figure out*), idioms (such as *swimming against the tide, raining cats and dogs, against the clock*), or any other phrases that constitute a single unit of meaning. (See "Learning in Chunks: The Lexical Approach" in chapter 3 for more examples.)

Note also that words are part of families. The four words *active, actively, activity*, and *activities*, for example, are part of the same word family, and it makes sense to learn these words together (at least to the degree that it is reasonable for a learner at a particular level).

When choosing vocabulary for classes, we must also consider relevance. Certain words, for example, are considered high-frequency words and should be learned as early as possible because they are the most useful. The eight hundred most-used word families, for example, are sufficient for everyday conversations, while the three thousand most-used word families are sufficient for understanding most conversations, movies, and radio programs, and the eight thousand most-used word families will allow students to read newspapers, magazines, and books. (A quick Internet search will reveal lists [of various lengths] of the most-used words or word families in English.)

As such, much of the vocabulary taught in language classes is drawn from the words and phrases used most by everyday speakers of the language, while terms sometimes encountered but not often used may need to be taught from time to time. A lesson on banking, for example, may need to include terms that are commonly used but have not yet been learned by the students (such as *deposit*, *withdraw*, and *cheque*), and these terms should be reused in class from time to time in order to familiarize students with their common uses. A newspaper article on banking, however, may use the word *derivatives*—an investment term not frequently used even by native speakers. This word can be taught once for the sake of understanding the article, but a better option might be to rewrite the article in order to avoid the word altogether.

In other classes—where the topics are academic, professional, or vocational, for example—the vocabulary taught is likely to be specialized. Some of those terms will form part of the students' **productive vocabulary**—that which they use correctly in speaking and writing; others will form part of their **receptive vocabulary**—that which they understand when reading or listening but do not use in their speaking or writing.

☞ Consider: What might be the effect of giving students reading material that contains numerous new words that they otherwise would not likely encounter?

SEMANTICS AND LANGUAGE LEARNERS

Learning vocabulary can be difficult, and it often involves much more than simply "learning new words" or phrases. Some words or phrases in one language, for example, do not have equivalents in another language, or if they do, they might differ in usage. Others may have a meaning similar to the nearest equivalent in another language, yet the differences are significant enough to cause confusion or misuse. Understanding such differences is important to both language teachers and learners if our goal is effective communication, and many of these differences are revealed by the field of **semantics**.

Semantics is the study of the meaning of words, phrases, **clauses**, and sentences, and it is useful to help us discover what rules allow meaning to be communicated and how those rules might present problems for language learners. The most relevant concepts in semantics, at least for our purposes, are as follows:

- *Sense*: The term *speaker-sense* refers to the meaning intended by the speaker, while *linguistic-sense* refers to the literal meaning of the words expressed. The difference is important. When teaching the word *job*, for example, we can explain that the phrase *Nice job!* is often used as a general comment on what someone has done (even if it is not an actual job), and that it might be a compliment (when spoken literally) or an insult (when spoken with sarcasm).
- *Lexical ambiguity*: When a word has more than one possible meaning, the intended meaning may not be clear. *Bank*, for example, can refer to a financial institution, the side of a river, or even a pile of snow, and although the intended meaning might seem clear in a particular context, it might not be clear to a language learner who knows only one meaning of the word.

    Worse yet, a single word may be used in the same way but with different (or even opposite) meanings. For example, British speakers *table* a topic for discussion, but Americans *table* a topic to postpone the discussion; and in British English, *homely* describes a place as being cozy and comfortable, but in American English it describes a person as being unattractive.
- *Synonyms*: Two or more words may have the same meaning. However, most synonyms are not perfect synonyms, as they may differ slightly in meaning or at least in nuance, and perhaps even more in usage. Consider, for example, the difference between *my big sister* and *my large sister*. A language learner may not understand the differences in nuance or usage, but your older sister certainly will.
- *Overlap*: Words are said to overlap in meaning if they share some, but not all, semantic values. The English words *beyond* and *behind*, for example, are both prepositions of location; in a few contexts, they can be used interchangeably, but in most contexts they cannot be.

    Overlap can cause problems for language learners because it can be difficult to know which word to use, particularly if overlapping words in one language are a single word in another. An English speaker, for example, is likely to confuse the French words *connaître* and *savoir*, both of which are translated as *know*.

- *No equivalent*: In some cases, a word in one language simply has no equivalent word or expression in another language.
- *Idioms*: Some expressions have a meaning other than the literal meaning of the words themselves, such as *out of the blue* or *in the nick of time*. Language learners generally cannot guess the meanings of idioms and may be further confused when an expression is used both as an idiom (such as *over the hill*, referring to age) and in its literal sense (such as *over the hill*, referring to location).

Keeping these concepts in mind when teaching new vocabulary will help us understand the struggles our students may have and may also help us to find better ways of explaining the meaning and usage of new vocabulary.

UNDERSTANDING MEANING AND USAGE

The study of semantics shows us that learning a new word or phrase may not be as simple as looking up the definition in a dictionary. Rather, it is the nuances of the word or phrase, including how and when it is used, that can be difficult. Understanding these nuances requires an understanding of four key elements:

- *Meaning*: Pictures, gestures, and dictionaries can all help clarify meaning, but sometimes the properties of a word or phrase can be explained to differentiate it from a similar word or phrase. The word *high*, for example, is used to indicate position, while the word *tall* is used to indicate height: *The balloon is high above the lake. The building is very tall.*
- *Grammatical context*: If the learners are well-versed in grammar, they will find it helpful to know the common grammatical usage of a new word or phrase. The word *deposit*, for example, is most often used as a transitive verb, as in *deposit the money*, though it is also used as a noun, as in *make a deposit*.
- *Common collocations and chunks*: It is essential to know that particular words or phrases are most commonly used with certain other words or phrases. The verb *deposit*, for example, is always followed by a noun (or equivalent) and is used most often in reference to money, while the noun *deposit* often follows the verb *make*. Consider also the word *about*. As a preposition, it is most often used in phrases such as *think about, learn about, talk about, worry about,* and *excited about*. As an adverb, it is most often used to mean *approximately*, as in the phrases *about five*

o'clock, *about two metres*, and *just about ready*. Without knowing collocations and chunks, students are likely to use new terms in ways that are grammatically correct but unnatural; as such, teachers should be sure to emphasize this step any time new terms are encountered.
- *Social context*: Knowing when to use (or when not to use) certain words or phrases is essential. Consider, for example, that although the word *deposit* can be used in a number of situations, the most common of those situations, by far, is banking; and although the idiom *over the hill* is often used to replace the adjective *old*, especially when referring to a person, it should be used only in a joking, friendly way with a person of close acquaintance, and it is considered rude in many contexts.

☞ *Try: Make a list of 10 terms related to a particular theme. Then write a simple definition, the grammatical context, the social context, and two sample sentences (using common collocations) for each.*

TEACHING VOCABULARY: GENERAL TIPS

Learning the correct meaning as well as the nuances of new vocabulary takes time, and committing those details to long-term memory takes even more time. Our job as language teachers, then, is to provide the conditions for students to learn and practice using new vocabulary items in their natural grammatical and social contexts. Furthermore, vocabulary should be taught in ways that encourage further vocabulary development. As such, keep the following in mind when planning any type of vocabulary activity for class:

- Choose vocabulary related to a specific theme (such as banking, travel, hobbies) so that new terms will be taught within their natural context and with other related words that can be remembered together.
- Teach and practice the correct pronunciation of any new vocabulary item—without it, the item is largely useless in speaking and listening.
- Teach the social contexts, grammatical contexts, and common phrases (or language chunks) in which new items are commonly used.
- When appropriate, teach words with their opposites so they can be remembered together (such as *big-small, tall-short, high-low, bright-dark*).
- When appropriate (depending on the students' level, time available, and class objectives), teach other forms of the same word roots (not only *build*, but also *building, builder*).

- Use the most natural form of expressions, such as *swimming against the tide*, not *to swim against the tide*.

VOCABULARY LESSONS

Sometimes we need an entire lesson to introduce students to a group of related terms and to help them develop their understanding of and ability to use those new terms. A lesson plan on banking vocabulary, for example, may teach terms such as *deposit, withdraw, cheque, teller,* and so forth before moving on to provide practice of these terms in a variety of oral and written exercises so that students can internalize them. A typical lesson contains these basic steps:

1. *Teach pronunciation and spelling*: Our first step is to ensure that students learn the correct pronunciation of new vocabulary. After all, a mispronounced word is sometimes as unintelligible as the wrong word. Focus, then, not only on the correct sounds but also on the correct word stress and on how the pronunciation might differ in the context of a sentence. (For more on pronunciation, see chapters 15 and 16.) Teach the spelling too, if appropriate. (Note that learners at lower levels, and young learners in particular, often learn vocabulary that they are not yet ready to spell.) In particular, draw attention to similarities of new words to previously learned words.
2. *Teach meaning*: Our second step is to ensure that students have a clear idea of the correct meaning of new vocabulary. There are numerous ways of doing this:
    - using flashcards for basic nouns, verbs, adjectives, numbers
    - using actions and gestures to demonstrate action verbs, basic adjectives
    - drawing pictures or diagrams
    - matching words with their definitions or opposites
    - explaining the meaning in simple words and short sentences, often by contrasting a new term with a known term (e.g., *a vest is like a jacket, but a vest has no sleeves*)
    - explaining the meaning by listing basic characteristics (e.g., *tractor: a large machine, powerful, has large tires, used by farmers, used in fields*)
    - using an ESL dictionary to find a definition in very simplified English, or eliciting such a definition from students
    - translating the word into the student's first language, particularly for unusual or abstract meanings

Note that while translation might seem the easiest of these, it is not necessarily the most useful because it reinforces students' tendency to think in their first language and then translate (while our goal is to have them think in the target language). Furthermore, the translation of a word may not be an exact equivalent, or may consist of more than one term in the other language, with each used in a different context. The English word *please*, for example, can be translated as *kudasai*, *dozo*, or *onegaishimasu* in Japanese, but these terms are used in very different contexts and relate very different intentions.

3. *Teach social and grammatical context, as well as common collocations*: Students will use new vocabulary more naturally if they know when and how the new vocabulary is commonly used. (See "Understanding Meaning and Usage" earlier in this chapter.)

4. *Give typical examples*: Meaning and usage can be explained using any number of methods, but they are often further clarified and internalized only through examples that demonstrate the term's natural use. The best examples, then, use the term in its natural context and with words it naturally occurs with. The term *disgusting*, for example, is clarified and memorable in the following example: *The three-month-old stew in my fridge was disgusting, so I threw it out.*

5. *Controlled written practice*: Once students have clarified the meanings and usage of the terms, they are ready to begin to commit them to memory through practice. Begin with written exercises such as the following that require students to use the new terms in their natural contexts:
    - labelling a picture using the new terms
    - word bingo (words on chart, hints or definitions given orally)
    - true-or-false sentences using new vocabulary
    - matching the new terms with pictures, definitions, synonyms, or antonyms
    - crossword puzzles (with definitions or sample sentences)
    - fill in the blanks with the new vocabulary
    - categorizing words under given headings
    - correcting written mistakes using the appropriate new vocabulary

6. *Controlled oral practice*: As students become more comfortable with the new terms, introduce oral practice activities that require students to use their new vocabulary without the aid of written material. The following are particularly useful:
    - identifying oral sentences as true or false (and providing corrections)

- naming the terms being described or acted out
- filling in the blanks (in a story or anecdote given orally)
- explaining the difference between two words or phrases
7. *Authentic written/oral practice*: Authentic practice allows students to use the new vocabulary with relative freedom to choose the context and usage. If students need a lot of additional practice, consider using authentic written practice followed by authentic oral practice; alternatively, a combination of the two in a single activity may be the best solution. Common activities include the following:
   - writing a short anecdote, essay, or letter using the new vocabulary
   - writing and delivering a short speech using the new vocabulary
   - developing and acting out a role play using the new vocabulary
   - small-group conversation using the new vocabulary

Committing new vocabulary to long-term memory requires not only immediate practice but also practice over time. In fact, students are unlikely to retain new vocabulary until they've met or used it a dozen times or more in various contexts. For this reason, new vocabulary should be used again in future lessons whenever appropriate.

INTEGRATING VOCABULARY IN VARIOUS CONTEXTS

Vocabulary activities are found in many types of lessons. A speaking lesson on international travel, for example, may use a short vocabulary activity to teach basic travel terms such as *passport, immigration, customs,* and so forth before moving on to discussion, role plays, and other activities where such words might be required. The new vocabulary in this case plays a secondary but vital role—without it, the students would not be able to achieve the lesson's objective.

In a similar way, a communicative lesson might include speaking, listening, reading, and writing activities to help students master a particular language function, but it might also include a vocabulary activity to introduce students to new terms relevant to that language function.

Content-based lessons often require new vocabulary in order to master the content and thus include vocabulary activities early in the progression. Without this support, students would struggle with the content and have difficulty achieving the lesson objective.

In each of these contexts, the other activities in the lessons provide a natural context (both grammatical and social) for the vocabulary, as well as common language chunks in which they are used, and are therefore very useful. As such, it is essential for language teachers to become adept at developing vocabulary activities that take advantage of the opportunities provided by the lesson.

Building Vocabulary through Extensive Reading and Listening

Reading for pleasure is an excellent way for students to build vocabulary on their own time. Ideally, they should choose texts, such as graded readers, that are set at an appropriate level and introduce a limited number of new words. The text, then, provides the natural social and grammatical contexts for the new words and phrases, and it will generally use new vocabulary numerous times, providing the practice needed to fully understand the proper use of the vocabulary and to commit it to long-term memory. (For more information on extensive reading, see chapter 10.)

Extensive listening is another good way for students to build vocabulary and to learn the natural use of new words and phrases. Again, students should choose listening material that is set at an appropriate level and introduces a limited number of new words—the audio CDs that come with many graded readers are ideal. As the students hear new vocabulary items used again and again, they will become more familiar with their natural usage and be more likely to commit them to long-term memory. (For more information on extensive listening, see chapter 9.)

THE REWARD

No matter which methods we use to help students build vocabulary, the time we spend is very worthwhile. A larger vocabulary allows students to express themselves more accurately and naturally when speaking and writing, and to better understand the meaning of what they hear and read. In other words, learning vocabulary enhances each of the language skills, and that, of course, is the usual reason for studying language in the first place.

QUESTIONS FOR REVIEW

1. Why is vocabulary arguably the first and most important step in learning a language?
2. In each sentence that follows, which of the underlined phrases is a single unit of meaning? Explain.

    a. *I <u>ran into</u> an old friend last week. I <u>ran into</u> the house to get my jacket.*
    b. *I <u>drove her up the hill</u>, and she <u>drove me up the wall</u>.*
    c. *I'd rather be stuck in <u>blueberry jam</u> than a <u>traffic jam</u>.*
3. Why might the following expressions cause trouble for language learners?
    a. *Way to go …* (Spoken while looking at someone's mistake.)
    b. *When the boss sees this, he'll hit the roof!*
4. Why is it helpful to learn vocabulary related to a particular theme (i.e., to learn related terms at once)?
5. Why is learning the correct pronunciation of a word almost as important as learning the word itself?
6. Why is it important to teach common collocations and natural use of new vocabulary?
7. What is meant by the "social and grammatical contexts" of vocabulary? Why should we teach these?
8. Why is it important to use a variety of activities to help students learn and practice using new vocabulary?
9. Explain how extensive reading and extensive listening can be used to help improve vocabulary.
10. Read through the sample lesson plan (appendix 12A). What are its strengths? What might you change if you were to use this lesson in a class?

FURTHER READING

I. S. P. Nation's *Learning Vocabulary in Another Language* (Cambridge, 2013) provides a systematic approach to learning vocabulary with specific strategies.

James Nattinger and Jeanette DeCarrico's *Lexical Phrases and Language Teaching* (Oxford, 1992) explores lexical phrases as the basis of language learning.

Norbert Schmitt and Michael McCarthy's *Vocabulary: Description, Acquisition and Pedagogy* (Cambridge, 1998) provides an accessible, comprehensive guide to relevant theory.

Penny Ur's *Vocabulary Activities* (Cambridge, 2012) provides numerous practical activities for vocabulary classes.

Stuart Webb and I. S. P. Nation's *How Vocabulary Is Learned* (Oxford, 2016) is a practical guide to issues and activities related to learning vocabulary.

CHAPTER 13
Understanding Grammar

Grammar—the word itself inspires dread among the masses—yes, even (or perhaps especially) among native speakers of a language. Students have been known to wring their hands in despair, while teachers have been seen hunched over grammar books late at night, trying to make sense of the grammar for the next day's lesson—but it needn't be like this. Grammar is simply the structure of the language, and we already know most of it—otherwise we wouldn't be able to communicate.

The challenge of grammar lies not in our ability to use it but in our understanding of why we use it the way we do. Subconsciously, we access grammar rules every time we speak: we know to use the plural form *children*, not *childs*, so it seems likely that we have a basic understanding of **morphology**, which is the study of how words are formed. Likewise, we know to say *Where are you going?* not *Where you are going?* as a standard question, so it seems we also have a basic understanding of **syntax**, which is the study of how words are arranged to form phrases, clauses, and sentences. Explaining grammar, then, is often a matter of finding the right words to express what we already know and use.

Before moving on, we should quickly dispel the myth that English grammar is unusually difficult because it has so many exceptions. It isn't, and it doesn't. English spelling, not grammar, is riddled with exceptions. English grammar rules are surprisingly logical and consistent, and though exceptions do occur, English grammar overall is no more difficult than the grammars of many other languages, and it is certainly easier than some.

WHAT SHOULD A TEACHER KNOW?

Most language teachers have no desire to explain the finer points of grammar, and thankfully, they will rarely—if ever—be called on to do so. They will need, however, a basic knowledge of how and when we use certain grammar forms—for example, how we form questions, or how we form and when we use present perfect tense or passive constructions. We use these forms regularly, and with a little preparation, we can likely explain them without confusing our students.

There are also times when a basic understanding of grammar terms and grammar theory is very helpful—grammar reference books, for example, often assume a certain level of knowledge. This chapter, then, introduces the basic structures of grammar for teachers (not for students, though some students will know them) under the following four categories:

1. *Words*: how they are formed; how they are categorized
2. *Phrases*: how words are combined into phrases
3. *Clauses*: how phrases are combined into and function within clauses; types of clauses
4. *Sentences*: how clauses form various types of sentences

Covering these basics in one chapter requires a certain efficiency, so this chapter is not intended as light reading. It may seem a bit overwhelming, in fact, so it should be read one section at a time, with a bit of time and practice between sections, and then later used as a reference. (See this book's companion website for practice.)

THE STRUCTURE OF WORDS

When we use words like *hopeful* or *strongest*, we recognize that these words are made up of more than one part: *hopeful* is made of *hope* and a suffix, just as *strongest* is made of *strong* and a suffix. In a similar way, we recognize that the word *went* is actually a form of the word *go*, even though it doesn't look the same. In each case, the word is a combination of smaller parts.

The smallest part of a word that retains key information about its meaning and/or function, even in different contexts, is called a **morpheme**. Morphemes include word roots, inflections, and derivational affixes.

A word **root** contains the word's core meaning; a free root can stand alone as a word, such as *truck*, *book*, or *eat*; a bound root is one that cannot stand alone, such as {clude}, as found in *include* and *exclude*, or {vert}, as found in *invert* and *convert*.

Inflections are properties that are added to a **stem** without significantly changing the stem's meaning or grammatical class. A stem may be inflected by adding an affix or by changing the stem itself. There are eight inflections in English: plural, possessive, comparative, superlative, (third-person singular) present, past, present participle, past participle.

- Most nouns become plural by adding *s* or *es* (though some are exceptions):
  toy + {PLU} = *toys*; *box* + {PLU} = *boxes*; *child* + {PLU} = *children*
- Nouns become possessive by adding *'s* or *'*, and pronouns by altering the pronoun itself:
  girl + {POSS} = *girl's*; *boys* + {POSS} = *boys'*; *they* + {POSS} = *their*
- Many adjectives become comparative by adding *er*:
  big + {COMP} = *bigger*; *tall* + {COMP} = *taller*
- Many adjectives become superlative by adding *est*:
  tiny + {SUPL} = *tiniest*; *hard* + {SUPL} = *hardest*
- Verbs form the third-person singular present by adding *s*:
  jump + {PRES} = *jumps*; *sing* + {PRES} = *sings*
- Verbs form the simple past tense by adding *ed* or by modifying the verb stem:
  walk + {PAST} = *walked*; *eat* + {PAST} = *ate*
- Verbs form the present participle by adding *ing*:
  do + {PRES PART} = *doing*; *try* + {PRES PART} = *trying*
- Verbs form the past participle by adding *ed* or by modifying the verb stem:
  walk + {PAST PART} = *walked*; *go* + {PAST PART} = *gone*

Derivational affixes are prefixes and suffixes that cause a new word to be derived from an existing word or root, thereby changing the meaning and, in many cases, the part of speech:

- Prefixes do not change the part of speech but modify the meaning:
  {re} + {do} = *redo*; {dis} + {allow} = *disallow*
- Suffixes generally change a word from one grammatical class to another; for example, *able* changes many verbs into adjectives, while *ful* changes many nouns into adjectives:
  {teach} + {able} = *teachable*; {hope} + {ful} = *hopeful*

Morphemes cannot be combined randomly; rather, their arrangement is governed by rules. For example, derivational suffixes (such as *ly*, which is sometimes used to change a noun into an adjective) always precede inflectional suffixes (such as *est*, used to form the superlative) when both are present: {friend} + {ly} + (SUPL} = *friendliest*.

An awareness of basic morphology helps us better understand the types of mistakes students make and how we can better teach the ways in which these words are formed. We'll address both these issues in the next chapter.

☞ *Consider: Numerous tenses are mentioned in the list of possible word inflections in English. Why are none of the future tenses mentioned?*

WORD CATEGORIES (PARTS OF SPEECH)

When examining how words combine to form phrases, clauses, and sentences, we note that words behave in a variety of ways: some words name things, others describe things, still others imply action, and so on. As such, we categorize words according to how they behave in a sentence. (In grammar books, these categories are often referred to as the **parts of speech**.)

Nouns

A noun is a word that names a person, place, thing, idea, or quality:

- person: *boy, girl, mother, king, princess, teacher, driver, dad, Lucy, Tom* …
- place: *town, city, river, mountain, island, post office, Rome, shop, school, kitchen* …
- thing: *computer, desk, lamp, car, building, tree, flower, grass, foot, eye* …
- idea or quality: *kindness, comfort, freedom, solitude, gratitude, peace* …

Language students sometimes struggle to learn the difference between **countable nouns** (which normally have a singular form and a plural form, such as *dog-dogs, child-children, city-cities*) and **uncountable nouns** (such as *art, bread, cream, furniture, milk, music, power*).

Language students may also struggle to recognize that words that are normally verbs may sometimes function as nouns:

- **infinitive** verb form as noun: <u>*To swim*</u> is to live. I love <u>*to swim*</u>.
- present participle as noun, called a **gerund**: <u>*Swimming*</u> is fun. I love <u>*swimming*</u>.

Adjectives

An adjective modifies a noun by describing a quality of the noun; in a sentence, it often appears just before the noun it modifies: *a tiny tomato, a green leaf, a long story, a significant decision, a delicious meal, an unbelievable story, an obvious mistake.*

Adjectives may also appear after a **linking verb**: *The dog was dirty, smelly, and tired. That lady seems pleasant and easygoing.*

Many adjectives have comparative forms (*bigger, shorter, taller*) and superlative forms (*biggest, shortest, tallest*), and they are often modified by degree adverbs: *very big, unbelievably short, incredibly tall.*

In some cases, the present participle or past participle of a verb can act as an adjective: *the sleeping dog, the untold story, the spilled milk.* Note that these **participle adjectives**, as well as certain other adjectives (such as *primary* and *favourite*, which already imply the utmost degree), do not have comparative or superlative forms, and many of them cannot be modified by a degree adverb (such as *very*).

Determiners

A determiner is a word that introduces a noun and helps determine what the noun refers to or the quantity of the noun, but it does not describe a quality of the noun. Determiners in English include the following subcategories:

- articles: *a, an, the*
- demonstrative determiners: *this, that, these, those*
- interrogative determiners: *what, which, whose*
- possessive form of nouns: *Tim's, book's, London's, dog's, moon's* ...
- possessive form of indefinite pronouns: *anyone's, everybody's, nobody's, someone's* ...
- possessive form of personal pronouns: *my, your, his, her, its, our, their*
- quantifier determiners: *all, any, each, every, few, many, more, most (of), some* ...
- cardinal and ordinal numbers: *one, two, three* ... ; *first, second, third* ...

Pronouns

A pronoun substitutes for and functions like a noun (or equivalent). Pronouns in English are often subcategorized as follows:

- personal pronouns: *I, me, you, we, us, he, him, she, her, it, they, them*

- possessive personal pronouns: *mine, yours, ours, his, hers, its, theirs*
- indefinite pronouns: *anyone, somebody, everywhere, nothing …*
- interrogative pronouns: *who, whom, whose, what, which*, used to form questions that a noun (or equivalent) is likely to answer: *<u>Who</u> are you? <u>What</u> is your name?*
- relative pronouns: *that, which, who, whom, whose*, used to join a relative clause to a main clause: *The man <u>who</u> sits by the window each week is my uncle.*
- demonstrative pronouns: *this, that, these, those*

Note that determiners and pronouns often appear similar, but there is a key difference: a determiner precedes a noun, but a pronoun replaces a noun:

- *<u>Many</u> people arrived late. <u>Many</u> will leave early.* (determiner, pronoun)
- *<u>My</u> book is on the shelf. <u>Mine</u> is on the shelf.* (determiner, pronoun)
- *<u>This</u> book is not mine. <u>This</u> is not mine.* (determiner, pronoun)
- *<u>Which</u> book is yours? <u>Which</u> is yours?* (determiner, pronoun)

Verbs

A verb expresses an action, an occurrence, or a state.

Many verbs express action: *run, sing, dance, eat, read, faint, fly, cry, swim, drive, complain, jump, type, sit, stand, write, read, study, sleep*, and many more.

Some verbs, called linking verbs, do not express action but instead link the subject of the sentence to something that describes it: *The test <u>is</u> difficult. It <u>seems</u> impossible. He <u>turned</u> green. I <u>feel</u> sleepy. She <u>became</u> ill. This soup <u>smells</u> delicious but <u>tastes</u> bad. They <u>feel</u> sad.* (Note that in each case, the word or phrase that follows the verb describes the subject of the sentence.)

Others, called **stative verbs**, express a state, not an action, and cannot be used in progressive tenses: *The soup <u>looks</u> good, <u>smells</u> good, and <u>tastes</u> good. I really <u>like</u> it! I <u>believe</u> you will <u>like</u> it too!*

There are also verbs, called **auxiliary verbs**, that are used mainly to add nuance to the main verb(s) in the sentence, such as tense, voice, or other conditions:

- tense: *He <u>is</u> running. He <u>will</u> run. He <u>has been</u> running all day.* (See appendix 13A for a list of verb tenses in English.)
- voice: *The cake <u>was</u> eaten early in the morning.* (passive voice)
- conditions such as necessity, ability, advisability, permissibility, possibility, or probability: *He <u>must</u> run! She <u>can</u> dance. They <u>should</u> go. He <u>may</u> go.* (These are known as **modal auxiliary verbs**.)

Adverbs

An adverb modifies a verb, an adjective, another adverb, or a group of words by giving information about time, frequency, place, manner, cause, or degree. In other words, adverbs generally answer the questions *when, how often, where, how, why,* or *to what extent.*

There are thousands of adverbs in English, including commonly used ones such as the following: *quickly, softly, gently, harshly, quietly, slowly, carefully, nearly, very, always, often, sometimes, occasionally, rarely, never, again, then, yearly, daily, yesterday, today, tomorrow, unfortunately, obviously, completely, consequently, thus, rather, indeed, finally, here, there* …

Some adverbs provide a smooth transition between two main clauses; they are called **conjunctive adverbs** and include words such as *furthermore, however, meanwhile, moreover, nonetheless, otherwise, then, therefore,* and *thus.* (Note that these words are not conjunctions and therefore cannot be used to grammatically join clauses.)

Interrogative adverbs (*where, when, why, how*) are used to form questions that an adverb (or a phrase or clause that acts like an adverb) is likely to answer.

Prepositions

A preposition normally appears before a noun (or equivalent) to form a prepositional phrase that modifies some other part of the sentence (such as another noun, a verb, or an adjective). Consider these examples: *The cat <u>on</u> the sofa often drinks <u>from</u> the fish tank. He is fond <u>of</u> cloudy water.*

- The preposition *on* forms the prepositional phrase *on the sofa*, which modifies the noun *cat*.
- The preposition *from* forms the prepositional phrase *from the fish tank*, which modifies the verb *drinks*.
- The preposition *of* forms the prepositional phrase *of cloudy water*, which modifies the adjective *fond*.

Some prepositions are noted for indicating direction or location: *above, across, around, below, beneath, beside, between, beyond, from, in, in back of, in front of, inside, into, near, next, of, off, on, onto, on top of, out, out of, outside, over, past, through, throughout, to, toward, under, underneath, up, upon, up to* …

Others are noted for indicating time (*after, before, during, by, since, until* …), while still others indicate other types of relationships: *about, according to, against, along, along with, among, apart from, as, as for, at, because of, before, behind, by means of, concerning, despite, except, except for, excepting, for, in addition to, in case of, in place of, in spite of, instead of, like, regarding, round, till, unlike, with, within, without* …

Conjunctions

Conjunctions are joining words, and they come in two types:

- A **coordinating conjunction** joins words, phrases, or clauses of equal importance. There are seven of them in English: *and, or, nor, but, for, so, yet*. Any coordinating conjunction can be used to join clauses, but only *and, or, nor, but,* or *yet* can be used to join words or phrases.
- A **subordinating conjunction** joins a less important clause to the main clause of a sentence. (See the section on clauses later in this chapter.) There are many of them, including *after, although, as, as if, as long as, as much as, as soon as, as though, because, before, even if, even though, if, if only, in order that, now that, once, rather than, since, so that, though, unless, until, when, whenever, whereas, wherever, while,* and many others.

Note that prepositions and certain subordinating conjunctions often appear similar, but a preposition joins a noun to another part of the sentence, while a subordinating conjunction joins a clause to another clause:

- *After lunch, we went to the park.* (preposition)
- *After we ate lunch, we went to the park.* (subordinating conjunction)
- *I stayed at work for an extra hour.* (preposition)
- *I stayed at work, for it was not yet time to go home.* (subordinating conjunction)

Interjections

Interjections are words like "Hey!" that are interjected into speech or writing.

Noting the Differences

Note again that parts of speech cannot always be determined by simply looking at the words themselves, as many words can function as more than one part of speech. The only way to determine the part of speech is to determine what the word is doing in the sentence. Consider the following examples:

- *He is <u>swimming</u>.* (main verb) *He likes <u>swimming</u>.* (gerund [see noun])
- *<u>Which</u> is mine?* (pronoun) *<u>Which</u> salad is mine?* (determiner)
- *Do you have a <u>three</u>?* (noun) *I have <u>three</u> books.* (determiner)
- *It <u>surprised</u> me.* (verb) *I was very <u>surprised</u>.* (participle adjective)
- *It is <u>about</u> six o'clock.* (adverb) *This chapter is <u>about</u> grammar.* (preposition)
- *This gift is <u>for</u> you.* (preposition) *I must go, <u>for</u> it is getting late.* (conjunction)

Also note that for each category, there are specific rules to describe how words in that category behave. For example, the following rules apply in English:

- A determiner must precede the noun it modifies (*a chair*), while an adjective may precede the noun or follow a linking verb (*the big chair; the chair is big*).
- If a noun is modified by a determiner and an adjective, the determiner must precede the adjective (*a big dog;* ~~*big a dog*~~).
- Articles, demonstratives, and possessive determiners cannot occur together in one phrase (~~*a his book, a this book, his this book*~~).
- Only verbs can be inflected with tense (*run, ran; walk, walked*).

These, of course, are only a few of the many rules describing how parts of speech behave. Many more can be found in grammar books, but for now, these will give us a taste of what we are describing. It is worth noting, however, that such rules are language specific, so the rules for another language may differ significantly.

☞ *Try: Visit this book's companion website for practice labelling words according to their parts of speech.*

☞ *Consider: The "parts of speech" are simply categories of words, and it is not necessary to know them in order to learn and use a language; they are necessary, however, to talk about a language and its grammar. When should students be taught these terms, if at all?*

PHRASES

When we combine words to make meaning, we do not combine them randomly but according to rules and into successively larger units. Words combine to make phrases, and phrases combine to make clauses and sentences.

A phrase is built around a **headword**. A noun phrase, for example, is built around a noun, just as a verb phrase is built around a verb, an adjective phrase is built around an adjective, and so on. These headwords may be combined with other words (of specific types) that complete the phrase. The words that are combined and the order in which they are combined are described by what we call *phrase structure rules*. The rules for the most commonly used types of phrases in English are as follows:

- A *noun phrase* must contain a noun (or the equivalent, such as a pronoun or gerund), which may be preceded by a determiner and/or one or more adjective phrases, and may be followed by a prepositional phrase (which itself contains another noun phrase). Examples: *the old man; they; him; the very silly boy; the big red dog by the flowering bush.*
- A *verb phrase* must contain a verb, which may be preceded by or followed by an adverb, and may be followed by one or more objects or complements (see the next section); it may end in a prepositional phrase. Examples: *ate; sat down slowly; quickly ate a sandwich for lunch.*
- A *prepositional phrase* consists of a preposition and a noun phrase (known as the object of the preposition) and acts like an adjective or an adverb. Examples: *near the tree; in the house; in an hour; until the next time.*
- An *adjective phrase* must contain an adjective, which may be preceded by an intensifier and/or followed by a prepositional phrase. Examples: *special; very pretty; very fond of chocolate.*
- An *adverb phrase* must contain an adverb, which may be preceded by an intensifier. Examples: *fortunately; very quickly.*

Note that one phrase can be embedded within another. In the verb phrase *very quickly ran over the hill*, for example, the noun phrase *the hill* is part of the prepositional phrase *over the hill*, and both the adverb phrase *very quickly* and the prepositional phrase *over the hill* are part of the verb phrase. We can see this structure by representing it as a tree diagram (see figure 13.1).

```
              Verb Phrase
            /     |     \
           /      |      PP
          /       |     /  \
         AdvP     |    |    NP
        /   \     |    |   /  \
      Adv   Adv   V    P  Det  N
      very quickly ran over the hill
```

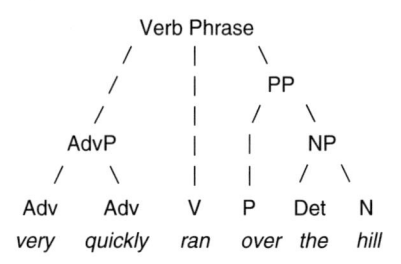

Figure 13.1: Tree Diagram of a Verb Phrase

☞ *Try: Visit this book's companion website for practice in identifying various types of phrases.*

CLAUSE STRUCTURE

Words join to make phrases, and phrases join to make clauses. A clause is a group of grammatically related words that contains a subject and a predicate.

The **subject** tells who or what the clause is about. It is a noun phrase—that is, it contains a noun (or equivalent) and may include modifiers such as determiners, adjective phrases, and prepositional phrases. Consider these examples:

- <u>Tom</u> ate his dinner. <u>He</u> is a good boy.
- <u>The very small bird by the shed</u> ate his dinner too.

Note that in the first example, the subject is a noun or pronoun alone; it has no modifiers. In the second example, however, the noun (*bird*) is modified by a determiner (*the*), an adjective phrase (*very small*), and a prepositional phrase (*by the shed*). In this latter case, we often refer to the noun alone (*bird*) as the *simple subject*, and the noun with its modifiers as the *complete subject*.

The **predicate** tells something about the subject, such as what it is or does. It consists of a verb and whatever completes the verb phrase, such as verb modifiers, objects, and complements:

- Verb modifiers include adverb phrases and prepositional phrases.
    - She ran <u>very quickly</u> <u>down the hill</u>. (adverb phrase + prepositional phrase)
- A **direct object** receives the action of the verb; that is, it tells whom/what is acted upon. It is a noun phrase and answers the question *whom* or *what* after the verb.
    - He kissed <u>the girl</u> on the cheek. (He kissed whom? The girl.)
    - I smelled <u>the flowers</u>. (I smelled what? The flowers.)
    - He gave his father <u>a new shirt</u>. (He gave what? A new shirt.)
- An **indirect object** is the recipient of the direct object; that is, it tells to whom/what or for whom/what the action is done. It is also a noun phrase.
    - I gave <u>her</u> a present. (I gave a present to whom? Her.)
    - Tina made <u>her parents</u> a nice dinner, and then she gave <u>them</u> some flowers.

Note that in some cases a prepositional phrase may serve the same logical function:
- Tina made a nice dinner *for her parents*.

- An **object complement** is a noun phrase or an adjective phrase that follows a direct object and renames it or tells what it is or has become.
  - I call my dog *Sam*.
  - I painted my shutters *green*.
  - I left my window *open* all night.
  - I saw him *sleeping*. (*Sleeping* in this case is a participle adjective.)
- A **subject complement** follows a linking verb and completes the idea by giving more information about the subject. It may be a noun phrase, an adjective phrase, a prepositional phrase, or an adverb phrase of time or place. (Note: As described earlier in this chapter, linking verbs do not show action but "link" the subject to a term in the predicate that describes or renames the subject.)
  - He is *quiet*. He feels *sick* today, and he seems *very tired*. (adjective phrases)
  - This dog is *my pet*, and she is *a faithful friend*. (noun phrases)
  - Your watch is *not here*; it is *on the counter*. (adverb phrase, prepositional phrase)

☞ Try: Visit this book's companion website for practice in identifying subjects, objects, and complements.

Word Order in Clauses

Unlike some languages, English does not mark or otherwise indicate the functions of sentence elements except by word order. As such, knowing and using the correct word order is imperative. For basic statements, the order is typically one of the following:

- [SUBJECT] + [VERB], often written as S-V:
  - *The dog slept*.
- [SUBJECT] + [VERB] + [SUBJECT COMPLEMENT], or S-V-C:
  - *My dog is a very silly mutt*.
- [SUBJECT] + [VERB] + [DIRECT OBJECT], or S-V-O:
  - *Timothy kicked his brother*.

- [SUBJECT] + [VERB] + [INDIRECT OBJECT] + [DIRECT OBJECT], or S-V-IO-O:
  - *Geraldine gave her parents some very pretty flowers.*
- [SUBJECT] + [VERB] + [DIRECT OBJECT] + [OBJECT COMPLEMENT], or S-V-O-OC:
  - *The man made his situation worse.*

The order of these sentence elements changes, however, when a statement is transformed into a question. For yes/no questions, the subject is moved to a position after the first auxiliary verb or linking verb. (If there is an action verb but no auxiliary verb, a form of the verb *do* is inserted.) This is called **subject movement** and is seen in these transformations:

- *He can jump across the stream.* → *Can he jump across the stream?*
- *I should have cut my grass earlier.* → *Should I have cut my grass earlier?*
- *We are late for supper.* → *Are we late for supper?*
- *They have two dogs and a cat.* → *Do they have two dogs and a cat?*
- *She ate her supper.* → *Did she eat her supper?*

Forming a wh-question (i.e., a question that begins with *what, when, why, who, where, which,* or *how*) is more complex, as it requires two types of movement: subject movement (as above, when the subject is moved to a position after the first auxiliary verb or linking verb) and **wh-movement** (when the desired information is replaced by a question word, which is then moved to the beginning of the clause). Both types of movement are seen in these examples:

- *She hid the toy under the sofa.* → *What did she hide under the sofa?*
- *She hid the toy under the sofa.* → *Where did she hide the toy?*
- *He wants this one.* → *Which one does he want?*
- *They left yesterday.* → *When did they leave?*
- *We ate it because we were hungry.* → *Why did you eat it?*
- *They gave her five coins.* → *How many coins did they give her?*

Interestingly, languages whose dominant sentence structure is verb-subject-object (V-S-O) almost always have wh-movement, while subject-verb-object (S-V-O) languages are very likely to have wh-movement (English and French do, though Chinese does not), and subject-object-verb (S-O-V) languages (such as Japanese and Korean) usually do not have wh-movement.

Diagramming Clause Structure

The overall structure of a clause—including its subject (a noun phrase), its predicate (a verb phrase), and the hierarchical nature of its phrases—is best represented in a tree diagram (see figure 13.2). In this example, we again notice that the clause contains a subject (NP1) and a predicate (VP1).

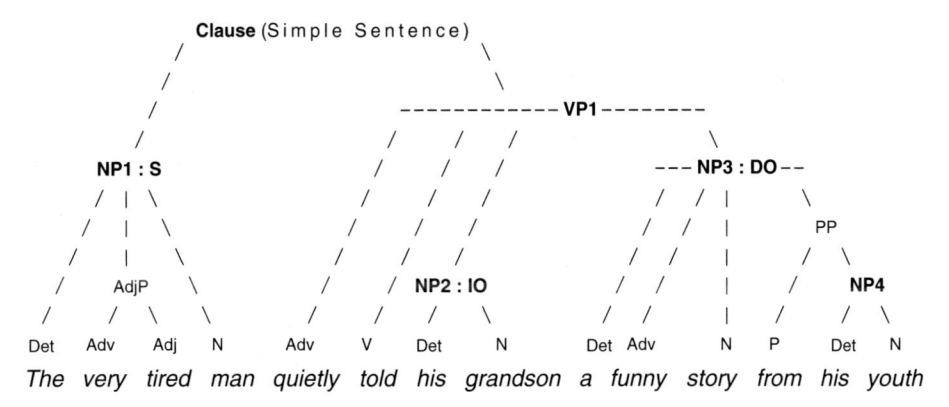

```
                Clause (Simple Sentence)
               /                         \
              /                           \
             /               ------------VP1--------
            /               /    /   /               \
         NP1 : S           /    /   /         ---NP3 : DO--
         / | \            /    /   /          / / |        \
        /  |  \          /    /   /          / / |          PP
       /   |   \        /    /   /          / / |          / \
      /   AdjP  \      /    /  NP2 : IO    / / |          /  NP4
     /   / \     \    /    /  /  \        / / |          /   / \
    Det Adv Adj   N  Adv  V  Det  N     Det Adv N   P  Det  N
    The very tired man quietly told his grandson a funny story from his youth
```

Figure 13.2: Tree Diagram of a Clause

- The subject (S) is a noun phrase (NP1) that includes a noun modified by a determiner and an adjective phrase.
- The predicate is a verb phrase (VP1) that includes a verb, an adverb, an indirect object, and a direct object. The indirect object (IO) is a noun phrase (NP2) that includes a noun modified by a determiner; the direct object (DO) is a noun phrase (NP3) that includes a noun modified by a determiner, an adjective, and a prepositional phrase, which of course contains a noun phrase of its own (NP4).

TYPES OF CLAUSES

Clauses are commonly named according to whether they can stand alone as a sentence or not. If the clause can stand alone as a sentence, it is considered an **independent clause** or a **main clause**:

- *I won the race.*
- *Although I won the race, I did not get a trophy.*
- *I won the race, but I did not get a trophy.*

If the clause cannot stand alone as a sentence (because it needs to be connected to something), it is considered a **dependent clause** or a **subordinate clause**.

- *Although I won the race*, I did not get a trophy.

Dependent clauses are further categorized by the role they play in a sentence: an *adverb clause* acts like an adverb, an *adjective clause* acts like an adjective, and a *noun clause* acts like a noun.

Adverb Clauses

An adverb clause begins with a subordinating conjunction and modifies the main clause by telling how, when, where, why, to what extent, or under what conditions something occurs:

- *Although I won the race*, I did not get a trophy.
- *As I crossed the finish line*, the spectators clapped and cheered.
- I was upset *because I did not get a trophy*.
- *Until the judges agree to investigate*, I will not be satisfied.
- The judges will investigate *if I make a formal request*.

To recognize an adverb clause, ask whether it meets three conditions: it can precede or follow the main clause (in most cases), it can be removed (and the main clause will still make sense), and it can be replaced by an adverb.

Adjective Clauses

An adjective clause (also called a *relative clause*) begins with a relative pronoun (*that, which, who, whom, whose*) or a relative adverb (*when, where, why*). It modifies the noun (or equivalent) that precedes it:

- That man, *who did not win the race*, stole my trophy. (*who* = subject of relative clause; the relative clause modifies *That man*)
- The race *(that) I won* was long and difficult. (Note: the relative pronoun is optional if it is not the subject of the relative clause.)
- Central Park, *where the race was held*, is a nice place for such an event. (*race* = subject of relative clause; the clauses are connected by relative adverb *where*)
- He couldn't run very quickly, *which surprised me*. (*which* = subject of relative clause; in this case the relative clause modifies the entire preceding clause)

Noun Clauses

A noun clause begins with a subordinating conjunction (though only certain ones: *if, that, whether*) or an interrogative word (such as *what, whatever, when, whenever, where, wherever, who, whoever, why, how*) and functions within another clause as a subject, subject complement, direct object, or the object of a preposition:

- *That he lost the race is no surprise to me.* (noun clause as subject)
- *What he did before the race was inexcusable.* (noun clause as subject)
- *Whoever helped him should be punished.* (noun clause as subject)
- *The truth is that he tried to cheat.* (noun clause as subject complement)
- *I don't know if he will enter the next race.* (noun clause as direct object)
- *I haven't heard when the next race will begin.* (noun clause as direct object)
- *The judges are talking about what he did.* (noun clause as object of a preposition)

Note that in the examples above, the noun clauses function as nouns, so they can be replaced by pronouns (such as *he, him, she, her, it, they, them*). However, there is one additional type of noun clause that cannot be replaced by a pronoun: it is the *appositional noun clause*.

An appositional noun clause follows a noun (usually a noun that names an idea, such as *assumption, belief, conclusion, explanation, fact, proposal*) and renames it or tells what it is. It is often confused with a relative clause because they look very similar. Compare the following:

- *The story that Jim had written isn't true.* (relative clause; Jim had written a story, and the events of the story were fictional. The relative clause modifies the noun *story*.)
- *The story that Jim had written a letter to the principal isn't true.* (appositional noun clause; there is a story (i.e., a rumour) circulating, but it's not true. The appositional noun clause does not modify the noun *story* but tells what that story is.)

Again:

- *The fact that Jim had misunderstood was actually not very difficult.* (relative clause; Jim misunderstood a particular fact, even though the fact was not difficult. The relative clause modifies the noun *fact*.)

- *The fact that Jim had misunderstood me was obvious to everyone.* (appositional noun clause; Jim misunderstood what I had said, and everyone knew that he did. The appositional noun clause does not modify the noun *fact* but tells what that fact is.)

☞ *Try: Visit this book's companion website for practice in identifying and forming various types of clauses.*

SENTENCES

A sentence is made of at least one clause, and sentence types are commonly named according to their component clauses:

- A **simple sentence** has one independent clause and no dependent clauses.
    - *My dog is a cute little Sheltie with an inferiority complex.*
    - *My cat is an ugly little beast.*
- A **compound sentence** is made of two or more independent clauses and no dependent clauses.
    - *My dog is friendly and gentle, but my cat is cold and aloof.*
    - *My dog is friendly and gentle; however, my cat is cold and aloof.*
- A **complex sentence** is made of one independent clause and one or more dependent clauses.
    - *If we didn't have pets, our house would be much cleaner.* (dependent + independent)
    - *Our house would be much cleaner if we didn't have pets.* (independent + dependent)
- A **compound-complex sentence** is made of two or more independent clauses and one or more dependent clauses.
    - *When my uncle bought a new house, he wanted to get rid of his dog, but his wife wouldn't let him.* (dependent + independent + independent)
    - *My uncle wanted to get rid of his dog when he bought a new house, but his wife wouldn't let him.* (independent + dependent + independent)

LOOKING AHEAD

In this chapter, we've covered the basic concepts and structures of morphology and syntax. As language teachers, we may never teach our students how to parse or diagram a sentence, but such knowledge helps us see the "big picture" of grammar as we teach the smaller details to our students. (That said, note that in some cases, understanding the structures is essential to understanding certain practical issues; a basic understanding of main clauses and dependent clauses, for example, is prerequisite to understanding the rules of punctuation.)

QUESTIONS FOR REVIEW

1. What is the difference between an inflectional affix and a derivational affix? (How does each function?)
2. Write five sentences, and label the parts of speech. (Try to use them all.)
3. Write examples for each of the tenses listed in appendix 13A.
4. Write five sentences, and underline and label each phrase. (Try to use all of the types named in this chapter.)
5. Write five sentences, and then underline and label the objects and complements. (Try to use all types.)
6. What are subject movement and wh-movement?
7. What is the difference between an independent clause (or main clause) and a dependent clause?
8. Name and explain, with examples, three common types of dependent clauses.
9. Draw tree diagrams for the following:
    a. *We live in a white house.*
    b. *Our pool is very clean.*
    c. *He gave me fifty bucks after I painted his fence green.*
10. Write one example of each type of sentence listed in this chapter. Label their clauses as independent or dependent.

FURTHER READING

Ronald Carter and Michael McCarthy's *Cambridge Grammar of English: A Comprehensive Guide* (Cambridge, 2006) provides theory, examples, and advice on avoiding common mistakes.

Ron Cowan's *The Teacher's Grammar of English* (Cambridge, 2008) is a comprehensive resource of grammar explanations.

Martin Parrott's *Grammar for English Language Teachers* (Cambridge, 2010) is a thorough reference with practice activities.

Leo Selivan's *Lexical Grammar: Activities for Teaching Chunks and Exploring Patterns* (Cambridge, 2018) includes both theory and suggested activities to explore the relationship between grammar and vocabulary.

Michael Swan's *Practical English Usage* (Oxford, 2005) provides a reference for problem areas in English grammar (as well as additional tips for vocabulary, pronunciation, and spelling).

Scott Thornbury's *About Language: Tasks for Teachers of English* (Cambridge, 2017) is a practical resource for training language teachers about how language works.

CHAPTER 14
Teaching Grammar

Many new English teachers start out with the belief (or hope) that they will not need to teach grammar—after all, don't most English teachers today teach something called "conversational English"? And aren't grammar classes the unfortunate result of outdated methodology that just won't die in spite of valiant attempts to kill it?

Before we answer those questions, consider the tale of two English students with similar abilities. At age 12, both began studying English for six hours per week. The first spent two hours per week studying grammar and four hours developing her fluency, while the second devoted all of her available time to developing her fluency, hoping that her grammar would improve over time as she learned to use the language. At the end of three years, who had the better command of English? Who was able to communicate more effectively?

WHY TEACH GRAMMAR?

Not long ago, many ESL teachers and authors suggested that studying grammar was dry and boring, and that it led to an understanding of a language without the ability to use it. As a result, new fluency-first methods of teaching language began to appear, focusing primarily on oral communication, with little or no grammar instruction. Such methods suggested that if students could learn to communicate, they would be better motivated to learn, and through practice they would eventually pick up enough grammar to speak correctly. (Some of these methods still included a limited amount of grammar practice, even if it was less explicitly taught).

The theory behind these methods would suggest that of the two students mentioned above, the second should have been better at speaking English at the end of three years; after all, she'd had more practice speaking and listening. In actual fact, she spoke more quickly, but her English was broken and sometimes difficult to follow. In contrast, the first student spoke at a slightly slower pace, but her English was generally correct and very easy to follow. She also demonstrated a much stronger overall command of English.

This is not to say that fluency-first methods of teaching language are completely wrong; in fact, they are probably more correct than incorrect. Teaching grammar alone can indeed be dry and boring, as many students do not find grammar particularly inspiring. Moreover, a focus on grammar without authentic communication generally leads to an understanding of the language without the ability to use it in practical, everyday situations.

Nonetheless, we have seen that most adult students who learn a language through practice alone, with little or no grammar instruction, generally do not "pick up" correct grammar; rather, they develop a type of pidgin English that rarely progresses beyond the low-intermediate level.

There is, of course, a healthy balance between these two extremes: while grammar needn't be the focus of a class, it shouldn't be ignored either. Teaching grammar as an integral component of a well-rounded class that also includes communicative practice can give students both the accuracy and fluency necessary for successful and competent communication.

Overall, there are a number of reasons why we must be well prepared to teach grammar:

- We cannot escape teaching grammar. Regardless of the focus of the class, students will ask questions that involve grammar. Why do we say *had gone* instead of *went* in a particular sentence? Why do we say *the man who fell* instead of *the felled man?* When do we use a colon or a semi-colon? Why do we say *I believe you* instead of *I am believing you?*
- Our students will know at least some grammar, and they will expect us to know (and teach) even more. In fact, many language students have studied grammar for years in school and perhaps also in university. They know many of the rules and complexities of the language, but they simply aren't used to using them in practical ways. As we guide them to do so, a strong knowledge of how the English language works is imperative, as is the ability to explain it.
- As we noted above, teaching (or learning) "conversational English" (properly known as communicative English) without a strong base in grammar often leads to a type of fluency without accuracy—a broken, mixed-up version of the language. Worse yet, students use the same basic (and often erroneous) structures over and over until those structures

begin to sound natural to them; at that point, their language habits are so ingrained that it becomes very difficult for them to fix their mistakes, and their ability to use the language progresses very little.
- Focusing on grammatical accuracy along with meaning and fluency generally leads to stronger language skills overall.

The need for grammar instruction and practice remains strong, then, and we as teachers need to make grammar lessons more relevant, more interesting, and more effective so that students can learn well and enjoy the process.

Grammar Issues for Language Learners

Studying a foreign language can often lead to confusion, particularly when trying to understand the rules of grammar. Although all languages have grammar rules, the rules are not necessarily the same from one language to another.

Consider, for example, that the properties of a particular part of speech or phrase may vary from one language to another:

- Most English nouns are made plural by adding *s*, but some nouns have irregular plurals (*children, geese*), and non-count nouns (*bread, milk*) do not have plural forms. Many other languages form plurals differently and do not have irregular plurals, and some languages do not have plural nouns at all.
- Most English nouns do not have gender; in many other languages, they do.
- English adjectives are not inflected; in many languages (such as French and Spanish) adjectives are inflected with gender and number; Japanese adjectives are inflected with tense.
- Most English personal pronouns vary by case: *I-me, he-him, she-her, we-us, they-them*; in some languages, they do not.
- English inflects some adjectives with comparative and superlative (*big, bigger, biggest*) but uses *more* and *most* with others; most languages use the equivalent of one form or the other, and in some languages, the same form is used for comparative and superlative.
- The rules for article use differ from one language to another, and some languages have no articles; as such, using English articles (especially *the*) correctly is difficult for many learners.
- English has phrasal verbs; many languages do not, and many language learners struggle to know where to use a direct object with a phrasal verb: *Please call back me later!*

- Where English uses gerunds (*Swimming is fun!*), some languages use the infinitive (*To swim is fun!*).
- In many languages, an indirect object requires a preposition, so learners of English may add one where it doesn't belong: *I gave to him a dollar.*

Verb tenses can be particularly difficult to master, as they vary in whether they exist, how they are formed, and when they are used. For example, where English uses future or present perfect progressive, some languages use only present, resulting in erroneous sentences (in English) such as *I go to work tomorrow* or *I work on this project since this morning.* Also, while many languages use inflection or auxiliary verbs to form tenses, English (though not only English) uses both.

Also note that the existence and order of basic sentence elements (subject, verb, object) vary from one language to another. Most languages use the order S-O-V or S-V-O (though some major languages, such as Arabic, use V-S-O), but other details may vary:

- In English, a direct object normally follows a verb (S-V-O). The same is generally true in Chinese, though the order is more flexible in simple sentences.
- In Japanese, an object precedes the verb, and the subject is often omitted: S-O-V or O-V.
- French uses the structure S-V-O if the object is a noun but S-O-V if it is a pronoun.
- German uses the structure S-V-O in main clauses and S-O-V in subordinate clauses.

Other sentence elements may vary as well. In some languages, for example, an object complement precedes the direct object (as in *I painted green the fence*), while languages such as Finnish and Spanish have highly flexible word order.

Question formation is another issue for language learners. English uses various combinations of auxiliary verbs, subject movement, and wh-movement to form different types of questions, but some languages do not have auxiliary verbs, and some do not use movement; in fact, some languages use only intonation to change a statement into a question. As a result, English question formation can seem surprisingly complex.

Finally, appropriate usage may differ from one language to another. In some languages, the imperative form is reasonably polite, while its grammatical equivalent in English would be considered too direct in many situations: *Give me a drink!*

When a language learner makes a grammatical error, the reason is often related to differences between one grammar system and another, and correcting the error requires a correct diagnosis of the problem and a clear explanation of the correction. As such, it is helpful for language teachers to have a good understanding of the types of mistakes students make, why they make them, and how we can explain the correct form and facilitate its practice. (See chapter 17 for more information on why language learners have trouble adopting the underlying rules of their new language.)

WHAT KIND OF GRAMMAR DO WE TEACH?

Most native speakers of a language know enough grammar to recognize sentences that are seriously ungrammatical, but we also use language that is ungrammatical. Consider the following question and answers: *Who is it? It is I. It's me.* Almost no one will give the first answer even though it is correct; almost everyone will give the second answer in spite of its poor grammar because it is the common and expected response.

Grammar, then, can be described as **prescriptive** (i.e., grammar rules determine correct usage) or **descriptive** (i.e., grammar rules describe common usage). Some languages, such as French and German, have official bodies that prescribe correct usage; but many languages, including English, have no such body, and rules change over time. Consider the following:

- There was once a rule, adopted from Latin, that a sentence should not end with a preposition, but almost no one cares today. (What more can we ask *for?*)
- There was another rule, also adopted from Latin, that infinitives should not be split; thus it was wrong *to boldly go* where no Latin grammarian had gone before.
- Not long ago, it was considered ungrammatical to use *they* (or its variations) as singular; today, in certain social contexts, a person refusing to use it as singular might find *themselves* in trouble.

Some usage is still considered incorrect even if it is surprisingly common, even (or especially) among native speakers of the language:

- Our express checkouts say "12 items or *less*" but should say *fewer*.
- We hear about a significant *amount* of people, as if they were an uncountable pile.

- People (and sometimes even newspapers) report that someone *should have went* (or even worse, *should of went*) instead of *should have gone*.
- People often say they *could care less* when they mean they *couldn't care less*.

There are also debates that are not quite settled but probably should be. The construction *try and* [verb], for example, is often used for *try to* [verb], as in *try and do it* and *try to do it*, but the first implies two actions, and the second just one. The difference is obvious in some past-tense constructions:

- *He tried and did it.* (He was eventually successful.) *He tried to do it.* (Result unknown.)
- *He tried and failed.* (He tried but was unsuccessful.) *He tried to fail.* (He failed deliberately.)

When teaching grammar, we may find ourselves teaching what is considered "correct" and what is common, along with an explanation of what is preferred in a particular context. After all, the grammar that language learners need most is the grammar that is most useful to them.

The Role of Corpora

Who decides which grammar forms are most common or useful overall? Fortunately, computerized analysis of large sets of text (**corpora**) have identified common patterns in speech and writing in various contexts, and newer grammar textbooks often include such information. Consider, for example, that although the modal forms *must* and *have to* have essentially the same meaning, the former is used most often in reference to rules or regulations, while the latter is used in everyday conversation—so for most language learners, *have to* is the more useful form. We might also note that the form *used to* is commonly used in affirmative statements but rarely used in negative statements or questions, so language learners would do well to practice accordingly.

Many new grammar textbooks are **corpus**-based and provide valuable insight into what we should teach and which areas deserve more focus. Keeping these insights in mind will help us make grammar lessons more effective for our students.

Considering Social Context

In addition to teaching what is common, we should also teach our students which forms are acceptable in specific contexts. Consider, for example, the following:

- Standard Written English (SWE) is relatively formal and is used in academic writing. It is highly structured and follows the rules of grammar and punctuation very closely.
- Business English is similar to SWE but is slightly less formal, though still professional. It is structured in a very straightforward way and follows the rules of grammar and punctuation closely.
- Polite English uses particular grammatical forms (such as modals or questions instead of direct statements) and vocabulary in order to show respect to the listener.
- Common English or Everyday English uses correct grammar most of the time but also common expressions that may bend or even break the rules of grammar. It is reasonably polite in most contexts but generally avoids very formal forms of politeness. This is the English that most people hear and use on a daily basis, and it is the English that most learners will need to understand and use most of the time.
- Very informal English, including slang, is used among many young people or close friends who accept such usage. It may use local expressions and unusual grammar, and it may be considered impolite or uncouth when used in more formal situations.

When teaching grammar, then, we must emphasize which forms are acceptable in particular situations. Consider again (see "Authentic Language: Communicative Language Teaching" in chapter 3) a simple request for a glass of milk:

- *Give me a glass of milk.*
- *Milk, please.*
- *Could I have a glass of milk?*
- *May I have a glass of milk, please?*

The first sentence might be acceptable among family members (depending on the family, perhaps), but many listeners would find it rude. The second sentence is acceptable as a reply but probably not as a request. The third is more polite, and the fourth is the most polite—note that both use modal verbs and are phrased as questions, not statements. Also note, though, that while using impolite forms in polite circumstances may come across as rude, using the most polite forms among friends would also sound unusual.

What kind of grammar do we teach, then? We teach grammar that is likely to be useful to our students and suitable to a given situation, and with higher-level classes, this may mean teaching a variety of ways to communicate the same message and explaining how each is used and when it should be used.

WHEN DO WE TEACH GRAMMAR?

Grammar is everywhere. When students ask why we say something the way we do, the answer involves grammar; when students ask when to use one tense instead of another, the answer involves grammar; when they get stuck in the middle of a reading passage because they do not understand how a particular sentence is constructed, the answer involves grammar; and when they ask how to word a sentence for a paragraph they are writing, the answer involves grammar.

Let's face it: most of the language questions students ask us will involve grammar. We cannot avoid it.

Answering grammar questions can be unnerving, especially for teachers who are not confident in their own knowledge of grammar topics. When asked a grammar question, we have two options:

- *Answer the question immediately with a quick explanation and a few examples on the whiteboard.* This option is suitable for grammar that the teacher knows well and the students are likely to learn quickly. It also satisfies the students' desire for an immediate answer. Be warned, however, that a quick explanation can easily become a long, confusing exercise in humility if the teacher is not absolutely clear on the grammar point.
- *Delay the answer until a later class.* This option works well if the teacher needs to double-check and clarify the details or if the students are likely to need written practice (such as grammar worksheets). Taking the time to adequately prepare often results in a shorter, clearer explanation and more effective practice.

Note that when a grammar question arises naturally from the content of the class, the discussion, reading, or writing activities that follow are likely to provide natural practice of that grammar. At other times, however, we may need to teach a grammar form that requires extensive practice in the form of an entire lesson that is scheduled for a later class.

When Do We Teach a Given Form?

Sometimes a student struggles with a particular grammar form simply because that form is much too difficult for the student's level. After all, there is a natural progression (more or less, with some flexibility) that begins with easier forms and moves through increasingly more difficult ones. Plural forms, for example, can be taught to beginners at the same time basic nouns are being taught; however, future tense should not be taught to beginners at the same time basic verbs are being taught, as it is normally acquired later. (For details on what grammar forms should be taught at each level, see appendix 2C.)

PREPARING TO TEACH GRAMMAR

Teaching grammar involves explaining a concept and facilitating its practice, but the process begins long before class. It begins with preparation. In fact, we might suggest that more than any other type of lesson in a language classroom, grammar requires preparation—and lots of it. After all, the ability to speak a language correctly does not automatically translate into an ability to explain it effectively. Teaching even simple grammar can be challenging when our explanations are limited by the vocabulary and the level of sentence complexity that our students can understand, and teaching difficult grammar may challenge our own ability to understand it.

In addition, nothing will kill the class mood more quickly than a convoluted grammar explanation that confuses and frustrates students. Such explanations are the natural result of inadequate preparation. In fact, the best grammar explanations are straightforward and simple only because the preparation was long and difficult—though of course it gets easier (and takes less time) with practice.

Preparing to teach grammar is a process that usually takes longer than teaching it. At the very least, consider the following steps essential:

1. *Research your topic*: Consult at least two good grammar books for easy grammar and three or more for difficult grammar. Why? The books not only provide a thorough overview of the grammar form but also present different ways to approach it. The more ways we grapple with it, the better we will be prepared to teach it.
2. *Ask two key questions: How is it formed? When is it used?* For example, when preparing to teach the modal *have to* in affirmative statements, we note that we use the form of *have to* that agrees with the subject, followed by the infinitive form of the main verb: *We have to go. He has to go.* We then note that we use this form in everyday conversation to express an obligation, a requirement, or a necessity.

3. *Limit the focus*: Don't teach all the rules and exceptions at once. Rather, focus on the key point(s) and save the rest for another class, or at least until students have mastered the first point.
4. *Write out your grammar explanation in advance*: Use simple words and short sentences. Then rewrite it to make it clearer. (If you don't think this step is necessary, try recording yourself giving a grammar explanation without written preparation, and see how confusing and mixed up you really are.) In most cases, it is helpful to begin with an example, and then refer to that example when explaining the grammar. It is also helpful to prepare a brief handout that explains (with examples) the grammar point, and to prepare diagrams and other visuals aids if appropriate.
5. *Prepare examples*: Write out at least five examples of the grammar point. Double-check them for accuracy.
6. *Choose appropriate practice activities*:
    - If the grammar point will be introduced briefly as preparation for a reading or writing activity, a few practice sentences on the board or a short written exercise might suffice.
    - If the grammar is difficult and is to be the focus of an entire lesson, begin with controlled activities that require students to use the grammar form in very specific ways, and gradually move on to activities that give students more choice in how to use the forms. (See "Grammar Lessons" later in this chapter.)
7. *Prepare materials*: Create or find whatever materials and handouts are necessary for the class.

☞ *Try: Choose a grammar point and look up at least three explanations; then use those to develop your own explanation in clear, simple English, with multiple examples.*

CONTROLLED GRAMMAR PRACTICE

Learning to use a new grammatical form requires practice, and since adult students generally prefer to "see" the new material they are learning, initial grammar practice is usually in the form of controlled written exercises. Such exercises isolate the target grammar so that students can focus on it alone: in other words, students have little choice in what to write or how to write it; rather, for each question they are required to provide a specific answer that demonstrates knowledge of the grammar. Such exercises may require students to fill in the blanks, choose the correct answer, correct the errors, or transform the sentence. Regardless of the format, good grammar exercises have certain features in common:

- Good grammar exercises include instructions that are accurate, clear, concise, and complete. Note the difference in these instructions for a worksheet on articles:
    - "Circle the articles in the sentences below." This exercise would be useless. Anyone with basic reading skills could simply circle the words noted, even with no knowledge of articles.
    - "Add articles in the blanks below." Better, but what if no article is needed in some blanks?
    - "Add the missing articles in the paragraph below." Logically correct, but could be better.
    - "Add the missing articles in the blanks below; if no article is needed, draw a line through the blank." These instructions spell out the details clearly.
- Good grammar exercises require knowledge of how to form the grammar and when to use it. Note the differences in these examples from an exercise on past perfect tense:
    - *When John arrived home late, his family (ate/had eaten) dinner already, so he ate alone.* This example requires knowledge of when to use the tense but not how to form it.
    - *When John arrived home late, his family _____ (eat) dinner already, so he ate alone.* This example requires knowledge of how to form the tense. It may also require knowledge of when to use the tense, but only if the instructions gave other tenses as possible answers.
    - *When John _____ (arrive) home late, his family _____ (eat) dinner already, so he ate alone.* This example requires knowledge of how to form the past perfect tense and when to use it. Even better, students must know how to use the past perfect tense with the simple past tense, as the two are often used together. (Note that we include simple past when teaching past perfect because the former is already known and relevant to the use of the latter; we would not include other tenses that are not relevant or have not yet been learned.)

- Good grammar exercises also provide sufficient context so that there is only one correct answer (or few correct answers, in some cases). Consider the difference:
    - *When John arrived home late, his family _____ (eat) dinner.* This example could be completed using simple past (*ate*), past progressive (*was eating*), or past perfect tense (*had eaten*), so it is not effective as grammar practice.
    - *When John arrived home late, his family _____ (eat) dinner already.* This example could be completed using past progressive (*was eating*) or past perfect tense (*had eaten*), so again, it is not ideal.
    - *When John arrived, his family _____ (eat) dinner already, so he ate alone.* This example requires the past perfect tense (*had eaten*) in order to make sense.
- Good grammar practice uses examples that are most likely to cause trouble for students and therefore need to be practiced. Consider these examples from an activity on subject-verb agreement:
    - *The instructions (is/are) posted on the wall.*
    - *The list of instructions (is/are) posted on the wall.*

  The first example may provide good practice for students learning how to conjugate verbs, but it is too easy for most students; the second, however, addresses a common error made by students at many levels (and sometimes by native speakers). To answer the second example correctly, students must understand that *list*, not *instructions*, is the subject of the sentence.

Controlled grammar activities can be custom-made by teachers to suit a class's particular needs, but they can also be found in grammar practice textbooks from major ESL publishers. Such textbooks usually include brief, clear instructions for each grammar point followed by multiple practice activities (with or without answer keys), and most are carefully designed to address language learners' most common needs.

Online grammar practice sites are also abundant, and they often have the advantage of giving immediate (or almost immediate) correction, so students can note their mistakes and try the activity again. Many sites are free, while others require a licence (often provided with a companion textbook). Most are of good quality, but because anyone can publish a website with minimal expertise, it is absolutely essential to try a website before recommending it to students.

Regardless of the format, controlled grammar activities are helpful in a variety of contexts, whether as preparation for a reading or writing activity, or as one step in a grammar lesson. In either case, they are most effective when students receive immediate feedback so they can correct their mistakes and attempt to master the form before moving on.

Controlled Oral Practice

Grammar worksheets help students "see" the grammar they are learning, but sooner or later students will need to form the grammar in their minds without the aid of writing. Learning to do this quickly and fluently takes practice—in this case, controlled oral practice, otherwise known as oral grammar drills.

Oral grammar drills have earned a poor reputation thanks to overuse in methods such as the Audio-Lingual Method, and we know that drills alone do not produce fluent speakers. Nonetheless, drills have their place, and they provide students with effective practice that is useful before moving on to more authentic uses of the grammar.

Common oral drills include transformation drills, single-slot substitution drills, multiple-slot substitution drills, and other drills that isolate the target grammar. (See activities from "Drilling It In: The Audio-Lingual Method" in chapter 3, as well as related appendixes; note also that some written grammar practice can be adapted for oral use.) As with written practice, they are most effective if the teacher gives immediate, honest feedback and has the students continue practicing until they master the form.

☞ *Consider: To what extent do the controlled grammar activities in appendix 3A conform to the guidelines given here?*

AUTHENTIC GRAMMAR PRACTICE

Controlled practice, whether written or oral, helps students master grammar forms within limited contexts; it does not, however, prepare them to use those same grammar forms in everyday conversations or writing. As such, we need to provide students with authentic practice as well.

Authentic practice gives students choice. The teacher may provide the topic and require use of a specific grammar form, but the rest is up to the students. Such practice includes conversations, speeches, role plays, debates, essays, letters, or any other speaking or writing activity in which students choose what to say and how to say it. These activities should be student-led, interactive, and as authentic as possible, with lots of choice in how to use the target language in natural ways. Moreover, the activities should be appropriate to the target grammar, as these examples illustrate:

- A conversation or writing assignment about what students did on the weekend provides natural, authentic practice for the simple past tense.
- A role play on a topic such as ordering food in a restaurant provides natural, authentic practice for modals used in polite speech.
- Having students follow and give task-based instructions provides natural, authentic practice for prepositions of location.

Providing feedback during authentic grammar practice is more challenging because teachers often do not wish to interrupt or discourage students. However, given that learning objectives for authentic grammar activities should include both accuracy and fluency, it is essential to ensure students use the grammar correctly. As such, teachers should have students correct their errors as soon as it is reasonable to do so—even during a conversation, though perhaps at the end of a role play (unless the teacher arranges in advance for a signal to cue students to self-correct as they perform). In doing so, the teacher should be encouraging students to improve their grammar, not discouraging them from using it. (See "Dealing with Errors" in chapter 6 for more information.)

☞ *Consider: When developing and using authentic grammar practice, how can we avoid sacrificing accuracy (which is a key objective of the activity) to fluency (which is also an objective of the activity)?*

GRAMMAR LESSONS

When a grammar point is sufficiently difficult to require an entire lesson, we can break that lesson into three general steps: teacher preparation, teacher-led explanation, and student practice. Of these, the explanation should be the shortest and practice the longest.

1. *Teacher preparation*: This step should not be underestimated. A good 5-minute explanation, with examples, may require 30 minutes (or more) of preparation, and developing effective practice activities takes even longer. (See "Preparing to Teach Grammar," "Controlled Grammar Practice," and "Authentic Grammar Practice" earlier in this chapter.)

2. *Teacher-led explanation:*
    a. Use an appropriate lead-in to interest students and activate their prior knowledge. Ideally, use a question, a skit, a story, or some other idea to introduce a typical situation in which the target grammar might be used.
    b. Teach the grammar using the prepared explanation. Begin with an example, and explain how the grammar is formed and when it is used. Keep the pace slow, and pause frequently to allow students to process the explanation. Use diagrams and visual aids when relevant.
    c. Move on to additional examples, further demonstrating the target grammar on the board.
    d. Distribute the explanation handout if there is one. (Give handouts after explanations, not before, so they will serve as **reinforcement** and not as a distraction.)
    e. Check for comprehension, and review (with examples) as necessary.
3. *Student practice:*
    a. Begin with controlled written practice, as described previously. Consider using more than one type of practice so that students can interact with the grammar in a variety of ways, and give immediate feedback that requires students to self-correct.
    b. When students have mastered the controlled written practice, move on to controlled oral practice, as described previously. Consider using more than one type of drill, and again give immediate feedback throughout the activity, not just after it is completed.
    c. When students are comfortable using the grammar orally, move on to authentic practice, either written, oral, or both, depending on the needs of the students and the natural use of the grammar form. As time allows, consider using a variety of authentic activities that require the students to speak, listen to, read, and write the target form in order to increase their overall ability to understand and use it correctly in a variety of situations, and be sure to emphasize both accuracy and fluency.

Note that variety is very useful at every step when learning grammar. More than one type of controlled written practice, more than one type of controlled oral practice, and more than one type of authentic practice will give students more exposure to how the grammar is formed and used, and will result in a better understanding of the grammar. Of course, even a whole class devoted to grammar has only so much time, so balance variety with realism in deciding what mix is best for a given group of students.

☞ *Consider: To what extent do the grammar lessons in appendixes 14A and 14B conform to the steps given here? What additional preparation might be necessary before using these lessons in class?*

INTEGRATING GRAMMAR IN VARIOUS CONTEXTS

Once again, we can see that language skills and subskills do not exist alone, and while a particular point of grammar might be isolated and studied on its own, it is often considered within a particular context. Speaking, listening, reading, or writing about a certain topic, for example, may require a grammar form not yet known to the students, so lessons that focus on any skill or integrate some or all of them may also introduce a grammar point; the rest of the lesson (largely skills practice), then, provides natural practice to reinforce the new grammar.

A content-based lesson on making good choices in life, for example, may require an understanding of conditional if-clauses in order to complete the required reading, and a follow-up writing activity may provide additional practice of the form.

MOTIVATED FOR GRAMMAR?

Some students enjoy learning grammar, but many struggle with it, so in all of this—the explanations, the examples, the activities—be sure to keep the mood light. Use facial expressions, gestures, and tone of voice to create an atmosphere of interest; choose unique and interesting sentences to use as examples of the target grammar; and encourage students by telling them that although mastering grammar doesn't always come quickly, it will come with practice. Recognize even their small steps of progress and have the class occasionally reflect on how far they've come.

Finally, encourage students to use their new grammar forms when communicating with one another in class. Grammar, after all, is really just a subskill that allows us to communicate, so using it in daily conversations is both natural and encouraging as it provides a very practical reason to continue to learn.

☞ *Consider: What is your attitude toward teaching or learning grammar? How will your attitude affect your students? How might you change your attitude, if necessary?*

QUESTIONS FOR REVIEW

1. For adult language learners, why is a balanced approach to grammar and fluency likely to result in a better command of a language than a "fluency first, grammar later" approach?
2. Why do we say that we cannot escape teaching grammar?
3. In a typical class of adults, do we teach "correct" grammar or common grammar? Or both?
4. What is meant by "the social context" of grammar?
5. Why is it a good idea to consult more than one grammar book when preparing to teach?
6. What is the difference between controlled grammar practice and authentic grammar practice? Give examples.
7. How do other types of lessons (skills based, content based) often provide a natural context for grammar practice?

FURTHER READING

Marianne Celce-Murcia and Sharon L. Hilles's *Techniques and Resources in Teaching Grammar* (Oxford, 1988) is a classic filled with practical advice.

Susan Conrad and Douglas Biber's *Real Grammar: A Corpus-Based Approach to English* (Longman, 2009) provides activities that reflect common usage.

Keith S. Folse's *Keys to Teaching Grammar to English Language Learners: A Practical Handbook* (Michigan, 2016) helps teachers identify and correct common errors in grammar.

Raymond Murphy's *Essential Grammar in Use* (Cambridge, 2019) is a multi-level series that provides brief clear explanations followed by practice.

Michael Swan's *Practical English Usage* (Oxford, 2017) provides clear descriptions of how the English language is used today.

Scott Thornbury's *How to Teach Grammar* (Pearson, 1991) is filled with practical tips.

George Yule's *Explaining English Grammar* (Oxford, 1999) is a practical guide to answering common grammar questions in the classroom.

CHAPTER 15
Understanding Speech Sounds

Eryk showed up at a local language school to enquire about classes. He spoke in English, slowly and carefully, asking about the types of classes the school offered. His pronunciation was poor, but his grammar was excellent. Eryk explained that he had studied English in school and university, had used English to do extensive research for his work, and had even published scientific articles in English. Reading and writing in English were not difficult for him, but he found oral communication much more challenging. His accent was strong, so even with excellent grammar he was often misunderstood, and when listening to native speakers of English, Eryk understood very little.

Eryk's situation is not unusual. Language learners who have studied in traditional classes that focused on grammar and reading can often read the language reasonably well, but they cannot speak it well, and they can barely understand the spoken language. Their difficulties are rooted in their unfamiliarity with the target language's sounds, particularly if they have studied in a class that gave little attention to sound perception and pronunciation.

Helping students with their sound perception and pronunciation requires an understanding of where the challenges lie and what causes them. In this chapter, we will examine how speech sounds are made, how they are combined into patterns, and how differences in these areas can create difficulties for language learners.

SPEECH SOUNDS

Phonetics is the study of human speech sounds (called **phones**) and how they are articulated. Such sounds are made by modifying the airstream that comes out of our lungs, and we are physically capable of making hundreds of them. Each language uses only a subset of these (usually about 35, though some dialects of English have more than 40), so many languages contain sounds that many other languages do not have. The sounds at the beginning of the words *think* and *this*, for example, do not exist in many languages. In contrast, some sounds, such as the initial sounds in *cat* and *man*, are common to most languages.

Human babies are capable of distinguishing all human speech sounds,[1] but within the first few years of life they focus on the sounds they commonly hear (i.e., the sounds of the language[s] spoken to them by others), and by the time they are adults, they can no longer distinguish many of the now "foreign" sounds.

This loss of ability is, of course, a significant challenge for adult language learners, for although they remain physically capable of producing all speech sounds, they must retrain their minds to accurately perceive those sounds and distinguish between them, and then develop the fine motor skills necessary to accurately produce them.

IDENTIFYING SPEECH SOUNDS: THE INTERNATIONAL PHONETIC ALPHABET

When discussing speech sounds, we need a way to visually represent those sounds—a way that can be used by speakers of any language with a minimum of confusion. After all, different languages write the same sound in different ways (using different letters or symbols), and they may read the same letter/symbol as a different sound. Not only that, but one language may write the same sound in different ways (consider the "ee" sound in *pea, see, key,* and *receipt*) and may have various sounds for one letter or set of letters (consider the various sounds of the English vowel written *a*, such as in *cat, father, about,* and *date* or the letters "ough" in *cough, rough, though,* and *plough*). A language may even have more than one pronunciation for the same written word, depending on dialect (compare Canadian and New Zealand pronunciations of *bread, ten,* and *garage*, or the Oxford, Toronto, and New York pronunciations of the word *drawer*).

The need for a common, agreed-upon, language-neutral way to write sounds has resulted in the development of the **International Phonetic Alphabet** (IPA), which has a single symbol for each human speech sound. For example, the long vowel sounds "ee" (as in *tree*) and "ay" (as in *hay*) are written as [iː] and [eɪ], respectively. (See tables 15.1 and 15.2 for the representation of North American English sounds.)

The IPA is convenient for language students (as well as singers and actors, incidentally) because it allows them to discover the pronunciation of a written word (using a dictionary) without hearing it; moreover, dictionaries usually

Table 15.1: IPA Symbols for North American English Vowels and Diphthongs

VOWELS					DIPHTHONGS		
i	ɪ	ɛ	æ	ə	eɪ[2]	aɪ[3]	aʊ[4]
beat green	bit silver	dress red	bat black	about cinema	bait ate, say	white high, my	loud brown
ɑ	ʌ	o[1]	ʊ	u	ɔɪ[5]	oʊ[6]	
job father	but, run love	or horse	book could	boot, do suit, hue	boy join	boat go, rose	

1. The [o] appears only in [oɹ] and [oʊ].
2. Some dictionaries use [ey] or [ej].
3. Some dictionaries use [ay] or [aj].
4. Some dictionaries use [au].
5. Some dictionaries use [ɔj].
6. Some dictionaries use [ou] or [ow].

Note that some American dialects have an additional vowel, [ɒ], found in words like *thought*, while others use [ɑ] instead. In addition, most North American dialects have r-coloured vowels, such as [iɹ] (as in *ear, deer, here*), [ɛɹ] (as in *air, care, bear*), [ɜɹ] (as in *fir, burn, earth*), [aɹ] (as in *are, star*), [ʊɹ] (as in *tour, pure*), and [oɹ] (as in *for, oar*). (See appendix 16A for more examples.)

Note also that these charts attempt to depict general North American English and do not include every sound from every North American dialect.

Table 15.2: IPA Symbols for North American English Consonants

CONSONANT PAIRS (VOICELESS/VOICED)								
Voiceless	p	t	tʃ	k	f	θ	s	ʃ
	pin nap	tin mat	chin nature	cap, kite unique	final, enough	thin author	sin, city pass	shin emotion
Voiced	b	d	dʒ	g	v	ð	z	ʒ
	bin nab	din mad	gin, joy edge	gap, gale beg	vinyl, love, of	then father	zip rose	pleasure beige
(VOICELESS)		**OTHER CONSONANTS (VOICED)**						
	h	m	n	ŋ	l	ɹ	j	w
	ham behold	map dim	nap din	ring ink	light play	right pray	yes papaya	we queen

English also includes the glottal stop, [ʔ], which is a momentary closing of the vocal cords, followed by an immediate opening, releasing air with force. It is the near-pause in *uh-oh*, as well as in *button* and *kitten* (in some dialects).

give the most common (accent neutral) pronunciation, which may be helpful for teachers who are uncertain just how their own accents differ from what might be considered a more neutral accent.

The IPA is also convenient for showing students that the same sound may be made by different letters, that the same letters may have different sounds, and that two similar sounds are actually different. In each of these cases, we can rely on the IPA to provide us with a unique and universal visual representation of a sound—something that regular letters cannot do.

Words transcribed into the IPA look like this:

- *cat* → [kæt], *play* → [pleɪ], *bite* → [baɪt], *phonetic* → [fənɛtɪk]

The diacritic mark ":" is used to indicate that a vowel is held longer:

- *seat* → [si:t], *blue* → [blu:], *two* → [tu:]

☞ Try: Visit this book's companion website for practice reading and writing in the IPA.

VOWEL SOUNDS

Standing in front of a mirror and saying *eeee, aaaah, ooooh*, we notice immediately that our mouth is continuously open, our voice is in continuous use, our tongue changes position, and our lips change shape. To be more precise, when making English vowel sounds, we use our lips and tongue to slightly modify the **voiced** airstream as it comes from our lungs; however, no parts of the mouth come into contact, so the airstream is restricted very little, thus allowing vowels to have greater stress and to form the centre of a syllable.

All English vowels are voiced (i.e., the vocal cords vibrate when these sounds are made), but they differ according to the position (vertical and horizontal) of the tongue and the roundness of the lips when the sound is made.

- *Vowel height* describes the vertical position of the tongue:
  - close (or high), when the tongue is positioned close to the roof of the mouth; or
  near-close (or near-high), when the tongue is slightly lower than the close (high) position;
  - mid, when the tongue is midway between the close and open positions; or

close-mid (or high-mid), when the tongue is slightly higher than mid position; or

open-mid (or low-mid), when the tongue is slightly lower than mid position;

- open (or low), when the tongue is as far as possible from the roof of the mouth; or

near-open (or near-low), when the tongue is slightly above the open position.

- *Vowel backness* describes the horizontal position of the tongue:
  - front, when the tongue is positioned at the front of the mouth; or near-front, when the tongue is slightly back from the front position;
  - central, when the tongue is midway between the front and back positions;
  - back, when the tongue is positioned at the back of the mouth; or near-back, when the tongue is slightly forward of the back position.
- *Vowel roundedness* describes the shape of the lips:
  - rounded, when the lips are rounded to form a circular opening;
  - unrounded, when the lips are relaxed or spread.

The vowel [ə], called **schwa**, deserves special mention. It is a weak, unstressed, toneless vowel that sounds a bit like a soft "uh" (the initial sound in *ago* and the final sound in *comma*) and is the most common vowel sound in English. In fact, many unstressed vowels in English, whether written *a, e, i, o,* or *u*, are reduced to schwa when spoken. Note how the unstressed vowels become schwa in this sentence:

- *I ate a banana while walking on a famous mountain.*
  [aɪ eɪt ə bənænə waɪl wakɪŋ an ə feɪməs mauntən].

Vowel sounds also include **diphthongs**, which are sounds that begin like one vowel but end like another. The beginning, called the nucleus, is generally longer and stronger than the end. Diphthongs in North American English are as follows:

- [eɪ], as in *eight, day*, begins like [e] and ends like [ɪ].
- [aɪ], as in *ice, my*, begins like [a] and ends like [ɪ].
- [au], as in *loud, now*, begins like [a] and ends like [ʊ].
- [ɔɪ], as in *toy, join*, begins like [ɔ] and ends like [ɪ].
- [oʊ], as in *oat, go*, begins like [o] and ends like [ʊ].

Table 15.3: Vowel Sounds in North American English

VOWEL, EXAMPLE	HEIGHT		BACKNESS	ROUNDEDNESS
[iː] as in b__ea__t, s__ee__d	close	(high)	front	unrounded
[ɪ] as in b__i__t, h__i__m	near-close	(near-high)	near-front	unrounded
[e] as in b__ai__t, m__a__de*	close-mid	(high-mid)	front	unrounded
[ɛ] as in b__e__t, dr__e__ss	open-mid	(low-mid)	front	unrounded
[æ] as in b__a__t, gr__a__ss	near-open	(near-low)	front	unrounded
[a] as in k__i__te, s__i__ght*	open	(low)	front	unrounded
[ə] as in c__o__mma, __a__bout	mid		central	unrounded
[ɑ] as in f__a__ther	open	(low)	back	unrounded
[ɔ] as in b__oy__, t__oy__*	open-mid	(low-mid)	back	rounded
[ʌ] as in b__u__t, m__u__d	open-mid	(low-mid)	back	unrounded
[o] as in b__oa__t, h__o__rse †	close-mid	(high-mid)	back	rounded
[ʊ] as in b__oo__k, w__ou__ld	near-close	(near-high)	near-back	rounded
[uː] as in b__oo__t, st__ew__	close	(high)	back	rounded
*Used only in diphthongs. †Used only in the diphthong [oʊ] or before [ɹ].				

For a visual representation of where in the mouth individual vowel sounds are made, see the IPA vowel chart in appendix 15A.

CONSONANT SOUNDS

Consonant sounds are made by restricting and modifying the airstream that comes from our lungs. There are three variables involved: the use of voice (or not), the place of articulation (i.e., the part of the mouth used to modify the airstream), and the manner of articulation (i.e., the way the airstream is modified).

Voiced or Voiceless

Consonants are said to be voiced if our vocal cords vibrate when the sound is made; they are **voiceless** if our vocal cords do not vibrate when the sound is made. For example, compare the final sounds in *bus* and *buzz* by holding your fingers on your throat while you say them aloud. You should be able to feel your vocal cords vibrating when saying the latter but not when saying the former.

In table 15.2, there are a number of consonant pairs such as [t, d] and [k, g]. The members of each pair differ only in whether the sound is voiced; otherwise, they are articulated in the same way.

Places of Articulation

Consonants may also differ in their places of articulation—that is, the various parts of the throat and mouth with which we restrict and modify the airstream from our lungs in order to make the sound. English consonants are described as follows:

- *Bilabial* sounds [b, p, m] are made by closing the lips together, as in *b̲an, p̲an, m̲an*.
- *Labiodental* sounds [f, v] are made using the bottom lip and top teeth, as in *f̲an, v̲an*.
- *Interdental* sounds [θ, ð] are made by placing the tip of the tongue between the front teeth, as in *t̲h̲ink, t̲h̲is*, or *teet̲h̲, teet̲h̲e*.
- *Alveolar* sounds [t, d, s, z, n, l, ɹ] are made by putting the tip of the tongue on or near the bony ridge behind the upper front teeth, as in *t̲ip, d̲ip, s̲ip, z̲ip, n̲ip, l̲ip, r̲ip*.
- *Alveopalatal* sounds [tʃ, dʒ, ʃ, ʒ] are made by placing the tongue on or near the area between the alveolar ridge and the palate, as in *c̲h̲in, g̲in, s̲h̲in, vis̲ion*.
- *Palatal* sounds, such as [j], are made by placing the tongue near the hard roof (palate) of the mouth, as in *y̲es*.
- *Velar* (sometimes called soft palatal) sounds [k, g, ŋ] are made by placing the tongue near the soft back portion of the roof of the mouth, as in the final sounds in *pic̲k̲, pig̲, ping̲*.
- *Labiovelar* sounds, such as [w], are made by rounding the lips while placing the tongue near the soft back portion of the roof of the mouth, as in *w̲et*.
- *Glottal* sounds, such as the glottal stop, [ʔ], are made by using the gap between the vocal folds, as in the near pause in the middle of *uh̲-oh*.

Manner of Articulation

Finally, the airstream from our lungs is also restricted and modified in different ways. For each English consonant sound, the manner of articulation is one of the following:

- *Stop*, or *plosive*: the airflow is completely interrupted when making the sounds [p, b, t, d, k, g], as in *pole, bowl, told, cold, gold* and in the glottal stop, [ʔ], as in *uh-oh*.
  ○ The strong release of air following the lag of a voiceless stop at the beginning of a word or syllable is called *aspiration*, represented in *pat* as [pʰ], in *tab* as [tʰ], and in *cap* as [kʰ]. Compare the [p] sound in *pin* (aspirated) and *spin* (not aspirated).
- *Fricative*: the airflow is interrupted to the point of causing audible friction when making the sounds [f, v, θ, ð, s, z, ʃ, ʒ, h], as in *find, vase, think, this, sing, zipper, ship, vision, hat*.
- *Affricate*: begins like a stop and ends like a fricative; the airflow is completely interrupted but then allowed through a slight opening that creates friction, when making the sounds [tʃ, dʒ], as in *church, jump*.
- *Nasal*: the airflow passes partially or entirely through the nose when making the sounds [m, n, ŋ], as in *mom, none, ring*.
- *Approximant*: the airflow is hindered but not enough to stop it or create audible friction when making the sounds [ɹ, j, w], as in *right, yes, wet*.
- *Lateral approximant*: the airstream is directed around the sides of the tongue but not hindered enough to stop the airflow or create audible friction when making the sound [l], as in *lip, pull*.

Note that many similar consonant sounds (including ones often confused by language learners) share two out of three properties:

- The sounds [p] and [b] are both bilabial stops, but [p] is voiceless and [b] is voiced.
- The sounds [f] and [v] are labiodental fricatives, but [f] is voiceless and [v] is voiced.
- The sounds [f], [θ], [s], and [ʃ] are all voiceless fricatives, but [f] is labiodental, [θ] is interdental, [s] is alveolar, and [ʃ] is alveopalatal.
- The sounds [ð] and [z] are voiced fricatives, but [ð] is interdental and [z] is alveolar.
- The sounds [s] and [ʃ] are voiceless fricatives, but [s] is alveolar and [ʃ] is alveopalatal.
- The sounds [n] and [l] are both voiced alveolar, but [n] is nasal and [l] is a lateral approximant.

☞ *Try: Choose five consonant sounds and practice explaining and demonstrating how they are made.*

Table 15.4: English Consonant Articulation

ARTICULATION									
↓Manner	Place→	BILABIAL	LABIO-DENTAL	INTER-DENTAL	ALVEOLAR	ALVEO-PALATAL	PALATAL	VELAR	LABIO-VELAR	GLOTTAL
Stops (Plosives)	voiceless voiced	[p] *pat* [b] *bat*			[t] *tip* [d] *dip*			[k] *cab* [g] *gab*		[ʔ] *uh-oh*
Fricatives	voiceless voiced		[f] *fine* [v] *vine*	[θ] *thin* [ð] *this*	[s] *sip* [z] *zip*	[ʃ] *ship* [ʒ] *vision*				[h] *hot*
Affricates	voiceless voiced					[tʃ] *chin* [dʒ] *joy*				
Nasals	(voiced)	[m] *man*			[n] *nip*			[ŋ] *sing*		
Approximant	(voiced)				[ɹ] *rip*		[j] *yes*		[w] *wet*	
Lateral approximant	(voiced)				[l] *lip*					

SPEECH SOUND PATTERNS

Phonology is the study of how speech sounds are selected, arranged, and modified in language. For example, we know that certain sounds can go together in a given language while others cannot: *twish* and *twank* are not real words in English, but they could be, while *srisht* and *tnapk* just don't sound right to English speakers' ears. We also know that when sounds are combined, one sound may influence another, resulting in a slight variation of that sound: the [p] sound in *spin*, for example, is slightly different from the [p] sound in *pin*.

Sound Combinations

There are phonological rules that govern which sounds may go together and which may not. For example, two or more sounds may combine to form a **consonant blend** (a combination in which each consonant sound is heard but blended with at least one other), but each language has specific rules about which sounds may blend with others. In English, consonant blends are fairly common, but most involve certain letters:

- The consonant sound [l] frequently follows [b], [c], [f], [g], [p], or [s] to form the consonant blends found in *black, claw, flop, glib, play,* and *slip*.
- The consonant sound [ɹ] frequently follows [b], [c], [d], [f], [g], [p], or [t] to form the consonant blends found in *brick, cry, dry, fry, great, prime,* and *try*.
- The consonant sound [s] frequently precedes [c], [k], [m], [n], [p], [t], or [w] to form the consonant blends found in *score, skip, small, snip, spin, stop,* and *swim*.
- Consonant blends involving [l], [n], [s], or [t] are often found at the end of words, such as those in *cold, elf, milk, elm, help, felt; end, ink, spent; desk, clasp, last; act, left, hint, kept,* and *last*.
- Consonant blends sometimes include three consonant sounds such as [skɹ], [spl], [spɹ], and [stɹ], as found in *scream, splash, spring,* and *street*.

Note that some languages have more consonant blends than English, while others have far fewer or even none at all.

Sound Variations

Phonemes are distinct sounds (such as [s], [t], [p]) in a language, while **allophones** are variations of a phoneme that occur because of the influence of the surrounding sounds. In other words, when sounds (phonemes) are combined to form words and sentences, they may change slightly; this variation of the sound is an allophone.

For example, hold your hand in front of your mouth and say the words *pin*, *spin*, and *tip*. What do you notice? In *pin*, the [p] sound is aspirated (written [pʰ]); that is, a puff of air is released as we say it. In *spin*, the [p] sound is not aspirated; there is no puff of air as we say it, although the air is released. In *tip*, the [p] sound is non-aspirated and also unreleased. In these three words, then, we recognize three allophones of the [p] phoneme. (And yes, the variations are so slight that we usually don't think about them, but we might notice the difference if someone speaking to us used the wrong one.)

We can also observe that if we change the phoneme in a word, the word itself changes (if [p] is changed to [b], then *tap* becomes *tab*), but if we change the allophone, the word does not change (though it might sound a bit funny, as in pronouncing *spin* with a [pʰ]).

The rules that govern how a particular phoneme varies are constant within a given language. For example, in English, the following rules always hold true:

- Voiceless stop consonants, [p, t, k], are aspirated [pʰ, tʰ, kʰ] when they begin a word or a stressed syllable, as in *pin, top, kin*, but are not aspirated when they follow [s] in a consonant blend, as in *spin, stop*, and *skin*.
- A vowel is lengthened when it immediately precedes a voiced consonant: compare the length of the vowel sounds in *beat* and *bead*, or *meat* and *mead*.
- A vowel followed by a nasalized consonant will itself become nasalized: compare the [ɪ] sounds in *chip* and *chin*.

In each of these examples, the specific variation of the sound is governed by the surrounding sounds. In some cases, however, two sounds might be interchangeable, regardless of the surrounding sounds. This phenomenon is known as **free variation**. In Korean, for example, the sounds [p] and [b] are interchangeable (as in the city of Pusan, also called Busan).

☞ *Consider: How will an understanding of how sound combinations and variations occur in language better enable us to diagnose pronunciation errors and help students produce intelligible speech?*

ISSUES FOR LANGUAGE LEARNERS

As we might expect, the differences in sounds and sound rules create problems for language learners. A sound in one language, for example, may not even exist in another, and the rules that govern which sounds can go together and which cannot are different for each language (though there is significant overlap between languages).

Phonemic Influences: Substitution

When language learners come across an unfamiliar sound, they tend to substitute a similar sound from their own language. The English consonant sounds [v], [θ], and [ð], for example, are unknown to many learners, so they tend to substitute known sounds:

- [v] is likely to be pronounced [b], [f], or [w], so *van* becomes *ban*, *fan*, or *wan*.
- [θ] is likely to be pronounced [s], [t], or [z], so *think* becomes *sink*, *tink*, or *zink*.
- [ð] is likely to be pronounced [d] or [z], so this becomes *dis* or *zis*.

Vowels can be even more problematic for many learners. English contains more vowels than many other languages, and two or more vowel sounds are often close in pronunciation. As a result, there is a strong tendency for learners to substitute a known vowel for an unknown vowel:

- [ɪ] is likely to be pronounced [iː], so *bin* becomes *bean*, and *ship* becomes *sheep*.
- [ʊ] is likely to be pronounced [uː], so *pull* becomes *pool*, and *look* becomes *Luke*.
- [æ] is likely to be pronounced [ɑ], so *band* becomes *bond*, and *cap* becomes *cop*.

The so-called r-coloured vowels, common in many North American English dialects, are often difficult simply because they do not exist in most other languages (or in many dialects of English, for that matter). Words such as *start*, *better*, and *turn*, for example, are likely to be pronounced with a lengthened vowel instead of the r-coloured vowel. While this type of substitution may simply sound like a quaint accent, it may also cause confusion when two words differ by only the vowel sound: the word *tarp*, for example, may sound like *top*.

Finally, not all languages have diphthongs, so some learners will find it extremely difficult to accurately pronounce relatively common words such as *buy*, *sight*, *loud*, or *toy*, likely substituting a simple vowel sound or two distinct vowel sounds for a diphthong.

Phonemic Influences: Allophones and Free Variation

Learners tend to be particularly confused when distinct sounds (i.e., phonemes) in one language are variations of the same sound in another. Consider the following examples:

- In English, the [l] and [ɹ] sounds are phonemes, but similar sounds in Japanese and Korean are allophones. As a result, Japanese or Korean speakers are likely to confuse words such as *play* and *pray*, or *light* and *right*.
- The English phonemes [b] and [v] are allophones in Spanish, so Spanish speakers are likely to confuse words such as *ban* and *van*, or *bent* and *vent*.
- The Mandarin phonemes [p] and [pʰ] are allophones in English, so English speakers are likely to confuse the sounds when learning Mandarin.

Voiced/voiceless pairs in English tend to be particularly troublesome because in many languages they are allophones, not distinct phonemes:

- [p] and [b] are likely to be confused, as in *buy* and *pie*, or *big* and *pig*.
- [t] and [d] are likely to be confused, as in *tad* and *dad*, or *time* and *dime*.
- [k] and [g] are likely to be confused, as in *kill* and *gill*, or *cash* and *gash*.
- [f] and [v] are likely to be confused, as in *fan* and *van*, or *ferry* and *very*.
- [s] and [z] are likely to be confused, as in *bus* and *buzz*, or *sip* and *zip*.

Phonological Influences

In addition to transferring sounds from their own language, language learners also transfer sound rules. The result is that they modify the language they are learning in order to make it conform to the rules of their own language.

For example, many language learners insert sounds or drop sounds in order to avoid consonant blends that do not exist in their first language:

- inserting sounds: *milk* become *milik*, *price* becomes *pirice*, *months* becomes *monthis*
- dropping sounds: *went* becomes *wen*, *instant* becomes *instan*, *test* becomes *tes*

In other cases, certain sounds or sound combinations occur only in particular positions. A particularly notable case is found in Spanish, where blends of [s] with another consonant never occur at the beginning of a word; thus Spanish speakers tend to modify English words accordingly: *stop* becomes *estop*, *Spain* becomes *espain*, *spoon* becomes *espoon*.

Final consonants are another issue worth noting. Some languages, for example, do not have voiced final consonants, but English does, and as noted earlier in this chapter, a vowel immediately preceding a voiced consonant is lengthened. Speakers of languages that do not have final voiced consonants, then, are likely to devoice a voiced final consonant and also shorten the preceding vowel, so *dog* becomes *dock*, *leave* becomes *leaf*, *sad* becomes *sat*, *pig* becomes *pick*, and so on.

Still other languages do not have final consonants at all, or very few, so speakers of those languages will avoid final consonants by adding or dropping a sound:

- adding: *wait* becomes *waito*, *rich* becomes *richi*, *post* becomes *posto*
- dropping: *can't* becomes *can*, *cart* and *card* become *car*, *kinship* becomes *kinshi*

In some cases, what appears to be a spoken grammatical error may in fact be a pronunciation error, such as when *worked* is pronounced *work* in a simple past sentence.

The situation is even worse when a language has no (or few) consonant blends or final consonants. Japanese, for example, has no blends and only one final consonant, so Japanese speakers tend to insert vowels in English words in order to avoid both. These issues, combined with others (especially the substitution of similar sounds for unfamiliar ones), result in what is often referred to as Japlish: *straight* becomes *sutoreito*, *building* becomes *birudingu*, *magic tape* (a.k.a. Velcro) becomes *majikku te-pu*, *classic* becomes *kurashikku*, and *McDonald's* becomes *makudonarudo*!

Spelling Influences

Because many language learners have more experience with the written language than with the spoken language, they frequently attempt to determine the pronunciation of a word from its spelling. In many languages, that would be perfectly reasonable, but English spelling is almost perfectly unreasonable:

- Many letters are silent.
- A single letter may represent many different sounds, such as the letter *o* in *got to go to or from work*.
- A particular combination of letters may represent different sounds at different times, such as *ough* in *cough, tough, plough, through, though*, and *ought*.
- Two letters may work together to represent a single consonant sound (not a blend), such as *ch* for [ʧ], *sh* for [ʃ], and *ph* for [f], or to represent two possible sounds, such as *th* for either [θ] or [ð].
- A single letter may represent two sounds combined, such as *x* for [k]+[s] as in *box* or *fix*.

As a result, students often guess incorrectly. For example, they might pronounce *cut* as *cute* or *coot*, *Phil* as *pill* or *p-hill*, *cot* as *coat*, and *said* as *say'd*; and no one expects *work* to sound like *werk* or *women* to sound like *wimmen*!

LOOKING AHEAD

The good news is that any human being can learn any human sound or combination of sounds; it just takes practice: first listening, then speaking. In the next chapter, we'll address some common and effective ways of facilitating such practice.

QUESTIONS FOR REVIEW

1. Why is it helpful for language teachers and learners to know the IPA?
2. What is the difference between vowels and consonants?
3. What three properties describe how vowel sounds are made?
4. What three properties describe how consonant sounds are made?
5. List the consonant pairs (i.e., pairs of consonants that are identical in manner/place of articulation but differ by whether they are voiced or not).
6. What are consonant blends? How might they differ from one language to another?
7. What is an allophone? Why might allophones be troublesome for language learners?

8. Why might some language learners (but not others) confuse *fan* and *van*, *sip* and *ship*, or *hit* and *heat*?
9. Why might some language learners (but not others) confuse *right* and *light*, *Ben* and *pen*, or *best* and *vest*?
10. Why might a language learner say *contrac* for *contract*, or *shipu* for *ship*?
11. Why might a language learner mispronounce written words that are unfamiliar?
12. "The rules of phonetics and phonology are largely responsible for the accents of language learners." Explain.

FURTHER READING

Philip Carr's *English Phonetics and Phonology: An Introduction* (Wiley-Blackwell, 2012) provides an accessible introduction to its topics and includes online resources.

William O'Grady, John Archibald, Mark Aronoff, and Janie Rees-Miller's *Contemporary Linguistics: An Introduction* (Bedford/St. Martin's, 2017) is a standard introduction to linguistics and provides an excellent overview of phonetics and phonology (as well as morphology, syntax, semantics, language acquisition, sociolinguistics, and other related topics).

Frank Parker and Kathryn Riley's *Linguistics for Non-Linguists: A Primer with Exercises* (Pearson, 2009) presents basic concepts of linguistics at a level suitable for beginners to the subject.

NOTE

1. Patricia Kuhl gives a fascinating talk on this topic. See her full presentation, "The Linguistic Genius of Babies," at http://www.ted.com/talks/patricia_kuhl_the_linguistic_genius_of_babies.html.

CHAPTER 16
Teaching Sound Perception and Pronunciation

Excellent grammar, extensive vocabulary, outgoing personality—and poor pronunciation. The result? Misunderstandings, frustration, and perhaps, depending on the context, social isolation. More than most language issues, poor pronunciation hinders language learners from experiencing meaningful interaction with others. Poor grammar can be deciphered, and even limited vocabulary is sufficient to communicate basic thoughts, but poor pronunciation is a barrier that can often make the simplest task seem impossible. Little wonder, then, that students who are concerned about their pronunciation are hesitant to speak up.

Poor pronunciation and its counterpart—an inability to distinguish between similar sounds—are common among language learners. Students of English in many parts of the world spend hours poring over grammar rules and vocabulary lists week after week, but they rarely have a chance to speak and hear natural English. As a result, they know a lot about the language but can barely use it, and many of them who write reasonably well are hesitant to speak at all.

As teachers, we must help students not only activate the English they have learned in the past but also polish it. Unfortunately, even classes that focus on authentic oral communication too often focus on fluency without addressing pronunciation, probably because pronunciation seems more difficult to teach. Listening practice also tends to focus on comprehension, with little attention given to accurate sound perception. But the latter is important, as inaccurate perception not only leads to confusion when listening but also influences pronunciation when speaking.

The methods for training students in sound perception and pronunciation are often repetitive and may not be as exciting as authentic use of language, but the payoff over time can be dramatic as language becomes a means to communicate effectively with others and not simply a subject of study. In this chapter, we will look at some of the issues related to accurate sound perception and pronunciation and suggest ways to address them.

WHICH PRONUNCIATION?

Before discussing the ability of language learners to perceive and reproduce sounds, we must consider which pronunciation (or accent) they should be trying to learn. Language textbooks are generally classified as "British English" or "American English," and students often want to learn one or the other, believing that these accents are more desirable or even superior—a belief that, in many countries, is carried over from their colonial past.

But both the United Kingdom and the United States contain a multitude of accents, and there are numerous other accents around the world. In fact, the majority of English speakers in the world speak English (often fluently) as a second language and have an accent that is neither British nor American. There is, then, no standard accent.

When teaching, we can approach this dilemma by attempting to use an accent that is fairly neutral. The catch, of course, is that not everyone agrees on what is neutral, and many speakers believe that their own accent is neutral and everyone else's is not! Perhaps the best we can do is this: learn about our own accent by comparing it with others, and then avoid strong tendencies that are specific to a particular area or group. We can also use a variety of accents in class—recordings are helpful—or we can focus on a particular accent if it is the one most likely to be encountered by our students.

Finally, keep in mind that our objective is not to make every student sound like the teacher, but to help students modify their accents so that they are easily understood by others.

☞ *Consider: How might accent be a social or political issue? How might clear pronunciation, regardless of accent, help empower a language learner?*

SOUNDS IN WORDS

As we saw in the previous chapter, language learners often have trouble distinguishing a particular sound from a similar one, either because the sound does not exist in their first language or because the two sounds exist as allophones in their first language. As a result, they often confuse one word for another when listening, and they pronounce words incorrectly when speaking.

We can help our students differentiate between similar sounds by teaching them how the sounds are made (see chapter 15), by teaching them to use the pronunciation guides in dictionaries, and by facilitating practice in class through a number of simple activities. Such activities help students accurately recognize and reproduce the correct sound (and therefore the right word) without hesitation.

Practicing Sounds, Step 1: Explanation

When students confuse similar sounds such as [b] and [v], explain and demonstrate the difference: *Both sounds use the voice, but [b] is made by pressing the lips together and then opening them to quickly release the air; [v] is made by pressing the top front teeth gently against the lower lip while releasing air to create friction.* Demonstrate the sounds a few times to help students see and hear the difference.

Practicing Sounds, Step 2: Perception

Even when students understand how a sound is made, they may not yet be able to perceive it correctly or pronounce it correctly; such skills develop over time. Begin practice, then, by using listening activities that help students learn to differentiate between commonly confused sounds. Such activities make extensive use of **minimal pairs**—that is, pairs of words that differ by only one sound, such as *play/pray*, *bit/beat*, or *sit/set*. (Recent studies have also investigated the advantages of minimal sets, such as *bit/beat/bet/bat/but*, or *sip/ship/zip*, which place the target sound in a larger context, thereby providing a greater number of contrasting sounds.) The following activities are particularly useful:

- *Minimal pair drill*: Choose pairs of words that target the problem sound(s), such as *light/right*, *play/pray*, and *lock/rock* for [l] and [ɹ], keeping in mind that the words in each pair should differ only in the targeted sounds. Write the pairs on the board, and then say a word from each pair and have students write (or point to) the word you are saying. This drill can also be used with minimal sets (instead of pairs) of words that target the problem sound(s), such as *bit/beat/bet*, *mitt/meet/met*, and *sit/seat/set* for the [ɪ] sound.
- *L1/L2 pair/set drill*: Do a minimal pair/set drill, but choose words from both the students' first language and English. For example: in French/English, *il/eel*; in Japanese/English, *mitsu/meets*.

- *Which is different?* The teacher asks, *Which is different? Lock, lock, rock, lock.* Students answer, *The third one.*
- *Which order?* Choose groups of three or four similar words that target the problem sounds (e.g., *think, sink, fink, shink*—note that they don't have to be real words). Have students write them down. Then read the words in random order and have students label the order in which you say them.
- *Word dictation*: Simply dictate words that include easily confused sounds, but be sure the words are already known to the students. (Otherwise, students will write the nearest known word rather than the one spoken.)
- *Sound families*: While minimal pairs/sets help students differentiate between similar sounds, sound families help students identify the same sound in a variety of words, regardless of spelling. The word *work*, for example, belongs to the same family as *dirt, bird, turn,* and *burp*, as they share the same r-coloured vowel, and the word *stew* belongs to the same sound family as *blue, two,* and *you*. Identifying a word with its sound family can help students quickly learn and remember the correct pronunciation even when the spelling is confusing or misleading. (See Pronunciation and Spelling later in this chapter.)

Keep in mind that a person's ability to accurately perceive sounds is developed through practice—plenty of practice—and because our class time is limited, we should aim to make the most efficient use of time spent practicing by creating somewhat ideal conditions:[1]

- To help students differentiate one sound from others, maximize their exposure by using multiple voices and multiple sets: rather than one speaker saying *sit/seat*, three speakers saying *sit/seat/set, mitt/meat/met,* and *bit/beat/bet.*
- Because individual sounds are influenced by surrounding sounds, teach a new sound using multiple examples from the same sound family, such as *bit, did, fit, him, hip, his, it, kick, kid, lip, mitt, rid, sit, tip,* and *zip* for the sound [ɪ].
- When using minimal sets or sound families, choose words that learners are likely to encounter on a regular basis.
- When practicing perception or pronunciation in class, focus intently on that alone. Avoid distractions such as grammar, vocabulary, or even background noise in the room.

- Give immediate feedback. Accuracy is key in each activity, so be sure to check students' answers after each question, and repeat the activity as necessary.

Practicing Sounds, Step 3: Repetition

As students become familiar with a sound, model the sound again and have students repeat the correct pronunciation. When necessary, review the correct place and manner of articulation. For example, the [θ] sound may become easier when we explain that it is made by placing the tip (and only the tip) of the tongue between the front teeth, with only a bit of air getting through and creating friction. (Keep in mind, however, that such an explanation is unlikely to lead to immediate success; the student may need countless reminders and plenty of practice, perhaps with a mirror.) Then have students practice by repeating a variety of words containing the target sound.

For vowels, it is often better to focus on imitation, not explanation. After all, few people can tell where their tongue is when making sounds such as [i] and [ɪ], so explaining the difference in position is not likely to help them, but they may be able to imitate vowel sounds that are held for a moment or two.

Practicing Sounds, Step 4: Pronunciation

Finally, have students read or say minimal pairs/sets, carefully differentiating between the targeted sounds. Continue modelling and practicing sounds as needed, keeping in mind that success usually doesn't come right away, and that success in one instance does not prevent students from reverting to their former pronunciation; old habits, after all, are hard to break. Also note that sometimes students simply need more time to develop their overall language ability before mastering the more difficult sounds.

☞ *Try: Choose five pairs of sounds that language learners are likely to confuse, and write five minimal pairs for each. (Example: [ɪ] and [i:]—bit/beat, ship/sheep, it/eat, wick/week, pit/Pete)*

SOUNDS IN SENTENCES

Students who master the individual sounds (or phones) and words of English are often surprised to discover that they still have difficulty understanding spoken sentences, largely because they do not understand the way native speakers verbally construct sentences. Individual sounds sometimes change slightly depending on the other sounds around them; at other times they might be minimized or almost dropped in a sentence, or they might be jammed together. Consider how the following sentences are commonly spoken in North American English:

- *I am going to go to the beach after lunch. (I'm gonna go t' the beach after lunch.)*
- *I want to go too, but I've got to study. (I wanna go too, but I've gotta study.)*
- *What do you think they are going to do about it? (Whaddaya think ther gonna do 'bout it?)*
- *Would you like a cup of coffee? (Wouldja lika cuppa coffee?)*

These sentences illustrate three common tendencies in spoken English:

- Some sounds are minimized. In particular, unstressed vowels are often minimized to [ə] (schwa), such as the vowel in the word *to* when spoken quickly in a sentence.
- Some common collocations are contracted, such as *want to (wanna), going to (gonna), what do you (whaddaya),* or *would you (wouldja).*
- Sometimes a word ending is linked to the beginning of the following word, as in *like a cup of (lika cuppa).*

In many cases we can see all three tendencies in a single phrase. For the language learner who has learned clear, distinct pronunciation for each word, this type of speech can be difficult to understand or reproduce.

Our objective, however, is to have our students *perceive* such speech correctly; the ability to reproduce it is not imperative. In fact, as long as language learners pronounce the individual sounds correctly, the pronunciation of their sentences will be correct and clear, and possibly easier to understand than the speech of many native speakers. Besides, the learner will begin to speak sentences more naturally (if less clearly) over time; accuracy is more important in the short term.

As such, we needn't teach our students how to say contracted forms such as *wanna, whaddaya,* or *gonna,* or linked forms such as *lika cuppa,* but we must teach them how to recognize them. The first step is explaining the reasons for difficulty:

- *English speakers often change, minimize, or drop certain sounds when speaking.*
- *English speakers often link the end of one word to the beginning of the next word.*

Next, provide practice: say the contracted form and have students guess what you are saying by repeating (or writing) the sentence in standard form. Initially, it may be necessary to speak the contracted form more slowly, perhaps as an isolated sentence, but increase speed and difficulty gradually to ensure students get used to hearing the natural way of saying the sentence. Eventually, you can use common contracted forms in normal class conversations and when giving instructions.

Also, although it is not necessary for students to be able to produce the informal, contracted pronunciation of a sentence, it might be valuable to have them repeat it after you so that they become more familiar with it and better able to recognize it, particularly when they are encountering such expressions for the first time. If they have difficulty saying the contracted form of a sentence, consider using a backwards buildup drill (see appendix 3C) to help them master it.

PRONUNCIATION AND SPELLING

We noted in the previous chapter that language learners run into trouble when they attempt to determine an English word's pronunciation from its spelling. Unfortunately, there is no simple rule to teach students; they must simply learn and practice the correct pronunciation of each new word they encounter. That said, we can create "sound families" to indicate that a new word may have a familiar pronunciation even if the spelling is unusual. By associating new words with known sound families, students will master their pronunciation much more quickly. (Appendixes 16A and 16B provide sound families for English vowels and troublesome consonants, respectively.)

WORD STRESS

When a word in English has more than one syllable, one of the syllables is given more stress—that is, the syllable is spoken higher, louder, and longer. In the word *textbook*, for example, the first syllable is stressed: *TEXT·book*, not *text·BOOK*.

In longer words, one syllable is stressed and another syllable might receive secondary stress. In the word *conversation*, for example, the third syllable is stressed and the first syllable receives secondary stress: *CON·ver·SA·tion*.

Word stress is an important factor in correct pronunciation, and understanding proper word stress is therefore important for accurate perception as well.

A simple case of missing or misplaced stress can make a word incomprehensible or, sometimes worse, misunderstood: consider introducing a man as *important* but stressing the first syllable instead of the second! (Canadians, and others who emphasize the [ɪ] sound more than many other speakers of English, may have to read this twice to get the joke.) Likewise, introducing the same man as *unique* but stressing the first syllable instead of the second could be equally embarrassing.

Language learners tend to stress syllables just as they do in their first language, which is problematic because many languages give equal stress to all syllables or stress some syllables in more subtle ways. Japanese speakers, for example, stress syllables by using a higher pitch but without making the syllable longer, while Cantonese speakers use a wide variety of tones without changing the syllable length. English stress (higher, louder, longer), then, must be taught and practiced.

There are certain patterns in word stress, but they are not absolute. About 80 or 90 percent of two-syllable nouns are stressed on the first syllable, while about 60 percent of two-syllable verbs are stressed on the second syllable. Patterns of stress in words with three or more syllables are complicated and subject to numerous exceptions. Word stress, then, must be learned through repetition and practice, preferably when new words are learned. One good practice is to have students mark stress on all new words and on any words they do not pronounce correctly.

☞ Try: Write 25 multisyllabic words: five nouns, five verbs, five adjectives, five adverbs; five others (prepositions, conjunctions). Then mark the primary stress for each.

SENTENCE STRESS

Compare the following two sentences: (a) *The mother robin feeds her babies.* (b) *Big boys play hard.* The first sentence has nine syllables, while the second one has four; yet they take roughly the same amount of time to say. Why? Both sentences have four stressed syllables:

(a) *The mother robin feeds her babies.* (b) *Big boys play hard.*

Sentence stress, like word stress, plays a significant role in pronouncing and perceiving English correctly, and it doesn't come naturally for many language learners because the way English speakers stress some syllables while minimizing others (in order to create a desirable **rhythm**) is not common. In fact, in many languages, all syllables carry equal weight, so a sentence with twice as many syllables as another will take twice as long to say.

For many language learners, this discrepancy makes English sentences difficult to hear since many of the words or syllables are minimized while others are stressed. As teachers, we must provide activities to help our students practice hearing all words and syllables:

1. *Explanation*: Teach the basics of sentence stress:
    - Content words (nouns, main verbs, adjectives, or adverbs) are usually stressed in a sentence. (In a multisyllabic content word, one syllable has primary stress. See the previous section, "Word Stress.")
    - **Function words** (pronouns, determiners, auxiliary verbs, prepositions, conjunctions) are generally not stressed and are often reduced.
    - New information is likely to be stressed more than information already known.
2. *Repetition*: Have students repeat a sentence, imitating your correct sentence stress. Also consider using a backwards buildup drill: Break the sentence into smaller chunks; say the final chunk and have the student repeat it; then add the previous chunk and repeat the process; continue adding chunks (working backwards) until the whole sentence has been repeated. Be sure to use natural sentence stress at each step.
3. *Dictation*: Read sentences using natural sentence stress. Have students write them. (Students will have to listen carefully to perceive unstressed words in the sentences.)
4. *Production*: Give students a list of sentences, and have them mark (with accent marks) the stressed syllables in the sentence. Then read the sentences aloud (with natural stress) and have them check their answers.

Once students get the idea, explain to them that sometimes we change the stress in a sentence in order to change the emphasis or contrast one element with another. Consider the sentence *I don't drink milk* with different words stressed:

1. *I don't drink milk* (but he does).
2. *I don't drink milk* (but I might use it for baking).
3. *I don't drink milk* (but I drink orange juice).

This type of stress is sometimes called *contrastive stress*. The simplest way to practice it is to say a given sentence in different ways and have students explain the meaning each time.

☞ *Try: Visit this book's companion website to practice marking sentence stress.*

SENTENCE INTONATION

Phrases in English sentences tend to rise or fall in pitch depending on the speaker's intent; this pattern of rises and falls is called **intonation**. Intonation is particularly important because an error in intonation could convey a very different intent or attitude. For example, the innocent question *You don't know what to do?* becomes almost an insult if spoken with flat instead of rising intonation.

There are a few basic rules for English intonation:

- Statements generally have falling intonation: *We don't have any classes next week.*
- Wh-questions generally have falling intonation: *What are you going to do next week?*
- Wh-questions used to double-check have rising intonation: *Huh? What are you planning to do?*
- Yes/no questions tend to have rising intonation: *Do you like kimchi?*
- Questions with choice normally rise on the first choice, then fall on the second: *Do you want to relax at home, or would you rather go someplace fun?*

Beyond these simple generalizations, intonation has many variations and gets tricky. A single statement, for example, might express seriousness, certainty, doubt, irony, or inquiry, depending on the intonation.

Intonation exists in most languages, so the concept is not difficult for language learners; however, the rules of intonation may differ significantly from one language to another, and learners may have difficulty adapting. For example, while English speakers use rising intonation for many questions and falling intonation for most statements, speakers of some languages use the opposite pattern, so English intonation will feel very unnatural to them. In other languages, speakers may use the same intonation for both statements and questions, or the intonation may differ depending on whether the speaker is male or female. Again, these life-long habits are hard to change.

Learning to use natural English intonation, then, requires practice in order to break previous habits. Extensive listening to natural English conversations (including those in movies and television programs) is particularly helpful, but there are also a few things we can do in class:

- *Intonation dictation*: Give students a list of sentences (including questions). Then say the sentences naturally as students mark the intonation with arrows. After checking their answers, say the sentences again and

have students repeat them after you. (This method works best for "standard" intonation such as simple statements and questions. It is usually used when teaching intonation for the first time.)
- *Correcting intonation*: Intonation is most easily recognized when it is incorrect. Consider gently correcting students' intonation, perhaps by writing the sentence on the board and using arrows to indicate correct intonation or to point out the difference in meaning caused by the change in intonation.
- *Intonation contrast*: In intermediate or higher-level classes, have students say the same word, phrase, or sentence using different intonation, and then discuss the differences. For example, have students say "Really?" with rising intonation (expressing surprise) and then falling intonation (expressing disbelief). They will soon get the idea. Also consider saying something in class using unusual intonation and having students correct you.
- *Intonation with attitude*: In intermediate or higher-level classes, say a given sentence using a particular intonation and have students guess your attitude or suggest a situation in which that intonation might be used.
- *Modelling intonation*: Model correct intonation in every class activity. (It may be necessary to exaggerate intonation a bit in order to draw students' attention to it, but avoid doing so to the point where your own intonation is no longer natural.)

Overall, keep in mind that intonation, like other aspects of pronunciation, is learned gradually and may require a lot of practice over a long period time, so be patient when progress seems slow.

☞ *Try: Visit this book's companion website to practice marking intonation on a variety of standard sentences.*

USING THOUGHT GROUPS

One very practical way of helping students speak more clearly is through the use of thought groups. A thought group is a phrase or clause, usually two to five words in length, that forms a unit of meaning within a sentence. Professional speakers often use thought groups to break their sentences into smaller chunks that are easier for listeners to process. Consider these examples, where the thought groups in each sentence are separated by slashes:

- *It was raining outside, / so we decided to stay indoors / and watch a movie.*
- *Whenever it snows, / we go outside / and build a snow fort.*
- *Professional speakers / use thought groups / to ensure clarity.*

Note that when these sentences are spoken clearly, the thought groups are separated by a slight pause. In writing, some of these pauses are indicated by punctuation, but others are not—they are added by the speaker in order to further break the sentence into smaller chunks.

There are three steps to teaching the use of thought groups to students:

1. *Introduce the concept*: Explain the basic characteristics of thought groups:
    - Speakers often use thought groups to break their sentences into smaller chunks that are easier for listeners to process.
    - Thought groups are separated by brief pauses.
    - A thought group has a focus word with more emphasis (usually the last content word). Particularly important phrases are also lengthened for emphasis.
    - The end of a thought group is often indicated by a drop in pitch and a lengthening of the final syllable.
2. *Listening practice*: Train students to recognize thought groups by listening to a reading or a recording while following along with a transcript.
    - The first time through, have them mark the pauses between thought groups.
    - The second time through, have them confirm their marks by listening for the drop in pitch and lengthened syllable at the end of each thought group.
    - The third time through, have them mark the focus words and any emphasized phrases.

    One particularly good source of material for this activity is the TED Talks website or app, which provides both videos (often of professional speakers who make good use of thought groups) and transcripts.
3. *Speaking practice*: Have students write sentences of their own, mark the thought groups, and practice saying them, pausing briefly between the thought groups—though beware of them sounding overly dramatic.

Finally, students should also be encouraged to take note of the pauses between thought groups when they are engaged in extensive listening.

INTEGRATING PRONUNCIATION PRACTICE IN VARIOUS CONTEXTS

While some teachers and courses specialize in pronunciation, most do not; rather, they integrate pronunciation practice into all their classes and many of their activities (especially those that focus on speaking, for obvious reasons), and occasionally dedicate entire lessons to specific aspects of pronunciation. Even a warm-up conversation at the beginning of class, for example, provides opportunities for teachers to provide good feedback (see chapter 6) on students' pronunciation, followed (when appropriate) by further practice.

In fact, it is only through long-term practice, in various contexts, that students can significantly improve their pronunciation. After all, pronunciation is largely about habit formation—in this case, replacing previous habits (often from the student's first language) with new habits (from the target language). However, as we mentioned at the beginning of this chapter, while students may try hard to understand spoken English, they are often shy to speak up because they fear they will not be understood. (Remember, many students have studied English grammar and writing in school but have had few opportunities to speak English and few good models of spoken English.) Furthermore, when students are asked to speak up in class, this fear of poor pronunciation is compounded by the stress of figuring out what to say and how to say it.

Practical Practice

Sustained, long-term practice, then, requires a bit of ingenuity. The best practice helps students focus on pronunciation without the distractions of other issues, and it helps students grow more confident in using their voices so they will begin to speak up more during other activities as well:

- *Audiobooks* provide extensive exposure to correct pronunciation, allowing students to gradually improve their perception of spoken language, which in turn influences their pronunciation. A graded reader with an accompanying CD or audio file at an appropriate level for the students is ideal. Have students listen to the audio while following along in the text; then have them listen to the audio without the text. Students can do this on their own time, and if they complete one book per week, they are likely to see significant improvement in their listening skills within six months; better pronunciation skills will follow, particularly when extensive listening practice is combined with the other types of teaching and practice described in this chapter.

- *Oral reading* for pronunciation (not comprehension) allows students to focus entirely on their pronunciation without the distraction of grammar, vocabulary, and so on. The text used should be one that is comprehensible to the students (and interesting, not dry, as tone is an important part of pronunciation), and the teacher should assist the students with only pronunciation—meaning is not important here. Reading play scripts (in particular those written for language learners at a particular level) is especially helpful because the material is written as dialogue, not prose, and with a particular social context in mind. As such, plays are particularly well-suited for practicing intonation.

- *Accent imitation*: Have students choose a model (a friend, actor, or any other model of natural English) and imitate that person's accent. Television personalities are particularly good because the students can listen to them regularly and practice imitating them. However, be sure the students choose realistic and "normal" accents to imitate, particularly if they are fans of old westerns.

- *Contrast similar sounds* during a class activity. For example, introduce a game by saying, "Okay, let's play—that's *play*, not *pray*—a game." Invite students to do the same when using words with difficult sounds. Of course, do so with a smile to keep the mood light, and don't overdo it by interrupting every conversation—find a balance that works for your class.

- *Listening comprehension activities* focus on content more than on sound, but they also help students notice and recognize difficult sounds and pronunciation features. (See chapter 9 for more information on teaching listening comprehension.)

- *Pronunciation feedback* during regular class activities is particularly helpful, even during those that involve authentic conversation. The guidelines here are simple: first, since there will be too many errors to correct, give priority to the most serious errors; second, if the pronunciation error is such that the student cannot be understood, offer assistance immediately, but if the error is obvious but the student is still intelligible, wait until the student has finished speaking, and then model the correct

pronunciation. In either case, have the student (and perhaps other students) repeat the correct pronunciation, and keep track of difficult words or phrases to be revisited in future classes. Be sure to offer all feedback as help, not judgment, and praise the students' efforts even when progress is minimal.
- *Smartphone apps* for learning and practicing pronunciation and listening are constantly improving, and many are free or inexpensive.

Overall, although teaching pronunciation and aural perception can be challenging and at times even frustrating, the effort is worthwhile over the long term, particularly as we watch students become more confident in their abilities and more integrated into English-speaking society.

QUESTIONS FOR REVIEW

1. "Poor pronunciation is as much a social issue as a language issue." Explain.
2. What is a minimal pair? Give four examples, each targeting a different sound.
3. How should we train students to deal with words that are minimized, contracted, or linked in a sentence?
4. How do word stress and sentence stress in English differ from those in most other languages? How can we help students learn correct word stress and sentence stress?
5. Why is intonation an important part of pronunciation? What makes it difficult to teach?
6. What are the most common patterns of intonation?
7. How might extensive listening help pronunciation?
8. How might oral reading be used to improve pronunciation?
9. How do we give feedback when teaching pronunciation?

FURTHER READING

Marianne Celce-Murcia, Donna M. Brinton, and Janet M. Goodwin's *Teaching Pronunciation* (Cambridge, 2010) contains both theory and practice activities.

Linda Grant's *Pronunciation Myths: Applying Second Language Research to Classroom Teaching* (Michigan, 2014) is a practical guide that addresses common misconceptions and suggests solutions.

Martin Hewings's *Pronunciation Practice Activities* (Cambridge, 2004) provides practical activities for class.

Jennifer Jenkins's *The Phonology of English as an International Language* (Oxford, 2000) explores mutual intelligibility (versus accent imitation) as the goal of pronunciation instruction in a post-colonial world.

Linda Lane's *Tips for Teaching Pronunciation* (Pearson, 2010) provides practical advice.

Peter Roach's *English Phonetics and Phonology* (Cambridge, 2009) provides thorough coverage of the subject along with activities and teaching suggestions.

Robin Walker's *Teaching the Pronunciation of English as a Lingua Franca* (Oxford, 2010) provides an overview of relevant techniques and materials.

Helpful Online Resources

Sounds of Speech: http://soundsofspeech.uiowa.edu/index.html#english

Ship or Sheep: http://www.shiporsheep.com

NOTE

1. The first four of these suggested conditions are adapted from Ron Thomson's presentation "Beyond Minimal Pairs: Research-Based Perspectives on Pronunciation Instruction" (TESL Canada Conference, Halifax, Nova Scotia, 2011).

CHAPTER 17
Linguistic Factors in Language Acquisition

Miguel was frustrated. He had been studying English for almost four years, but he felt that his English was not very good. He still made frequent errors in grammar, his pronunciation made it difficult for others to understand him, and he often had trouble finding the right words to express what he wanted to say. He wondered if he was wasting his time.

When Miguel asked his teacher why his English was not improving, his teacher smiled and began to shuffle through her files. After a few minutes, she showed Miguel an assignment that he had written two years earlier. Miguel laughed at the errors that he had made and could now easily correct. His teacher then showed him a video she had made of Miguel giving a presentation 16 months earlier, and again Miguel laughed at himself and acknowledged the progress he had made since then. His teacher's point was clear: while he still made errors when speaking English, he had improved significantly over the past few years. Nonetheless, Miguel was left with a simple question that does not have a simple answer: *Why was it so difficult to improve his English?*

INTERLANGUAGE

In earlier chapters, we learned that every language has certain rules that govern which sounds are used, how sounds are arranged, how words are formed, and how words are arranged to form phrases, clauses, and sentences. (The study of such rules falls under phonetics, phonology, morphology, and syntax, respectively.) Speakers of a language know these rules and subconsciously access them every time they use the language. However, we also know that the rules of one language are not the same as the rules of another.

When adults like Miguel attempt to learn a new language, they must learn the rules of the language. They are likely to master some of the rules quickly but misunderstand many others, resulting in a modified form of the target language. This modified form is called an **interlanguage**; it is an intermediate stage in the process of learning the new language.[1]

A learner's interlanguage, like any other language, has rules that govern which sounds are used, how sounds are arranged, how words are formed, and how words are arranged to form phrases, clauses, and sentences. The rules of an interlanguage are a bit of a hodgepodge, however:

- Some of the interlanguage rules are from the target language, acquired through the learner's observation and study of the language.
- Some of the interlanguage rules are from the learner's first language, and they have not yet been replaced with the equivalent rules from the target language.
- Some of the interlanguage rules are from neither the learner's first language nor the target language; rather, they are based on the learner's incorrect assumptions or deductions about how the target language works.

The learner will use these rules in a very systematic and consistent way, but over time, through correction and practice, the learner's interlanguage should become more like the target language as the erroneous language rules are gradually replaced with the correct ones. However, in some cases an interlanguage stops developing because there is no new learning or correction. In such a case, the language learner uses the erroneous forms over and over until they become so "natural" that they are very difficult to correct, and the interlanguage is said to have **fossilized**.

In Miguel's case, correction and practice have helped improve his English significantly: his accent, while still influenced by the pronunciation rules of his first language, is steadily improving through practice arranged by his teacher; his grammar, while still influenced by his first language and by his mistaken assumptions about English, is also improving as he studies and practices the correct forms; and his usage of English words is beginning to sound more natural as he expands his vocabulary and no longer overuses certain basic vocabulary.

Overall, Miguel's interlanguage is becoming more like standard English. Nonetheless, the question remains: Why is language so hard to learn? To this question we might add a few more: *How does a person's first language influence the acquisition of another language? Why are some language rules more difficult to learn than others? Why do we learn language rules or properties in a particular order?*

LANGUAGE TRANSFER

When the rules of the target language are similar to the equivalent rules of the learner's first language, we might expect that learning the target language will be easier; after all, the rules will feel familiar. This is called *positive language transfer*. Spanish speakers, for example, generally learn French more quickly than English speakers do because Spanish and French have more in common than English and French.

However, when encountering rules that are similar but not identical, learners may not recognize the small differences or may not easily adapt to them. Likewise, learners who simply do not know the rules of the target language may simply substitute the equivalent rules from their first language, resulting in errors. This is called *negative language transfer*. Many languages, for example, do not have the sound [θ], so speakers of those languages will often substitute a similar sound from their first language.[2]

LANGUAGE UNIVERSALS AND MARKEDNESS

When two properties of a target language are significantly different from the equivalent properties in the language learner's first language, are they equally difficult to learn? Not necessarily. One may be much more difficult to learn than the other. For example, learners encountering the sounds [θ] and [t] for the first time, with no similar sounds in their first language, will likely find [θ] much more difficult to acquire. We know this from the study of **language universals** (also called *linguistic universals*) and **markedness**.

Linguists have observed that there are certain properties and rules that (nearly) all human languages have in common. These properties and rules are called language universals. Language universals that are without exception are called *absolute universals* and include the following:

- All languages have consonant-vowel syllables.
- All languages have the sound [ɑ].
- All languages have nouns and verbs.

- All languages have pronoun categories that include three persons (first person, second person, third person) and two numbers (singular, plural), though some languages have additional pronoun categories as well.
- When wh-movement exists, the wh-word always moves to the beginning of the clause.
- No language has voiced stops without also having voiceless stops.
- No language has more than 11 basic colour terms.

Language universals that are very common but not without exceptions are called *universal tendencies* (also called *relative universals* or *statistical universals*) and include the following:

- Most languages have nasal consonants.
- In the overwhelming majority of languages, the sentence subject precedes the object.
- Verb-initial languages generally have prepositions, but verb-final languages generally have postpositions. (Latin is an exception, as it is verb-final but has prepositions.)

Generally speaking, universal language properties are common for a reason: they are easily learned. As such, we can hypothesize which language properties are easy to learn based on how common they are in the world's languages. The sounds [n] and [k], for example, are very common, so they are likely easy to acquire even by someone learning them for the first time. These and other common (and easy-to-learn) language properties are said to be *unmarked*.

In the same way, certain language properties are relatively rare because they are not easily learned, so we can hypothesize which language properties are more difficult to learn based on how rare they are in the world's languages. The English sounds [θ] and [ð], for example, are not common at all, so they are likely difficult to acquire. These and other less common (and more difficult-to-learn) language properties are said to be **marked**.

Markedness, of course, is relative. One language property might be more marked (more unusual, more difficult to learn) than another but less marked (less unusual, less difficult to learn) than still another:

- [ɹ] is more marked than [l], which is more marked than [d].
- [θ] is more marked than [t].

- The consonant blend [st] is more marked than [sn], which is more marked than [sl].
- The sentence structure S-O-V is more marked than the structure S-V-O.
- Voiceless stops are unmarked; voiced stops are marked.

Linguists have further posited the **markedness differential hypothesis**,[3] which suggests that when a property of the target language is different from the equivalent property of the learner's first language and is more marked, it will be difficult for the learner to acquire—and the more marked the target property is, the more difficult it will be to acquire; but when a property of the target language is different from the equivalent property of the learner's first language but is not more marked, it will not be difficult for the learner to acquire.

As we mentioned above, a language learner encountering the sounds [θ] and [t] for the first time, with no similar sounds in their first language, will very likely find [θ] much more difficult to acquire. We now know why: although both are new to the learner, [θ] is significantly more marked than [t].

DEVELOPMENTAL PROCESSES

We know that young first-language learners generally acquire some grammar forms before others, master the pronunciation of certain sounds before others, and learn certain words before others. Linguists have discovered that adult language learners go through stages of learning similar (though not identical) to those of a first-language learner.

Language lessons, courses, and course books are designed according to these observations: they begin with forms and content that are more easily acquired and gradually progress to more difficult forms and content. Although it is possible that some students could succeed in mastering forms beyond their level, in many cases an attempt to do so would create difficulty and confusion.

PATTERNS IN LANGUAGE ACQUISITION

Language acquisition, then, is influenced by language transfer, markedness, and developmental processes, but not all areas of language acquisition are influenced in the same way or to the same degree.

In Phonetics and Phonology

Language transfer is the most significant factor in acquiring correct pronunciation. When the learner's first language shares sounds and sound combinations with the target language, those features are transferred quickly and easily, resulting in faster acquisition. However, as we saw in chapter 15, language learners will often modify the target language to make it conform to the rules of their first language: for example, they will substitute known sounds for unknown ones, break up unfamiliar consonant blends, and avoid final consonants by dropping them or adding a vowel.

Language learners may also transfer rules related to word stress, particularly where the target word is similar to the equivalent word in the speaker's first language. A French speaker, for example, will often pronounce *different* with the stress on the final syllable (like the French *différent*) instead of the first syllable. In a similar way, Polish speakers tend to place stress on the second-last syllable of English words because the Polish language requires such stress.

The influence of language transfer is strong because the rules that allow us to speak our first language are largely subconscious, so when we attempt to speak another language, we tend to access those first-language rules. To do otherwise requires retraining our minds with a new set of rules.

The degree to which language transfer contributes to a speaker's accent is directly related to the degree of difference between equivalent properties: the greater the difference, the stronger the accent. Consider, for example, that the substitution of [pʰ] for [p] will barely be noticed, but the substitution of [ʃ] for [s] will be much more noticeable (as in *shine* for *sign*), as will [s] or [t] for [θ] (as in *sink* or *tink* for *think*), or [d] or [z] for [ð] (resulting in *den* or *zen* for *then*).

Secondary to transfer influences are developmental influences. Beginners are more likely to transfer sounds and sound rules from their first language, such as simplifying consonant clusters (*tay* for *stay*) or breaking them up (*supin* for *spin*) in order to simplify pronunciation, while students who are further along in learning a language are likely to learn new sounds and sound combinations with less difficulty, overcoming the tendency to transfer sounds or rules erroneously.

Finally, markedness also plays a role in phonetics and phonology, often in combination with language transfer. As we noted above, a language learner who encounters both [t] and [θ] for the first time may struggle with both (and may initially substitute a known sound for each) but is likely to acquire [t] before [θ] because the latter is more marked.

In Morphology

The language learner's understanding of word formation appears to be influenced primarily by developmental processes. As such, a language learner who struggles with a particular aspect of word formation (such as plurals, possessives, or tense inflection) may simply need more time to develop, just as a child learning a first language needs time to develop.

In general, certain patterns in this developmental process are common to both first-language and second-language learners:

- the acquisition of the plural morpheme "-s" before the possessive morpheme "-'s" and the third-person singular morpheme "-s"
- re-pluralizing non-standard plural forms (*teeths, sheeps*)
- the use of object pronouns (such as *me*) as subjects (*Me want this*)
- the use of temporal markers to indicate time and place in the absence of verb morphology (*Yesterday I go to the store*)
- the acquisition of inflectional affixes before derivational affixes (*taller* before *singer*)

In Syntax

A language learner's understanding of syntax is influenced by language transfer, markedness, and developmental processes.

In some cases, when the rules of the target language are similar to those of the learner's first language, language transfer is likely to have a positive influence on sentence formation:

- English, French, and Spanish share a basic subject-verb-object (S-V-O) sentence structure (when the object is a noun), so speakers of one language will easily transfer this structure to another: *I ate the bread. = J'ai mangé le pain. = Yo comí el pan.*
- French and Spanish speakers generally have no difficulty learning wh-movement in English because wh-movement also exists in French and Spanish.

However, language transfer may negatively influence sentence formation when the rules of the target language are different from those of the learner's first language, and these differences will be more difficult to overcome if the target form is more marked than the equivalent form in the learner's first language.

- Chinese, Japanese, Korean, and Vietnamese do not use articles, so speakers of these languages are likely to drop articles or misuse them when speaking English.
- Chinese and Vietnamese use the same forms for subject and object pronouns, so when speaking English, they tend to use a subject pronoun when an object pronoun is required.
- Japanese, Korean, and Spanish speakers may drop the subject of a sentence—saying *Is sunny*, for example, instead of *It is sunny*—because those languages allow the subject to be dropped in some situations.
- French and Spanish use S-O-V when the object is a pronoun, so the English S-V-O structure used in the equivalent sentence will be unfamiliar to French and Spanish speakers. Nevertheless, they can easily acquire the S-V-O structure because S-V-O is less marked than S-O-V.
- English speakers learning French or Spanish will not recognize the S-O-V structure used in French and Spanish (when the object is a pronoun), and they are likely to erroneously transfer the S-V-O structure because S-O-V is more marked. Consider these attempts to translate *I ate it* (S-V-O) into French and Spanish:
    - *J'ai mangé le.* (Erroneously transferred S-V-O. Should be S-O-V: *Je l'ai mangé.*)
    - *Yo comí lo.* (Erroneously transferred S-V-O. Should be S-O-V: *Yo lo comí.*)
- Language transfer may negatively influence sentence formation when certain words co-occur in the learner's first language but not in the target language.
    - French speakers may say *I obey to my parents*. The erroneous use of the preposition is a direct transfer from French: *J'obéis à mes parents*.
    - English speakers may say *J'écoute à mes parents* instead of *J'écoute mes parents* because the former is a direct transfer from English: *I listen to my parents*.
    - English speakers learning French tend to say *Je suis faim* instead of *J'ai faim* for *I'm hungry* because English uses *am hungry*, not *have hunger*, in the corresponding statement.

Developmental processes also play a role. Language learners are better prepared to learn more complex syntactic structures once they have mastered simpler ones:

- Beginners acquire lexical morphemes (those that have meaning on their own, including nouns, verbs, adjectives, and adverbs) before grammatical

morphemes (determiners, prepositions, conjunctions, inflections, and affixes) and often construct sentences accordingly: *He is nice boy.* (Note that in this example, language transfer may also play a role if the learner's first language does not use articles.)
- Learners whose first language forms questions without wh-movement or subject movement are likely to acquire wh-movement before subject movement (*Why I can't go?*).
- Beginners may soon be ready to learn simple past tense, but the future perfect progressive tense will likely be too difficult until the learner has progressed much further.

In Semantics

Language learners' correct use of words largely depends on their stage of development. While those whose vocabulary is well developed have a wide range of words to choose from in order to express their intended meaning, learners in early stages of development show particular tendencies related to their limited vocabulary:

- They overgeneralize by using **superordinates** (words that represent general classes) instead of more specific words, such as *animal* for *bear* or *bird* for *pigeon*.
- They overuse or misuse common words such as *good, bad, big, small, very,* or *many* where other words would normally be used.
- They misuse approximate synonyms, especially if they are the same word in the speaker's first language (e.g., *tall* for *long; work* for *job, occupation,* or *career*).
- They misunderstand idioms, which generally cannot be understood without being specifically learned.

THEORY IN PRACTICE

Numerous times in this book we have discussed options for giving feedback during student activities—feedback that includes both encouragement and correction. An understanding of linguistic factors in second-language acquisition gives us further insight into the struggles students face as well as the kinds of mistakes they make, the reasons they make them, and the methods we might use to help correct those mistakes. As a result, we are better informed and more likely to make effective decisions when giving feedback.

QUESTIONS FOR REVIEW

1. What is interlanguage?
2. What is language fossilization, and how might it be avoided?
3. What are positive language transfer and negative language transfer? Give examples.
4. Explain the relationship between language universals and markedness.
5. In what way is the developmental process of a second-language learner similar to that of a first-language learner? Give examples.
6. Of language transfer, markedness, and developmental processes, which is most likely to influence pronunciation? morphology? syntax? semantics?
7. Write out five sentences that contain common mistakes made by language learners. Then try to explain the influence of language transfer, markedness, and developmental processes for each of those errors.

FURTHER READING

Steven Brown and Jenifer Larson-Hall's *Second Language Acquisition Myths: Applying Second Language Research to Classroom Teaching* (Michigan, 2012) challenges common misconceptions.

Rod Ellis's *Understanding Second Language Acquisition* (Oxford, 2015) provides a comprehensive overview of relevant theories.

Susan Gass, Jennifer Behney, and Luke Plonsky's *Second Language Acquisition: An Introductory Course* (Routledge, 2013) is a thorough and practical introduction to the field.

Patsy Lightbown and Nina Spada's *How Languages Are Learned* (Oxford, 2013) makes the connection between theories of language acquisition and classroom activities.

Lourdes Ortega's *Understanding Second Language Acquisition* (Routledge, 2008) provides a thorough overview of theories and concepts.

Michael Swan and Bernard Smith's *Learner English: A Teacher's Guide to Interference and Other Problems* addresses specific problems caused by a speaker's first language interfering with their acquisition of English.

Bill VanPatten and Jessica Williams's *Theories in Second Language Acquisition: An Introduction* (Routledge, 2014) provides a survey of major theories still considered relevant.

NOTES

1. The concepts of interlanguage and fossilization were first discussed by Larry Selinker in "Interlanguage," *International Review of Applied Linguistics in Language Training* 10, no. 3 (1972): 209–231.
2. Language transfer was first described by Uriel Weinreich in *Languages in Contact* (Mouton, 1953).
3. The markedness differential hypothesis was first proposed by Fred Eckman in "Markedness and the Contrastive Analysis Hypothesis" in *Language Learning* 27, no. 2 (1977): 315–330.

CHAPTER 18

Intercultural Communication

AYAKO'S STORY

Ayako is Japanese. Like most people from her country, she studied English for many years at school; like some people from her country, she also studied English at university and took private English lessons in her free time. Nonetheless, when she visited Australia at the age of 22, she found that she could not communicate effectively and frequently became confused. Given the amount of time she had studied English, she wondered how this could have happened.

When Ayako had first begun learning English in school, her most significant difficulty was learning the correct pronunciation. The English she heard on recordings had many sounds that were unfamiliar to her; she could not reproduce them and instead spoke basic English with a "katakana" pronunciation—for example, *straight* became *su-to-re-i-to* (pronounced *su-toe-ray-ee-toh*).

As her class content progressed from simple phrases and pronunciation exercises to more complex grammatical forms, Ayako discovered that English grammar is very different from Japanese grammar. English indicates sentence functions by order and context, not by grammatical markers or particles; verb tenses are more numerous and use a variety of helper verbs with a confusing word order (whereas Japanese uses fairly simple suffixes to indicate tense and mood); and articles, whether definite or indefinite, made little sense at all, since they do not exist in Japanese.

While all this was going on, Ayako's class also progressed from simple words with "standard" spelling to a plethora of words with non-standard spellings, or, more accurately, non-phonetic spellings. "If English letters have sounds, why don't all words use the same letters to make the same sounds?" she would ask. "What is the point of having spelling rules if many words are exceptions?"

Through years of memorization and drills, Ayako eventually became familiar with English grammar and learned to spell at least reasonably well, but the school curriculum's emphasis on written English and simplistic drills meant that she had almost no experience actually communicating in English. She could speak formulaic English and could answer surprisingly complex grammar questions, but she had difficulty carrying on even a basic conversation.

By the time she finished university, Ayako had decided that she wanted to speak English more naturally and fluently, so she enrolled in an English language program in Australia. Her first week there, a total and immediate immersion in English, was a bit like jumping into a cold bath on a hot Australian day, but it did have the effect of forcing her to communicate in English.

Ayako's early experiences in Australia brought even more surprises. Initially, she couldn't decide if Australians were friendly or rude. On the one hand, they were always smiling and joking; on the other hand, they seemed to lack politeness, opting for a very direct, casual style of interaction. Even their apologies were short and quickly forgotten, as were expressions of thanks. For Ayako, who was used to apologizing or expressing thanks in a much longer, indirect fashion with many more words, such behaviour seemed odd. The Aussies were also quick to address any type of problem, even with teachers or leaders, while Ayako preferred to keep quiet on such matters.

Ayako also struggled with group work in her language classes. The Aussie teacher was very focused and keen to see things done quickly and done well, which was fine for Ayako, but some of her fellow students from other countries seemed constantly distracted; they were more interested in talking to one another than in getting their work done. And when they addressed the teacher, they used very formal language even more formal than what Ayako was used to while the teachers laughed and insisted they be called by their first names. It was all very strange.

When socializing after class, Ayako learned many new words and began using them in ways she thought would make her English sound more natural, but she discovered that certain words seemed to evoke a strong reaction from others—a look of amused shock, it seemed. Some kind friends soon explained to her that these words should not be used at all in most social situations.

Over time, Ayako learned to adjust. As she became used to hearing natural English and practiced communicating her thoughts in English, her confidence increased and her ability to communicate improved. At the same time, she tried to be open-minded about the different behavioural expectations and even enjoyed noting the differences between Australian culture, her own culture, and the various cultures of her classmates.

Today Ayako lives in Canada with her Canadian husband and three trilingual children. She still has difficulty with the meanings of idioms and the syntax of certain phrasal verbs, but she communicates very effectively. In fact, she admits that spoken English has become almost easy (though less so in large groups) and that written English is now her weaker point. Asked about the challenges she has overcome and what advice she would give others, she answers directly: "Work hard at learning the language, and keep an open mind about the culture. Both can be challenging but also an adventure."

Ayako's experience is not unusual. Like other language learners, she found that in order to communicate effectively, she had to learn not only the nuances of another language but also those of another culture. Much of what she learned is explored in a more general way through the studies of **sociolinguistics** and intercultural communication.

☞ *Consider: What non-linguistic challenges did Ayako face during her time in Australia? Why did they surprise her?*

LANGUAGE AND CULTURE

Like Ayako, language learners must learn not only the grammar and vocabulary of a language but also the cultural norms of those who use the language. Without such an understanding, even higher-level language learners are likely to experience confusion and frustration caused by miscommunication, whereas a strong understanding of these cultural norms leads to clearer, more effective communication and better social integration of the language learner.

What Is Culture?

The term *culture* is broad and not easily defined, but for our purposes, it is a set of agreed-upon norms that define a particular social group. These norms, mostly subconscious, consist of and influence our behaviour, beliefs, values, priorities, perspective, traditions, and observances. They are the unspoken assumptions that guide our thoughts and influence our actions as we interact with other members of society. Consider, for example, the assumptions that underlie your responses to these questions:

- Do you smile when you meet a stranger while walking down the street? Why or why not?

- Under what circumstances, if any, do you greet someone with a handshake?
- Do you speak to your teachers the same way you speak to your friends?
- Do you feel awkward during pauses in a conversation?
- How much personal space do you expect when talking to an acquaintance?
- What body language do you consider aggressive?
- How do you give bad news to someone you care about?
- When you are running late for a meeting and you suddenly see an old friend, do you prioritize the meeting or the friendship?
- What is appropriate to wear to a wedding? a funeral? a language class? the beach?
- What holiday traditions do you observe, and how?
- What foods are typical breakfast foods?
- Which is more important: individual reputation or family reputation?
- How do you express gratitude after having a meal at someone's house?
- Is it appropriate for a man to compliment a female colleague on her appearance?

Although individuals may vary, most people from a given culture will have similar answers to these questions; however, their answers may differ significantly from those given by people from another culture. Both groups tend to assume that their own norms are standard and those of other cultures are different, strange, or even wrong.

This last point is key: we all have a natural bias toward the societal norms that we have learned and adopted over a lifetime, and it is difficult for us to accept alternative norms; worse yet, we tend to judge the words and actions of others according to our own norms, not theirs.

Consider, for example, Ayako's reaction to Australian ways of showing gratitude or apologizing: she found them too direct, too informal, and perhaps even rude. Australians, meanwhile, would likely see the equivalent Japanese expressions as wordy, overly formulaic, and perhaps even insincere. In both cases, we note a tendency to judge others according to one's own cultural norms.

In a multicultural classroom or community, the solution to this predicament comes in two steps: first, we acknowledge that our cultural biases are real and powerful, and that they often cause us to misunderstand and misjudge others; then, we do our best to learn about (and, if possible, experience) the norms of other cultures, with an open mind. The more we do this, the more accepting we will be of differences.

CULTURAL NORMS: COMMUNICATION

We discover the communication norms of a culture (or a speech community) by studying the language within its social context; this study is known as *sociolinguistics*. In particular, sociolinguistics examines how utterances are put together by speakers. This type of study, known as **discourse analysis**,[1] attempts to discover the nuances of language functions, the rules and conventions of conversation, and the overall styles of communication. We will look at each individually.

Language Functions

When we speak, we are not only saying something but also doing something. This is the basic premise of speech-act theory. Consider, for example, that promising, requesting, and apologizing are actions as much as they are speech, and the method of performing each, as well as the significance attached to the action, can vary significantly from one culture to another. Consider these differences:

- In some cultures, it is important to apologize profusely numerous times with particular words or even formulaic expressions, while in other cultures it is considered better to apologize once but with sincerity.
- In some cultures, speakers hesitate to say "sorry" unless they are at fault, while in other cultures, speakers will use the word *sorry* almost every time they inconvenience another person, even if the other person is more at fault.
- In some cultures, a quick "thanks" is considered polite, while in other cultures, multiple (and perhaps more formal) verbal expressions of thanks are expected, perhaps followed by a card.
- In some cultures, "yes" is used to indicate agreement with the speaker's point or a willingness to fulfill a request, but in other cultures it is used to simply acknowledge that the request or the point has been made.
- In some cultures, honesty is valued highly and is considered a reflection of character, though "little white lies" might be acceptable when sparing someone's feelings; in other cultures, truth may quickly be sacrificed for the sake of convenience or to avoid awkward moments.

- In some cultures, promises are taken very seriously, even if implied rather than spoken; in other cultures, even an explicit promise may be taken lightly depending on the context.
- In some cultures, it is considered polite to refuse an invitation indirectly by offering an excuse such as "Sorry, I already have an appointment that day" (even if no appointment exists), while in other cultures, a more direct reply is preferred.
- In some cultures, it is common to verbally accept an invitation but not show up for the event; in other cultures, this type of behaviour may be considered very rude.
- In some cultures, an offer should not be accepted immediately but refused once or twice and then accepted, while in other cultures, the offer might not be made a second time.

In each of these cases, the intended act may be carried out very differently from one culture to another, even if the same result is desired, and a lack of understanding of the relevant social nuances can lead to serious miscommunication and even embarrassment.

Language teachers may wish to have a reference book that outlines some of these cultural differences, not only to know what kind of background students are coming from, but also to review the cultural norms in their own society.

The Rules of Conversation

Using a method known as **conversation analysis,** linguists attempt to discover what types of utterances are made in conversation, how they are organized, and what components make up such utterances. The study of such components and rules are of interest to language teachers and language learners because many of them are culture-specific.

Consider that a typical conversation (in almost any language) has a distinct opening (that may influence whether the conversation will continue) and a distinct closing (that signals the end of the conversation), but the details of each vary by culture. For example, speakers from one culture may use certain verbal clues (such as a particular phrase or a drop in tone) or physical gestures (such as looking at one's watch) to indicate a desire to end a conversation, but speakers from another culture may be accustomed to very different clues and therefore miss the other speaker's intention.

There are also distinct social rules that govern turn-taking in conversation, again varying by culture. Speakers in many Western cultures, for example, take brief turns in a conversation, with minimal silence between speakers because they find silence awkward. Speakers from many other cultures, however, take slightly longer turns, and they allow (and expect) a brief pause after each speaker to give time for thoughtful consideration of what has been said. In still other cultures, speakers regularly interrupt one another and expect overlap. Note how a speaker from one of these cultures might react when conversing with speakers from another:

- A speaker from the first group might find a conversation with the second group awkward because of the frequent pauses, and might find a conversation with the third group difficult because of a lack of opportunities to speak.
- A speaker from the second group might find the other groups aggressive and lacking in consideration.
- A speaker from the third group might find the pace of conversation painfully slow with either of the other groups.

Conversations may also include **adjacency pairs**, which are pairs of utterances in which the first is normally followed by the second, but once again the details may differ from one culture to another:

- A question normally requires an answer, just as a greeting requires a response, but occasionally the rules change, such as when a greeting of "How are you?" receives a reply of "Hey, how ya doing?"
- An offer (of a gift) normally requires acceptance or refusal, but as noted above, in some cultures it is polite to initially refuse a few times before accepting.
- An offer (in business or sales) normally requires acceptance or refusal, but further negotiation may or may not be appropriate, depending on the culture and the specific situation.
- A compliment normally requires acceptance or at least acknowledgement, but not all compliments are appropriate in all situations, and these conditions again may vary by culture and change over time.

Through text analysis, linguists have also discovered other conventions in speaking. Most conversations, for example, include various **discourse markers**—that is, words or expressions that do not change the meaning of the utterance but may serve one or more broader functions. (Review appendix 8A for a list of common discourse markers used in English.)

As we might expect, differences in the rules of conversation can lead to awkward moments, missed turns, perceived interruptions, frustration, and so on. As language teachers, we must be aware of these differences and help our students understand what to expect. We can begin by teaching specific conversation conventions to our students and explaining how they are used. Then, in future classes, we can use them in our class conversations and even when giving instructions, occasionally pausing to check whether students understand their use.

Styles of Communication

When we communicate with another person, our communication is more than just a continuous flow of words. Rather, in order for us to communicate effectively, we must have not only a shared grammar and vocabulary but also a shared set of rules that tell us what is or is not appropriate to the situation. What tone is appropriate? What level of formality? Which phrases or words? What overall style (or **register**) does the other participant expect?

Sociolinguists analyze communication to discover these rules. Such study has revealed the following tendencies in some cultures' communication:

- During rituals (such as weddings, funerals, and religious ceremonies), most cultures will use formal language and archaic words that may not be known by someone from another culture.
- Young people frequently use slang or other expressions that may be appropriate in some contexts but not in others.
- Technical writing often uses specific terminology (jargon) not common in other contexts, and it may exclude individuals not familiar with such terminology.
- English-language newspaper headlines usually omit articles and forms of the verb *to be* ("Man Arrested in Local Diner").
- English-language recipes or cooking instructions often omit determiners and pronouns ("Add milk and stir").
- Apologies in business are likely to include formal language and may include a promise to correct the mistake or an offer of compensation (such as a gift), and they may also avoid admitting direct responsibility.

As language teachers, we must realize that our students may be confused or even frustrated by such situations until they learn about them.

CULTURAL NORMS: SOCIAL INTERACTION

As we've seen above, many facets of communication, whether verbal or non-verbal, are cultural, as are many of the assumptions that underlie our communication. For language teachers, an understanding of how culture affects communication (and of the variety of cultural norms that exist) can help us understand the issues our students face and perhaps even assist them in overcoming such differences.

High-Context and Low-Context Cultures

Although each culture differs from others in numerous ways, there are also some generalizations we can make to help identify similarities between cultures. For example, most cultures can be categorized as *high context* or *low context*. High-context cultures (such as Japanese, Korean, and many other Eastern cultures) say things less directly and rely on context for clarity. They may even drop parts of a sentence (such as the subject or object) that are understood from the context. Low-context cultures (including those of many Western countries) says things more directly and with more detail, relying much less on context for clarity.[2]

Persons from a low-context culture will often have difficulty communicating in a high-context culture because they are unable to fill in the gaps in information that locals will understand from the context. Persons from a high-context culture will usually have less trouble fitting into a low-context culture, as details are spelled out; however, they may be surprised at the directness in conversation, particularly if it involves confrontation.

Relationships and Social Roles

Cultures are often defined by the way individuals within the culture understand their relationship to others.[3] Some cultures, for example, are described as being more **task oriented** than **relationship oriented**. When working in a group, individuals from task-oriented cultures expect other group members to remain focused on the task and to avoid unnecessary chit-chat or other distractions until their work is done. In fact, they will likely view such distractions as a lack of commitment to the group, and they may confront the "less-focused" members of the group to remind them that there is work to do. They are also likely to recognize individuals who make significant contributions to the group's success.

Individuals from a relationship-oriented culture, however, will see things very differently. They will emphasize relationships within the group, even if that means taking longer to get things done; as such, they may expect to have conversations that are not relevant to the task at hand, seeing them as necessary to building unity, trust, and loyalty within the group, and they are likely to avoid confrontation, choosing instead to focus on the group's results rather than on the specific contributions of individuals.

Note that both groups believe they are doing what is best for the group, even though their expectations are very different.

Cultures also differ in their understanding of social and political **power**. Some cultures, for example, accept social hierarchies and inequality as natural; they believe that superiors must be obeyed and respected and that consultation with subordinates is unnecessary. Cultures on the other end of this spectrum, meanwhile, stress equality and believe that power must be used responsibly, often in consultation with subordinates or constituents.

Gender roles vary in a similar way. In many traditional cultures, men are admired for strength, hard work, and material success, and they are expected to show little emotion, while women are defined by their feelings and their role as nurturer within the family, often with few rights as an individual. In other cultures, however, gender roles are less defined: both men and women are likely to work outside the home, and women enjoy the same rights and freedoms as men (at least in theory).

Politeness

There is a joke that asks how to recognize a Canadian among a group of international journalists. The answer? The Canadian is the one who waits for a chance to speak and then apologizes for interrupting.

Indeed, Canadians are often noted for their politeness. They are said to be less pushy than Americans about their beliefs, more likely than Europeans or Asians to wait in line, and perhaps more likely than most people on earth to strike up a friendly conversation about the weather.

Regardless of how true such statements are, they do imply a "standard" of politeness. That standard, however, is not universal; rather, politeness, like other aspects of communication, is expressed in many ways and is culturally specific, and expectations of politeness vary widely.

Canadian politeness, for example, has much to do with informal friendliness based on a strong sense of egalitarianism. This is especially true in Atlantic Canada, where people generally value sincerity over formality. A formal expression of thanks or appreciation is much less common than a warm smile and a knowing nod or hearty handshake.

Such informality, however, may be seen as "too direct," "too casual," or even "rude" by other cultures whose idea of politeness requires the speaker to use very formal language and to show humility by addressing the listener as someone higher in status. To them, style and form is just as important—or perhaps even more important—than sincerity.

The difference becomes noticeably greater when we consider that in many Western cultures (and especially in North America), formal language is often used for what we call *negative politeness*—a form of politeness that increases the distance between the speaker and the listener (and is often used as a form of condescension or to express distaste). At the same time, *positive politeness*—which brings the speaker and the listener closer together—is often created by using informal language and humour. In this sense, the Western use of formal language is almost upside down from the Eastern use, and we can see how an Asian listener might reply very positively to a Western speaker who is actually being very condescending.

Classroom Expectations

Cultural differences are frequently obvious in the classroom as well. In Western cultures, students are expected to participate verbally in class and ask questions when they do not understand the material being taught; in fact, teachers often assume that students' questions are an indication that the students are interested in and engaged by the material. Students from some Eastern cultures, however, may be less likely to speak up in class, having grown up in a system where students speak only when asked a question by the teacher, and where asking a question of their own might imply that the teacher was not sufficiently clear—which, of course, would not be polite at all, and might even be seen as confrontational. When such students join a class where speaking up is expected, it may take some time (and some persuasion) before they feel comfortable speaking without first being spoken to.

Worse yet, such students may be even less inclined to speak up if they disagree with something someone else has said, because while some cultures value healthy debate, others may deliberately avoid what they see as confrontation.

To put it another way, in some cultures it is common and acceptable to politely disagree—in fact, freely disagreeing in a friendly manner can even indicate a certain level of comfort between speakers—but in other cultures, disagreement of any kind may be considered impolite, and the speakers may speak very indirectly or not at all in order to avoid such disagreement.

Forms of Address

It seems that every generation bemoans the "lack of respect" shown by the generation that follows. The younger generations, however, are not always at fault, particularly when they receive mixed messages from the adults around them. How should they address a police officer, for example? (He was introduced as "Officer Tim" when he gave a speech at school but called something else when he gave Dad a speeding ticket.) Why is one teacher *Mrs. Baker* while another is *Ms. Janet* and still another *Jim*? Why are the local clergy called *Father Debow*, *Reverend Smith*, and *Pastor Tom*? Why does one restaurant server ask, "Would you like to order, sir?" while another asks, "What can I getcha, bud?"

In many cultures, however, the rules of respect remain much clearer. Students in Asia, for example, are often expected to stand and bow when the teacher or principal enters the classroom, and in some UK universities, entering the dining hall without removing a cap or bowing to the head table may quickly earn the student a monetary fine.

Such differences, however, are only the beginning. In some Eastern cultures, students have special forms of address not only for instructors but also for older students, and even adults often avoid addressing each other by first name. Even at home, children may be expected to address their older siblings using an appropriate term (often translated as "older sister" or "older brother") rather than using their names, and women are likely to address their husbands as "father," especially when speaking in front of the children.

When students from such cultures enter a language classroom where Western cultural rules are followed (such a class may exist in a language school in their own country), it may take some time to get used to a level of informality that they would normally consider odd or even rude.

Non-Verbal Communication

Some types of non-verbal communication are universal—that is, they are common to almost all cultures; most types, however, are culture-specific, and for that reason they can once again lead to miscommunication and confusion.

Western cultures, for example, are often very expressive in their use of gestures and body language, while Eastern cultures are not. Moreover, while East Asians are merely surprised by the expressiveness of Western gestures and body language, South Asians are often not only surprised but also perplexed as they search for the meaning behind such "strong" body language.

Even common non-verbal communication may be used in different ways. In many Western cultures, making eye contact during a conversation is important, and lack of eye contact may indicate guilt, shame, or untrustworthiness; in some Eastern cultures, however, maintaining eye contact with someone of a higher status is rude and inappropriate, and in some Middle Eastern cultures, maintaining eye contact with someone of the opposite sex (outside one's own family) is considered inappropriate.

Likewise, although a friendly smile is common to all cultures, it is not always used or expected in the same circumstances. A North American may smile at a stranger on the street, particularly in a small town; a person from northern Europe is much less likely to do so.

Other Cultural Differences

A few additional cultural differences are worth noting:

- A language may reflect certain beliefs or attitudes of its society; for example, its speakers may use certain vocabulary depending on whether they are male or female, or depending on what socio-economic class they are from.
- Some languages have words that are clearly taboo, such as swear words; other languages may have strong words but no such taboo words.
- Some cultures have a strong concept of time and schedules; others may not, and as such may be less concerned about punctuality.
- In many Western cultures, a person is likely to deal with conflict by addressing the other person directly in hopes of solving the problem; in many Eastern cultures, both parties are more likely to act in ways that allow the other to save face, and a third party is likely to act as a go-between.

GENERALIZATIONS AND STEREOTYPES

When discussing cultures, we must remember that any generalization we make is just that: a generalization, not an absolute truth. We may generalize about

Asian culture, for example, but we must also realize that while various groups in Asia share certain cultural traits, they differ in many others, and even at the local level, where people seem more culturally homogeneous, individuals often vary. In fact, in many societies today, we see a growing diversity of beliefs, values, and perspectives.

Time is also a factor, as culture is not fixed or static. It is constantly changing, so what might be true in one generation might not be in another, and similarities that exist between cultures today might not exist in a decade; conversely, significant differences between one culture and another might be minimized over time through regular interaction.

We must also be careful not to confuse similarity with sameness. Two cultures might both be task oriented, for example, but one might be more task oriented than the other, just as two cultures might be high context, but one more so than the other. These descriptors are not absolute categories but general descriptions that exist on a continuum.

Finally, we must carefully note the difference between a generalization and a **stereotype**. A generalization is based on the observation of similarities; it is meant to be descriptive and helpful, and it acknowledges exceptions. A stereotype, however, is an oversimplified perception based on assumptions, not facts; it limits how we see something or someone, it generally does not recognize exceptions, and it is judgmental and harmful. Noting, for example, that people in a particular culture "typically work only 30 hours per week" (based on census data) is a generalization, but suggesting that those same people are "lazy" is a stereotype based on a misinterpretation of that data.

INTERCULTURAL COMPETENCE AND ACCOMMODATION

When working and teaching in a cross-cultural environment, and when preparing students to interact in the same, we must not only develop our cultural knowledge but also our **intercultural competence**.[4] In other words, knowledge is not enough: if we are to communicate successfully with people from other cultures, we must develop certain skills and habits to facilitate that communication. A few key reminders might help:

- *Recognize our own ethnocentrism*: We all tend to believe that our norms are the correct ones, but we must recognize that there are many other valid norms that may differ significantly from our own.

- *Remember that the goal is successful communication*: Once we recognize our own cultural biases, it is easier to consider what adjustments can be made in order to facilitate successful communication.
- *Understand and respect differences*: There is a human tendency to oversimplify anything that is complex and difficult to understand, and culture is no exception. Worse yet, we often stereotype others in order to protect our own way of understanding the world. Instead, we should recognize not only the differences but also the fact that our understanding of them will always be incomplete; only then can we approach these differences with the kind of humility that leads to deeper understanding.
- *Tolerate ambiguity*: There will be times when we are unsure of the intentions of others, but we must resist jumping to conclusions and instead give them the benefit of the doubt.
- *Cultivate interest, patience, and empathy*: Cultural differences can make communication difficult and frustrating—on both sides—but they can also make it interesting and rewarding. We need to remember that.
- *Interact appropriately and respectfully*: If our goal is successful communication, then any act that knowingly violates the norms of the other culture is very likely at cross purposes with our goal. Instead, we must consider how we can interact in a way that respects both cultures.

Are there exceptions? Of course there are. In a culture where bribery, corruption, and oppression are expected, for example, we may find it impossible to respect such norms; but even then, if we wish to communicate successfully, we must consider how we might adapt in other ways in order to begin bridging the cultural gap without sacrificing our own values.

The term **accommodation** is used to describe the altering of one's language or customs to suit another person's style, culture, or ability, or the altering of one's expectations to allow for differences in the other person's style of communication or cultural norms. In both cases, the communicants adapt in order to help minimize frustration and misunderstanding. Such accommodation often includes the following:

- simplifying vocabulary and grammatical structures when speaking or writing
- avoiding the false association of linguistic ability with level of intelligence; even a genius, after all, may struggle with certain languages

- learning about other cultures, respecting their differences, and cultivating intercultural competence
- recognizing that cultural differences exist on both sides, and avoiding false conclusions of cultural superiority
- remembering that not every individual is typical of their culture, and that no individual is a perfect match for the generalizations (hopefully not stereotypes) we hold about other cultures
- recognizing that our perception of others and of other cultures is always incomplete and often inaccurate

WE'RE ALL DIFFERENT

In 1956, Horace Miner published an article entitled "Body Ritual among the Nacirema"[5] in which he described "the magical beliefs and practices" of a particular tribe as "an example of the extremes to which human behavior can go." He gives various details about the culture and its ways: household "shrines" dedicated to rituals and ceremonies meant to arrest aging and bodily deterioration; medicine men and herbalists who concoct various potions for the body; "holy-mouth-men" who use various objects "in the exorcism of the evils of the mouth," causing "almost unbelievable ritual torture of the client"; men who insist on "scraping and lacerating the surface of the face with a sharp instrument"; women who "bake their heads in small ovens for about an hour" at a time; a special temple, called a *latipso*, where the very ill willingly undergo "protracted ritual purification" in spite of discomfort, embarrassment, and even torture; and "women afflicted with almost inhuman hypermammary development" who are "so idolized that they make a handsome living by simply going from village to village and permitting the natives to stare at them for a fee."

Miner concludes that "it is hard to understand how they have managed to exist so long under the burdens which they have imposed upon themselves." Miner's readers tend to concur, but the sharper minds among those readers soon discover that *Nacirema* is the reverse spelling of *American*, and that the rituals described are common health and beauty practices in North America, described from an outsider's point of view.

Miner's clever exposition of our own prejudices reminds us that there is no "normal" culture, and that just as someone's behaviour may seem strange to us, our behaviour might seem even stranger to them. Overall, then, keeping an open mind is imperative. The sooner we learn to adapt to and accept the "different" customs of others, the sooner we can enjoy the variety and adventure that comes with intercultural experiences.

QUESTIONS FOR REVIEW

1. Explain the possible cultural differences for the following: apologizing, promising, expressing thanks, accepting an offer, declining an invitation.
2. What kinds of rules guide our conversations? How might they differ from one culture to another?
3. How might silence be used or interpreted differently in different cultures?
4. What are language registers? Give examples.
5. What is the difference between a high-context culture and a low-context culture? How might these differences cause confusion between speakers?
6. How does a task-oriented culture differ from a relationship-oriented culture?
7. How do cultures differ in their understanding of power?
8. How is Canadian politeness different from that of many other cultures?
9. What is negative politeness? How might it confuse someone from another culture?
10. Why might students from some cultures be hesitant to speak up in class, even when they don't understand the teacher's explanation?
11. How might forms of address differ from one culture to another?
12. Why might eye contact or a smile be misinterpreted by someone from another culture?
13. What is the difference between a generalization and a stereotype?
14. How might individuals accommodate one another regarding language and culture?

FURTHER READING

Michael Byram's *Teaching and Assessing Intercultural Communicative Competence* (Multilingual Matters, 1997) provides an overview of intercultural competence and its importance.

Joe McVeigh and Ann Wintergerst's *Tips for Teaching Culture* (Pearson, 2010) is a helpful resource with practical activities.

Erin Meyer's *The Culture Map: Decoding How People Think, Lead, and Get Things Done across Cultures* (Public Affairs, 2016) is filled with clear explanations, helpful anecdotes, and practical advice for navigating cultural differences.

Patrick Moran's *Teaching Culture: Perspectives in Practice* (Heinle ELT, 2001) provides a good overview of culture and teaching culture with helpful anecdotes and examples.

James W. Neuliep's *Intercultural Communication: A Contextual Approach* (Sage, 2017) provides a thorough overview of relevant theory.

Sonia Nieto's *Language, Culture, and Teaching: Critical Perspectives* (Routledge, 2017) explores the role of culture in the language classroom.

Bernard Spolsky's *Sociolinguistics* (Oxford, 1998) is a brief but thorough introduction to the subject.

Stella Ting-Toomey and Leeva C. Chung's *Understanding Intercultural Communication* (Oxford, 2011) is an accessible and thorough introduction to the field.

NOTES

1. This type of discourse analysis, called ethnography of communication, was first described by Dell Hymes in his article "The Ethnography of Speaking" in *Anthropology and Human Behavior*, eds. Thomas Gladwin and William Sturtevant (Anthropology Society of Washington, 1962).
2. The concept of high-context and low-context cultures was first discussed in Edward Hall's book *Beyond Culture* (Anchor, 1976).
3. This description of social roles and relationships is based very loosely on Geert Hofstede's dimensions of culture (https://geerthofstede.com), though similar models and descriptions can be found in numerous textbooks used for business classes in intercultural communication.
4. The concept of intercultural or cross-cultural competence is explored in depth in numerous articles by Claire Kramsch. See, for example, "Culture in Foreign Language Teaching" in *Iranian Journal of Language Teaching Research* 1, no. 1 (2013): 57–78.
5. Horace Miner's "Body Ritual among the Nacirema" first appeared in *American Anthropologist* 58 (June 1956): 503–507.

CHAPTER 19
Frequently Asked Questions

1. *What are the most common mistakes that new teachers make?*
   - They talk too much. They give long explanations that should be short, they explain content that should be presented in a handout or discovered by students through an activity, and they add a running commentary during activities. All this chatter is distracting and at times confusing for students.
   - They spend too little time preparing and try to do things on the fly. Good teaching requires careful planning.
   - They choose topics and activities that interest themselves rather than those that best meet the needs of their students.
   - They don't make full use of available materials. A single reading, for example, can often be used to generate five related activities, so why use it for only one?
   - When teaching content-based material, they focus almost exclusively on content-related objectives and forget to consider language-related objectives.

2. *What are the most common mistakes that experienced teachers make?*
   - They talk too much. (See the first answer for the previous question.)
   - They lose sight of long-term goals—topics, lessons, and activities should be part of an overall progression, but far too often they seem almost random.

3. *Is it helpful to show movies or videos in class?*
   Short videos are useful for listening activities, and videos in general can be used to present specific content on a given topic, but watching an entire movie

in class is generally a waste of valuable time. However, if the movie or video is at a reasonable level for the students, it can be viewed by the students, at home, for extensive listening practice.

4. *Do you recommend using textbooks or planning courses from scratch?*

If you are an expert at designing courses that are tailored to the needs of your students and you have the time to do so, then do so. If you have trouble designing an effective long-term progression and the activities to support it, or if you have a tendency to be a bit random in your planning, then a well-designed textbook will likely be better, particularly if you supplement it with additional activities that help meet your students' specific needs.

5. *What textbooks do you recommend?*

The selection of textbooks is always changing and the needs of students vary widely, so it is impossible to recommend particular textbooks. Ask a colleague who is familiar with the type of class you are teaching, and when choosing a textbook, be sure to try it out first by going through a chapter/unit or two as if teaching it. Major publishers often provide sample pages on their websites, and local libraries may have copies of various texts.

6. *I have heard that there is a debate about whether language teaching should be skills based or content based. What is that all about?*

Some language teachers (and other experts) believe that the focus of a language class should be the actual skills (speaking, listening, reading, writing), while others believe that those skills are best practiced by focusing on specific content. (See "Dual Purpose: Content-Based Instruction" in chapter 3.) There is no simple answer, but a few general comments might help:

- Skills-based instruction is often simpler to use at lower levels and (obviously) keeps the focus on skill improvement; however, some students may not be motivated by skills practice alone, particularly if it feels repetitive. (Note that communicative methods attempt to address this issue by insisting on authentic use of language, not repetitive tasks.)
- Content-Based Instruction is often more interesting (depending on the content, of course) and provides a natural context for skills practice. It is particularly effective at the higher levels, but only if skills practice is truly integrated into the lessons. (In other words, the focus must not be on the content alone, and skills practice must not be limited to reading

and writing; rather, the teacher must deliberately provide practice in all four skills as a way of reinforcing the content.)

7. *What advice do you give new teachers?*
   Remember the basics:

   - Plan your class carefully: base your goals and objectives on the needs of the students, and plan lessons and activities that meet those objectives by keeping the students focused and on task.
   - Generate and maintain interest by using a strong lead-in to begin the lesson and effective transitions between activities.
   - Keep explanations short and clear. Elicit details from students whenever possible, and write key terms on the whiteboard.
   - Distribute handouts after giving instructions, not before. (Otherwise students will focus on the handouts and miss the instructions.)
   - Check for understanding by having students explain things back to you.
   - Use pairs and small groups to increase individual **student talk time (STT)** during speaking activities.
   - Give lots of feedback. Help students correct their own mistakes.
   - Never forget that in most cases, your job is to set up, facilitate, and give feedback. Your students should be doing most of the work during class.
   - Break these rules whenever there is a very good reason to do so.
   - Reread this book every three or four months in your first year of teaching, and at least once a year thereafter.

8. *What advice do you give language learners?*
   Top tips for learning a language efficiently include the following:

   - Practice extensive listening. Choose videos, audio files, and social situations (when possible) that are interesting and at a comfortable level.
   - Practice extensive reading. Choose books, articles, or any other reading material that is interesting and at a comfortable level. Consider keeping a journal (in the target language) about what you read.
   - Don't simply study the language; use it to communicate as much as possible.
   - Find a language partner and speak only the target language to that person. Chat (in person, on the phone, online) about whatever is of interest.

- Associate new words with their meaning, not their translation, and try to use them in conversation right away.
- Do all the above regularly.

9. *What qualifications are needed to teach language overseas?*

While there is no formal international standard, most countries now require language teachers to hold a university degree (in any major). Specific schools or organizations may require further qualifications such as a certificate, diploma, or degree in TESL/TEFL/TESOL or the equivalent, or they may offer additional pay for such.

Countries may also have their own accreditation system(s) for language teachers and language schools. Volunteer positions, however, often require few qualifications beyond the ability to speak the language.

10. *Where can I find information about teaching jobs overseas?*

Good sources of information vary over time, and some of the best online sources have already disappeared (or been corrupted with false information). Even worse, while a quick Internet search will find thousands of websites with job listings, not all are reputable. Consider a few tips to help sort the good from the bad:

- Overseas teachers frequently write about their experiences in blogs, on-line forums, and other websites, so do a little informal research to consider where you might like to teach and in what context (such as a school system, university, private language school, or business).
- When considering and comparing job details, note that *teaching hours* (typically 15 to 30 per week) are not the same as *working hours* (typically 30 to 40 per week). Also note class size, curriculum (provided or not), working days (five or six per week), holidays and vacation days, pay scale, and other possible perks (health insurance, travel reimbursement) and obligations (such as taxes).
- Be wary of recruitment agencies that make promises that sound too good to be true, even when those promises are put in writing.
- Be very, very wary of any offer that requires you to pay a fee up front, unless it is a fee for a work visa; even then, the fee should be paid to the visa office, not an individual, company, or school.

- Search online for "overseas teaching scams" to find information about specific scams and warning signs to take note of. Don't let them scare you away from teaching overseas, but be informed.
- Keep in mind that online lists of "best places to teach overseas" may or may not be real. Note carefully where the information comes from. (If it is part of an article in a reputable online magazine, it might be good; if it is linked as an ad to that same magazine, it might not be good. When in doubt, be suspicious.)
- Look for government websites during a web search, as some countries have a government department that specifically recruits language teachers for government-sponsored programs (such as JET in Japan or EPIK in South Korea, or similar programs in France and Spain). Even then, such programs may use recruitment agencies that vary in quality.
- Ask the coordinator of your TESL/TEFL/TESOL (or equivalent) training program if they offer guidance on finding teaching jobs.
- If you find a job offer that appeals to you, search for more information on the school or company to find out if it is legitimate and reasonable. Whenever possible, speak with a teacher who has taught there, and ask detailed questions about the work conditions, the classes, the curriculum, and so on. All the while, be inquisitive, think critically, and get another opinion; even good schools have disgruntled teachers, and scams can look very real.
- Remember that although sorting through the maze (or mess) of information can be time-consuming, it is all very worthwhile; after all, teaching overseas is a serious commitment that should never be taken lightly.

APPENDIX 1A
Common Acronyms

LANGUAGE LEARNING

- ESL: English as a Second Language
- EFL: English as a Foreign Language
- EAL: English as an Additional Language
- ESOL: English for Speakers of Other Languages
- EIL: English as an International Language
- EAP: English for Academic Purposes
- ESP: English for Specific Purposes
- ELL: English Language Learner

Note that "ESL" has, at times, referred specifically to English language learned in a context where it is commonly used as a second language (such as former British colonies) or where it is learned by immigrants to a country where English is spoken, while "EFL" has often been used to denote English language learned in a context where it is not commonly used and is seen as "foreign" (yet useful). At other times, however, they have been used almost interchangeably.

More recently, terms such as EAL and ESOL have been used in an attempt to be more inclusive of all contexts in which English language is learned by individuals who already speak one or more languages.

The same variation occurs with the related terms (TESL, TEFL, TEAL, TESOL) outlined in the following section.

TEACHER TRAINING

- ALT: Assistant Language Teacher
- ELT: English Language Teaching or English Language Teacher
- TESL: Teaching English as a Second Language
- TEFL: Teaching English as a Foreign Language
- TEAL: Teaching English as an Additional Language
- TESOL: Teaching English to Speakers of Other Languages

APPENDIX 2A
Student Details

Complete the chart using the student descriptions found in chapter 2.

	Where?	Why?	Level?	Strengths	Weaknesses	Preferences
Hiromi						
Sung-Hoon						
Mario						
Amelia						
Aliya						
Lucia						
Ana						
Nellie						

APPENDIX 2B
Common Frameworks for Describing Language Proficiency

- The American Council on the Teaching of Foreign Languages developed the ACTFL Proficiency Guidelines to describe foreign-language proficiency levels.
- The Common European Framework of Reference for Languages (CEFR) describes various levels of competency in European languages.
- The Canadian Language Benchmarks (CLB) describe language proficiency levels for living and working in Canada.
- The Interagency Language Roundtable (ILR) scale describes language proficiency levels for the US federal government.
- The World-Class Instructional Design and Assessment (WIDA) standards are widely used by K–12 educators in the United States.

See this book's companion website for more information and relevant links. See also appendix 7A for language proficiency tests and a comparison of various scales.

APPENDIX 2C
Appropriate Instruction for Particular Language Levels

While there is no definitive list of what should be taught at a given level, the following is compiled from a survey of language textbooks from major publishers. As such, specific textbooks or proficiency frameworks may differ, and the details given here should be taken as a rough guide only.

- *Low-beginner*: the alphabet, numbers, and other very basic vocabulary (everyday items, simple verbs, and basic adjectives)
- *Beginner*: basic nouns, regular plurals, personal pronouns, basic action verbs, verbs *to be* and *to have*, modal verb *can*, basic adjectives and colours, common daily expressions, prepositions of location, simple present, imperative present, simple past, present progressive, basic questions and answers, *there is* and *there are*
- *High-beginner*: countable versus uncountable nouns, irregular plurals, basic adverbs that describe action, adverbs of frequency, adverbs of sequence, definite and indefinite articles, other determiners and demonstratives, common prepositions, conjunctions, past progressive, present perfect, basic modals, simple future
- *Low-intermediate*: comparative and superlative forms, conjunctions, compound sentences, phrasal verbs, *some/any*, adverbs of quantity, past perfect, present perfect progressive, basic conditional, infinitives, gerunds, tag questions, modals
- *Intermediate*: passive voice, reported speech, participle adjectives, relative clauses, compound sentences, complex sentences, past modals, passive modals, past perfect progressive
- *High-intermediate*: appositives, future progressive, future conditional, past conditional, past reported speech, punctuation nuances
- *Advanced*: parallel structures, future perfect, future perfect progressive, modal perfect, adverb clauses, noun clauses, reduced subordinate clauses, and almost any other common grammatical structure

APPENDIX 2D
Sample Needs Assessment

NEEDS ASSESSMENT

Objective: To discover students' personal and educational backgrounds, expectations, and overall level of English proficiency, as well as their specific strengths and weaknesses.

Time: Approximately 45 minutes.

Outline:
1. *Welcome students*: Write the word *learn* on the whiteboard and explain that you would like to learn a little about them and their use of English.
2. *Grammar check*: Distribute Handout 1 and have students complete it.
3. *Dictation*: Give each student a sheet of paper and ask them to write exactly what they hear. (Do an example if necessary.) Then read each of the following sentences at normal speed and with natural intonation. Pause for 20 to 30 seconds after each sentence (longer if students need more time to write), and then repeat it once.
   a. *I have 28 coins in my pocket.*
   b. *Do you like apple pie with ice cream?*
   c. *I wanted to go to the beach last weekend, but I was too busy.*
   d. *Next week my friends are going to throw a party for me.*
   e. *My sister's friend is from Vancouver, but she has lived in many places.*
   f. *I have no idea what you are talking about, so please explain it to me again.*
4. *Reading comprehension and writing*: Distribute Handout 2 and have students read and complete it. (Complete step 5 concurrently.)
5. *Oral interviews*: While students are completing step 4, meet with them individually to conduct a brief interview using the following questions. Begin with the more difficult version of each question and normal

speaking speed; then adapt as necessary. Make notes on their listening and speaking (accuracy, fluency).

   a. *What's your name? Where are you from?*
   b. *What is your highest level of education? // Have you studied in university? college? high school?*
   c. *Where have you previously studied English, and for how long? // Where did you learn English? How long did you study English?*
   d. *What do you hope to achieve in this class? // Why do you want to learn English?*
   e. *What do you enjoy and not enjoy about learning English? // Is English difficult? fun? Why?*
   f. *Are you fluent in more than one language? // What languages do you speak?*

6. *Wrap-up:* Thank students for participating and congratulate them on their work.

HANDOUT 1: GRAMMAR CHECK

Complete the sentences below using the correct forms of the verbs provided.

1. Jim is a baker. He _____ (work) hard every day, and he _____ (get) home very late every night. He _____ (not, have) much free time.
2. Jim _____ (like) making cookies and sweets, but he _____ (not, like) making bread or pizza. Last week, he _____ (make) more than five hundred cookies, but he _____ (not make) any pizzas. Right now, he _____ (bake) a cake for his daughter's birthday.
3. Jim is always busy. He _____ (bake) cookies when we _____ (visit) his shop yesterday, and he _____ (clean) his kitchen when I _____ (call) last night.
4. Jim _____ (be) a baker for more than 10 years, and he _____ (bake) more than 30,000 cookies in his lifetime.

In fact, by the time he was 12 years old, he _____ (already bake) more than 1,000 cookies.
5. Jim is very tired because he _____ (not take) a vacation for many years, but he _____ (take) a long vacation next month.
6. Jim _____ (leave) soon because he _____ (be) tired. He _____ (work) since five o'clock this morning.
7. Yesterday, when I _____ (visit) Jim's shop early in the morning, he _____ (be) already busy. He _____ (work) for more than four hours.
8. Poor Jim. He really _____ (need) a break. He _____ (work) too hard for many years.
9. If he _____ (take) a vacation last year, he _____ (not, be) so tired now.
10. If he _____ (take) an extra-long vacation next year, he _____ (feel) much better.

ANSWER KEY

1. *works, gets, does not have*
2. *likes, does not like, made, did not make, is baking*
3. *was baking, visited, was cleaning, called*
4. *has been, has baked, had already baked*
5. *has not taken, is going to take* (or *will take*)
6. *will leave* (or *is going to leave*), *is, has been working*
7. *visited, was, had been working*
8. *needs, has been working*
9. *had taken, would not be*
10. *takes, will feel*

HANDOUT 2: READING AND WRITING

Read the passage below, and answer the questions that follow.

Thomas is a 16-year-old high school student. He gets up at 7:00 each weekday morning. He goes to school from 8:45 until 3:15, and plays soccer or baseball with his friends after school. In the evenings, he does his homework, plays his guitar and drums, and watches television. Then he goes to bed at 10:30.

On Saturdays, Thomas sleeps in until 10:00 and has a late breakfast. He then works at a delivery company from noon until 4:30, where he packs boxes onto trucks. In the evenings, he goes out with his friends. Sometimes they go to the movie theatre or a fast-food restaurant, but usually they play tennis for a few hours first.

Today is Friday, and Thomas is looking forward to the weekend because he has been studying hard all week. Final exams are just around the corner, and he wants to do well. After all, when he finishes high school, he wants to study at university to become a veterinarian, so he must earn very high grades. If he doesn't, he will not be able to achieve his dream.

Thomas is busy, but he enjoys his life. He knows that if he wants to succeed in life, he has to work hard; but he also knows that life must include a good balance of work and recreation, so tonight he will finish studying a bit earlier than usual and meet his friends for some well-deserved fun.

Questions:
1. How many hours does Thomas spend in school on a typical weekday?
2. How long does Thomas sleep on Wednesday nights?
3. When does Thomas work? What does he do?
4. When does Thomas play sports? What sports does he play?
5. Is Thomas musical? How do you know?
6. What do Thomas and his friends do on Saturday evenings?
7. Why is Thomas tired today?
8. What is Thomas's dream? What is required to achieve it?
9. Why does Thomas not spend all his time studying and working?
10. What is unusual about tonight?

11. What do you usually do on weekends? (Write 3 to 5 sentences.)
12. What do you hope to do in the future? (Write a short paragraph about your plans or dreams.)
13. If you had a lot of free time and plenty of money for the next two months, what would you do?

APPENDIX 3A
Sample GTM Grammar Worksheets

USING ARTICLES (A, AN, THE) AND SOME

Write a, an, the, or some in the blank as appropriate; draw a line if no article is needed.

1. Don't let _____ dog in. He is too dirty.
2. I wish I had _____ apple to eat.
3. _____ apples are green, while others are red or yellow.
4. James bought _____ sweater that I wanted to buy.
5. Can you lend me _____ money until next week? I just need a few bucks.
6. The mixing bowl is made of _____ stainless steel.
7. I didn't go to _____ school picnic on Saturday because I had to work.
8. Would you like to watch _____ movie with me tonight?
9. I'll meet you at _____ post office at 5:00.
10. I need to buy _____ grapes for tomorrow's lunch.
11. Oh no! My radiator has _____ leak.
12. Can you repair _____ leak by tomorrow morning?
13. Do you have _____ pet?
14. I want to have _____ time to myself, please.
15. Who broke _____ clock in the kitchen?

ANSWER KEY

1. *the*
2. *an*
3. *Some*
4. *the*
5. *some*
6. —
7. *the*
8. *a*
9. *the*
10. *some* or —
11. *a*
12. *the*
13. *a*
14. *some*
15. *the*

USING PAST PERFECT TENSE

Complete the sentences below by using the simple past tense or the past perfect tense of the verbs given in parentheses.

1. When Tim _____ (arrive) home last night, his family _____ (eat) already.
2. Tim _____ (be) late because he _____ (forget) to check the time when he was playing soccer with his friends.
3. Even though Tim _____ (not, arrive) on time for supper, his mother _____ (save) some casserole for him.
4. By the time Tim _____ (finish) his supper, his little sister _____ (go) to bed already. He was sorry that he _____ (miss) their playtime.
5. When Tim _____ (wake up) in the middle of the night, he wished that he _____ (not, eat) a second helping of casserole. His tummy hurt!
6. Tim _____ (get up) and _____ (drink) a glass of water. Once his stomach _____ (settle), he _____ (fall asleep) again.
7. When Tim _____ (wake up) the next morning, he _____ (not, remember) getting up during the night. He _____ (think) that he _____ (sleep) through the night!

ANSWER KEY

1. *arrived, had eaten*
2. *was, had forgotten*
3. *did not arrive, had saved*
4. *finished, had gone, had missed*
5. *woke up, had not eaten*
6. *got up, drank, settled* OR *had settled, fell asleep*
7. *woke up, did not remember, thought, had slept*

APPENDIX 3B
Sample GTM Reading Activity

BASIN HEAD

Read the following passage and answer the questions below.

In eastern Prince Edward Island, there is a beach that has been very popular among locals for many years. They often referred to it as their best-kept secret. Recently, though, it has become popular among tourists as well, and in 2013 it was named the best beach in Canada.

The beach is located in an area called Basin Head. The name comes from the shape of the surrounding land, which looks like a wide, deep basin with a river system at the bottom. The river runs through the beach and into the ocean, and a bridge over the river provides a popular spot for jumping and diving into the water.

The beach is also known by its nickname, the Singing Sands. The name comes from the noise that the sand makes when a person walks on it, causing the sand particles to rub together and make a squeaking sound.

Beachgoers love the area for its clean water, its white beaches, and its beautiful sand dunes, but they also love it for its size. Getting away from the crowds is as simple as walking further up the beach, enjoying miles and miles of unspoiled nature at its best.

Questions:
1. Why is Basin Head no longer a secret among the local people?
2. Why was the area named Basin Head?
3. What other name is used for the beach? Why is this name used?
4. What makes this beach special?
5. Would you like to visit this beach? Why or why not?

APPENDIX 3C
Sample Audio-Lingual Drills

SAMPLE BACKWARDS BUILDUP DRILL

Teacher:	*I am going to the park on Thursday.*
Student:	(hesitates)
Teacher:	*... on Thursday.*
Student:	*... on Thursday.*
Teacher:	*... to the park on Thursday.*
Student:	*... to the park on Thursday.*
Teacher:	*... going to the park on Thursday.*
Student:	*... going to the park on Thursday.*
Teacher:	*I am going to the park on Thursday.*
Student:	*I am going to the park on Thursday.*

SAMPLE CHAIN DRILL

Teacher:	*I'd like pizza for lunch. What would you like, Mario?*
Mario:	*I'd like lasagna for lunch. What would you like, Aliya?*
Aliya:	*I'd like meat and potatoes for lunch. What would you like, Hoshi?*
Hoshi:	*I'd like sushi for lunch. What would you like, Erin?*
Erin:	*I'd like fried chicken for lunch. What would you like, Lucia?*
Lucia:	*I'd like pizza too!*

SAMPLE SINGLE-SLOT SUBSTITUTION DRILL, LEVEL 1

Teacher:	I am going to the bank.	(Teacher: *post office* ...)
Student 1:	I am going to the post office.	(Teacher: *arena* ...)
Student 2:	I am going to the arena.	(Teacher: *pool* ...)
Student 3:	I am going to the pool.	(Teacher: *supermarket* ...)
Student 4:	I am going to the supermarket.	

SAMPLE SINGLE-SLOT SUBSTITUTION DRILL, LEVEL 2

Teacher:	I am going to the bank.	(Teacher: *He* ...)
Student 1:	He is going to the bank.	(Teacher: *She* ...)
Student 2:	She is going to the bank.	(Teacher: *We* ...)
Student 3:	We are going to the bank.	(Teacher: *They* ...)
Student 4:	They are going to the bank.	(Teacher: *Jim* ...)
Student 5:	Jim is going to the bank.	(Teacher: *Tina and Tim* ...)
Student 6:	Tina and Tim are going to the bank.	(Teacher: *I* ...)
Student 7:	You are going to the bank!	

SAMPLE MULTIPLE-SLOT SUBSTITUTION DRILL

Teacher:	I am going to the bank.	(Teacher: *She* ...)
Student 1:	She is going to the bank.	(Teacher: *post office* ...)
Student 2:	She is going to the post office.	(Teacher: *walk* ...)
Student 3:	She is walking to the post office.	(Teacher: *They* ...)
Student 4:	They are walking to the post office.	(Teacher: *Jim* ...)
Student 5:	Jim is walking to the post office.	(Teacher: *river* ...)
Student 6:	Jim is walking to the river.	(Teacher: *in* ...)
Student 7:	Jim is walking in the river.	(Teacher: *swim* ...)
Student 8:	Jim is swimming in the river.	(Teacher: *Tina and Jim* ...)
Student 9:	Tina and Jim are swimming in the river.	

SAMPLE TRANSFORMATION DRILLS

Affirmative to Negative, Simple Present

Teacher:	I like apples.
Student 1:	I don't like apples.
Teacher:	I swim every day.
Student 2:	I don't swim every day.
Teacher:	He visits Paris every month.
Student 3:	He doesn't visit Paris every month.
Teacher:	She has three eyes.
Student 4:	She doesn't have three eyes.

Present Progressive to Simple Past

Teacher:	He is taking a walk.
Student 1:	He took a walk.
Teacher:	She is singing her favourite song.
Student 2:	She sang her favourite song.
Teacher:	They are eating pizza again.
Student 3:	They ate pizza again.
Teacher:	You are speaking too quickly.
Student 4:	You spoke too quickly.

Statement to Wh-Question, Simple Past

Teacher:	He went to the store.
Student 1:	Where did he go?
Teacher:	They ate pizza for lunch.
Student 2:	What did they eat for lunch?
Teacher:	She left home at three o'clock.
Student 3:	When did she leave home?
Teacher:	They ate pizza because they were hungry.
Student 4:	Why did they eat pizza?

SAMPLE QUESTION AND ANSWER DRILL

Simple Past

Teacher:	What did John do yesterday?
Student 1:	He studied English.
Teacher:	What did Tina do yesterday?
Student 2:	She baked cookies.
Teacher:	What did Tim do yesterday?
Student 3:	He played soccer.
Teacher:	What did you do yesterday?
Student 4:	I slept.

Personal Information

Teacher:	How are you?
Student:	I'm fine, thanks.
Teacher:	Where are you from?
Student:	I'm from Romania.
Teacher:	How old are you?
Student:	I am 23 years old.
Teacher:	What are your hobbies?
Student:	I enjoy swimming and cycling.

APPENDIX 3D
Sample Communicative Lesson

ASKING FOR INFORMATION

Lesson Objective: Students will be able to ask for information using polite language appropriate to a variety of social contexts.

Methods: Students will complete the following:
- discuss ways to ask for information
- analyze sample dialogues in which people ask for information
- write questions that ask for information in a particular context
- perform dialogues in which they ask for information in a particular context

Materials and Preparation:
- Handouts 1 and 2 (one copy of each per student)
- Paper and pen for each student

Level: Low-intermediate
Time: Approximately 75 minutes

I. Lead-In (5 minutes)
1. Ask students:
   - *Have you ever asked someone for information? Give an example.*
   - *Are there polite and impolite ways to ask for information? Give examples.*

II. Noticing and Practicing the Language Function (20 minutes)
1. Distribute Handout 1 and have students work in pairs to read the dialogues and answer the questions. Circulate and monitor their work, and assist as necessary.

2. Have each pair team up with another pair to quietly compare their answers.
3. Distribute Handout 2 and allow students to read the first part; then have them use that information to discuss, as a class, their answers for Handout 1.
4. Have students complete the "Try" section on Handout 2. When they have finished, give them time to compare answers with others before going over the answers as a class.

III. Guided Production of the Language Function (25 minutes)

1. Distribute paper (as necessary) and have students write a request for the following situation:
   - Situation: *You need to know what time the train leaves. Ask the attendant.*
   - Sample answer: *Excuse me, can you tell me what time the train leaves?*
2. Have students share their answers with the class. Choose a few good examples and write them on the board. As necessary, discuss why some examples are particularly well suited to the context.
3. Repeat the process for these situations:
   a. *You want to know how to get to the CN Tower. Ask the hotel reception.*
   b. *You want to know where to find books for young children. Ask the librarian.*
   c. *You want to know where your father is. Ask your brother.*
   d. *You want to find a present for your nine-year-old niece. Ask the store clerk for ideas.*
   e. *You want to know what time it is. Ask your friend.*

IV. Authentic Production and Practice (20 minutes)

1. Choose one of the situations from Part III, and have two students come to the front of the class and perform a brief, impromptu dialogue (without using any notes).
2. After they have finished, have other students in the class comment on ways to improve their dialogue, especially regarding the language used to ask for information.
3. Repeat the process until each student pair has performed a dialogue.

V. Conclusion (5 minutes)

1. Congratulate students on their performances.
2. Ask students about the lesson: *What was difficult? What was helpful?*
3. Wrap up the class.

HANDOUT 1

Work in pairs to practice the following dialogues. Then answer the questions below.

Dialogue A:

Customer: Excuse me, where can I find a public restroom?

Attendant: There is one across the street, near the entrance to the library.

Customer: Okay, great—thanks very much!

Dialogue B:

Brother: Where's the milk?

Sister: It's in the fridge, of course.

Dialogue C:

Visitor: Excuse me, could you tell me how to get to the theatre?

Local guy: Sure, just keep going down this street two more blocks; then turn left at the traffic light. You'll see the theatre just ahead on your right.

Visitor: Thank you!

Questions:

1. Which of the requests was the most formal (or polite)? Which was the most informal?
2. What is the relationship between the speakers in each dialogue? How does this affect the way they speak?
3. How do the three requests differ in grammar?

HANDOUT 2

Note that in English, there are a number of ways to ask for information:

- A direct statement is not very polite: *I need to know where the library is.*
- A question is a bit more polite: *Where is the library?*
- A question with a modal verb is polite: *Could you tell me where the library is?*

There are also different ways to begin a request. For example, "hey" is very informal, "hi" is informal but friendly, and "excuse me" is polite.

Try: Order these requests from least polite to most polite.

_____ Excuse me, could you tell me where the library is?
_____ Excuse me, please tell me where the library is.
_____ Hey, where's the library?
_____ Uh, hi. Can you tell me where the library is?
_____ Hi, I need to know where the library is.

APPENDIX 3E
Sample Content-Based Lesson

THANKSGIVING

Lesson Objectives: Students will be able to write about and discuss Thanksgiving traditions and compare them to traditions of their own.

Methods: Students will complete the following:
- take notes on an oral reading about Thanksgiving and reconstruct a version of it
- work in pairs to prepare a better version of their writing and give feedback
- list the strengths and weaknesses of their version after comparing it to the original
- discuss Thanksgiving traditions and compare them to traditions of their own

Materials and Preparation:
- Prepare two pictures (a cooked turkey, a cornucopia) to show the class.
- Pre-read Handout 1 and prepare definitions and explanations necessary for your group. Keep a good ESL dictionary on hand.
- Handout 1: The Thanksgiving Holiday (one copy per student).

Level: Intermediate
Time: 75 minutes

I. Lead-In (10 minutes)
1. Show the students pictures of a cooked turkey and a cornucopia. Ask them what they are and what holiday they might represent.
2. Ask students what they know about Thanksgiving Day in North America.

II. Dictogloss, Part 1: Listening and Note-Taking (15 minutes)

1. Have students listen for the main idea as you read aloud Handout 1. Then have them discuss the main idea in pairs and report to the class.
2. Have students take detailed notes as you again read aloud Handout 1. (Read at a steady but reasonable pace. Pause for about 10 seconds after each paragraph. If the students are having trouble, repeat this step.)

III. Dictogloss, Part 2: Writing and Revision (20 minutes)

1. Have students individually reconstruct the article from their notes.
2. Have students work in pairs to compare and combine their work in order to construct a better version.
3. Have each pair exchange their version with another pair for feedback and suggestions.
4. Have student pairs make final revisions to their own version of the article.

IV. Reading and Comparing (20 minutes)

1. Distribute Handout 1. Have students read it individually and underline any vocabulary or expressions they do not understand. Clarify these as a group.
2. Have students compare their version to the original. Which details did they have correct? Which were incorrect or missing?

V. Discussion and Conclusion (10 minutes)

1. Ask students: *Do you have a similar tradition or holiday? How is it similar? How is it different?*
2. Ask students: *What was most interesting about this lesson? What was most difficult?*
3. Congratulate students on a job well done.

HANDOUT 1: THE THANKSGIVING HOLIDAY

Thanksgiving Day is a national holiday celebrated primarily in Canada and the United States, though similar celebrations are observed in other countries. Originally, people gathered on Thanksgiving to celebrate and give thanks for a successful harvest; today, Thanksgiving has become a time to gather with family for a special meal that often includes a roasted turkey, mashed potatoes, turkey stuffing (also called dressing), vegetables (especially peas and carrots), gravy, pickles, cranberry sauce, pie, and apple cider.

The origin of Thanksgiving Day is a matter of debate, though several events and traditions seem to have played a role. Martin Frobisher, a 16th-century explorer, held a thanksgiving celebration in what is now Canada to give thanks for his successful voyage. Other settlers from England and France brought with them traditions related to autumn festivals during which they gave thanks for the harvest.

Thanksgiving Day is always in the fall season, around the time of harvest. In Canada, it is observed on the second Monday of October, while in the United States, it is observed on the fourth Thursday of November.

Because many North Americans wish to be with family on Thanksgiving, the holiday often involves travel to "grandma and grandpa's house," where grandparents, parents, and children enjoy a large meal and other activities together as a family. The meal is often preceded by a special prayer of thanks and followed by the breaking of the wishbone by two family members. Later, activities may include going for a walk to enjoy the beauty of autumn, watching sports events or a parade on television, playing games together, or taking an afternoon nap.

APPENDIX 3F
Sample Lexical Approach Activities

Suggest at least three words or phrases to complete each of the sentences below.

1. I have a broken _____.
2. Have you ever _____?
3. I think that _____.
4. The real problem is that _____.
5. I've never _____.

Which word or phrase does not naturally complete the language chunk?

1. I have to _____ the course in order to graduate. (pass, take, complete, study)
2. He is always _____ trouble. (asking for, getting into, constructing, causing)
3. She has to _____ an essay by Monday. (write, take, revise, proofread)
4. What are you _____ ? (doing, waiting for, watching, saying, seeing)
5. He likes to _____ money. (save, make, earn, spend, invest, waste, acquire)

APPENDIX 7A
Commonly Used (International) Proficiency Tests

- IELTS: International English Language Testing System measures English proficiency for academic study, immigration, or work.
- TOEFL: Test of English as a Foreign Language measures English proficiency for studying in a college or university.
- TOEIC: Test of English for International Communication measures English proficiency for working in an international environment. There are currently two separate tests: one for reading and listening, and one for speaking and writing.

See also appendix 2B for Common Frameworks for Describing Language Proficiency.

IELTS	TOEFL*	CEFR†	ILR	CLB†	DESCRIPTION
9.0	118–120	C2	4+	12	Very advanced; expert
8.5	115–117	C2	4	11	
8.0	110–114	C1	3+	10	Advanced; sufficient for graduate-level academic study
7.5	102–109	C1	3+	10	
7.0	94–101		3	9	High intermediate; sufficient for college or university study
6.5	79–93			8	
6.0	60–78	B2	2+	7	Intermediate
5.5	46–59		2	6	
5.0	35–45	B1	1+	5	Low intermediate
4.5	32–34	B1	1+	5	
4.0				4	High beginner
3.5					

*Comparisons provided by Educational Testing Service (ETS). † Comparisons provided by IELTS.

Notes:
- Because test methods and level descriptions vary, the details of this chart should be taken only as rough guidelines.
- While charts comparing TOEIC scores to other test scores exist, the significant variation among them suggests that a definitive, reliable comparison may not exist.

APPENDIX 8A
Common Discourse Markers

- adding information: *above all, additionally, also, as well as, furthermore, in addition, moreover, not only … but also, too*
- assessing negatively: *regrettably, sadly, unfortunately*
- assessing positively: *amazingly, astonishingly, fortunately, hopefully, ideally, incredibly*
- changing topic: *by the way, incidentally, just to let you know, now, on a different note, speaking of which, while we're on the subject*
- comparing: *in comparison, in the same way, likewise, similarly, too*
- contrast: *although, but, conversely, however, in contrast, on the contrary, on the other hand, unlike*
- emphasizing truth: *absolutely, actually, as a matter of fact, assuredly, certainly, definitely, doubtless, genuinely, in actuality, in reality, in truth, indisputably, undeniably, undoubtedly, without a doubt*
- explaining cause or result: *as a result, because of this, consequently, for some reason or other, for that reason, somehow, then, therefore, thus, since, so, so that*
- expressing expectations: *inevitably, ironically, oddly, predictably, surprisingly*
- expressing certainty or uncertainty: *arguably, conceivably, evidently, likely, perhaps, possibly, presumably, seemingly, supposedly*
- giving an example: *for example, for instance*
- including the listener: *you know, you think*
- indicating order: *after that, at the same time, to begin, before that, earlier, later, next, simultaneously, subsequently, then, finally, last, lastly*
- indicating time: *after a while, afterward, in the meantime, meanwhile, previously, when*
- reformulating: *i.e., in other words, namely, specifically, that is, that is to say*
- suggesting an alternative: *alternately, in lieu of, in place of, instead, on second thought, rather*
- summarizing: *all in all, in brief, in closing, in conclusion, in general, in short, in summary, to conclude, to sum up, to summarize, on the whole*
- using fillers: *well, oh, I mean, eh?, kind of, actually, basically, like,* and many expletives

APPENDIX 8B
Sample Simulation and Role-Play Scenarios

BUSINESS LUNCH SIMULATION

Situation: A manager from a mid-sized company is treating two new employees to lunch at a nearby restaurant.

- *Student 1*: You are the company manager. You want your new employees to feel comfortable around you, so you try to be friendly and ask them about themselves.
- *Students 2 and 3*: You are new employees, and you want to make a good impression on your new boss.
- *Student 4*: You are the server in the restaurant. It is your first week on the job, and you want to get everything right, so you are careful to double-check everything.

RESTAURANT ROLE PLAY

Situation: Two old friends are ordering food in a restaurant.

- *Student 1*: You are a customer in a restaurant. You are very hungry, but you are a fussy eater, and you often change your mind about what you want to eat. You also get frustrated when people tell you to hurry up.
- *Student 2*: You are a customer in a restaurant. You are good-natured and friendly, and you like to tease your friend about being a fussy eater and taking too long to order. You also enjoy teasing the server.
- *Student 3*: You are the server, and you think these two old friends are hilarious. You joke around with them as you take their order.

APPENDIX 9A
Sample Listening Activities

RESTAURANT CONVERSATIONS, PART I

i. Listen to Jack, Tina, and Sally talking in a restaurant. What are they discussing?

ii. Listen to the conversation again, and check the menu items that they decide to order.

__ lobster	__ chicken	__ steak	__ fish	__ pasta
__ ice cream	__ pie	__ cake	__ salad	__ tomatoes
__ cheesecake	__ milkshake	__ chocolate	__ milk	__ soup

TRANSCRIPT

Tina: So, have you guys decided what to order yet?

Jack: I'm still thinking. I wonder if the steak here is good.

Sally: I've heard it's kind of tough. Maybe you should try the fish. That's what I'm having.

Jack: Actually, I don't eat fish. I think I'll try the chicken. What about you, Tina? Chicken? Fish?

Tina: I'm a vegetarian. I think I'll have pasta with tomato sauce, and perhaps a small salad.

Sally: That sounds good too. What about dessert? They've got cake, pie, ice cream ...

Jack: Pie sounds good, but I'm on a diet, so I don't think I'll have any dessert.

Sally: Yeah, I'm on a diet too, but I hear they have cheesecake. I've got to have some.

Tina: Ooh, that sounds good. But the pie with ice cream sounds good too. It's hard to decide!

Jack: Why don't you just order both? If you can't finish them, I'll help you.

Sally: I thought you were on a diet!

Jack: I am ... but I'm always willing to help a friend!

Tina: Of course you are, but I think I'll have a chocolate milkshake instead.

RESTAURANT CONVERSATIONS, PART II

i. Now listen to the rest of the conversation. What happens?
ii. Listen again, and complete the chart.

	Meal	Drink	Dessert
Jack	_____	_____	_____
Tina	_____	_____	_____
Sally	_____	_____	_____

TRANSCRIPT

Server: Good evening. Are you ready to order, or would you like a few more minutes?

Jack: We're ready. Sally, why don't you go first …

Sally: Okay. I'd like the fish dinner please. Wait, no, I think I'll have the chicken instead.

Server: Chicken dinner? And would you like gravy on the chicken?

Sally: Could I have gravy on the side?

Server: Of course. And what would you like to drink?

Sally: A glass of ice water would be fine.

Server: And would you like to order dessert now?

Sally: I'd like two slices of cheesecake, please.

Server: Okay … And you, madam?

Tina: I think I'll have the pasta with tomato sauce, and a small salad.

Server: And to drink?

Tina: I'd like water with my meal please, and a chocolate milkshake later, for dessert.

Server: Perfect. And you, sir?

Jack: I'll have the chicken dinner—no gravy—and a large glass of milk.

Server: And for dessert?

Jack: I'll have the pie and ice cream, and a slice of cheesecake.

Tina: Jack! What about your diet?

Jack: I'll start again tomorrow …

APPENDIX 10A
Sample Reading Lesson

LETTER TO THE EDITOR

Lesson Objectives: Students will be able to predict the content of a letter to the editor, analyze and explain its content, and write a response to it.

Methods: Students will complete the following:
- predict the content of a letter to the editor by reading the introduction and skimming the body
- answer short-answer questions and write a summary about the letter
- answer critical reading questions
- write a response to the letter

Materials and Preparation:
- Handout 1: Letter to the Editor (one copy per student)
- pre-read the letter and prepare definitions and explanations for any words or expressions that might be new to this class

Level: Intermediate
Time: 75 minutes

I. Lead-In and Introduction (5 minutes)

1. Ask students: *Do you read the newspaper? Which sections do you read? What is a letter to the editor?*
2. Explain: *A letter to the editor is a short letter written by a reader. It expresses an opinion.*

II. Pre-Reading for Overview (5 minutes)

1. Distribute Handout 1. Have students read the title and the first paragraph. Then ask: *What do you think it will be about? Does the letter have a specific purpose?*

2. Have students skim the rest of the letter. (Allow only 1 minute.) Then ask: *What did you discover? Were your predictions correct?*

III. Reading for Comprehension (25 minutes)

1. Have the students read the entire letter and underline any unknown words or phrases. Then have students clarify them for each other. Assist as necessary.
2. Have students reread the letter silently and answer the "Comprehension Questions" on the handout. When they finish, have them compare answers in pairs.
3. Go over the answers as a group, and help students clarify each other's misunderstandings.
4. Have students write five sentences that summarize the key points of the letter in their own words. When they finish, have students read aloud some of their sentences, and write a sample answer (five sentences) on the board.

IV. Reading Critically (20 minutes)

1. Have students answer the "Reading Deeper" questions on the handout. When they finish, have them compare answers in pairs.
2. Go over the answers as a group, and help students clarify any misunderstandings.

V. Written Response (15 minutes)

1. Instruct students: *Imagine you are one of the teenagers who uses the park, and you disagree with Mr. Grumps. Write a letter in response, exposing the weaknesses of his argument.*

VI. Conclusion (5 minutes)

1. Ask students: *Which activities were most helpful? How were they helpful?*
2. Congratulate students on a job well done.

HANDOUT 1: LETTER TO THE EDITOR

Dear Editor,

I would like to add my voice to the many others asking that Cedar Park be closed each night at 9:00 pm. I live near the park, and I am sick and tired of the noise of rowdy teenagers on Friday and Saturday nights.

Almost every Friday night, the noise begins around 8:00 pm. It escalates until around 9:30, and then continues non-stop, often until midnight or later. Those of us who live nearby have no choice but to close our windows and doors, even on a warm night, if we are to enjoy a bit of peace and quiet. Saturdays are no better, and often worse, and in summer, the same scene is repeated almost every night.

Furthermore, there are other reasons to close the park earlier in the evening. In particular, the teenagers there are undoubtedly engaging in activities such as smoking, drinking alcohol, swearing, and who knows what else. I believe it is our duty as a society to curtail such behaviour.

Some writers to this newspaper have suggested that a closing time is not necessary, that simply posting "clear and reasonable rules" will change young people's behaviour. Such opinions are ridiculous, and those who hold them obviously have little understanding of human behaviour.

In conclusion, I would like to reiterate my call for Cedar Park to be closed at 9:00 pm. Nothing less will solve our ongoing problems of excessive noise and rowdy teenage behaviour.

Sincerely,
Charles B. Grumps

Comprehension Questions:
1. According to paragraph one, what is the purpose of this letter? (What does the author hope to accomplish?)
2. How are neighbours affected by the noise in the park?
3. According to the author, what other problems occur in the park?
4. Why does the author believe that closing the park early is the only solution to the problems?

5. According to the author, has anyone else written about this issue? How did their opinions differ?

Reading Deeper:
1. In the first paragraph, how does the author establish his right to speak about this issue?
2. In the second paragraph, the author uses words such as "almost," "around," and "often." How do these words relate to whether the statements are factual or not?
3. In the third paragraph, the author discusses the behaviour of teenagers in the park. Are his statements fact or conjecture? Does he give any evidence for his claims? What phrases might suggest that these statements are his assumptions, not his observations?
4. In the fourth paragraph, the author suggests that other writers are wrong about this issue. Does he support his claims by providing evidence or reasons?
5. In the final paragraph, the author claims that "nothing less" than his proposal will solve the problem. Can such a claim be proven?

APPENDIX 11A
Sample Writing Lesson

LETTER OF COMPLAINT

Lesson Objective: Students will be able to write a persuasive letter to the customer service department of a company.

Method: Students will follow a standard process to plan, write, and revise their letter while helping others to do the same.

Materials and Preparation:
1. Handout 1: Product Problems (one copy per student)
2. Handout 2: Sample Letter (one copy per student)
3. Handout 3: Feedback Checklist (one copy per student)

Level: High-intermediate
Time: 75 minutes

I. Lead-In and Introduction (10 minutes)
1. Ask students: *Have you ever bought something and had problems with it? What did you do? (Return it to the store? Call or write the company that made it? Forget about it?)* Encourage students to share their stories with the class.
2. Distribute Handout 1: Product Problems, and have students read it. Then have them explain the situation back to you.
3. Explain to students that they will each write a letter, but they will also help each other.

II. Gathering, Developing, and Organizing Ideas (15 minutes)
1. Have students use these questions to decide on the details of their letter. Circulate and monitor their work, assisting as necessary.
    a. What is the product that you will write about?
    b. What problem(s) does the product have?
    c. Has the product negatively affected your life? If so, how?
    d. What would you like the company to do?

2. Have students organize their ideas into an outline (introduction, problem and details, suggested solution).
3. Have students work in groups of three or four to review each other's ideas and suggest ways to improve them.

III. First Draft and Feedback (20 minutes)

1. Distribute Handout 2: Sample Letter, and ask students to explain the purpose of each paragraph. Once they have done this, have each student use the letter as a model to write their first draft (individually). Give basic assistance as necessary.
2. When they have finished, have them exchange their letters with two partners and give feedback on the content using Handout 3: Feedback Checklist. Circulate, monitor, and give hints or suggestions as necessary.
3. If applicable, write common errors on the board and address them as a class.

IV. Revisions (15 minutes)

1. Have students revise their own work according to feedback received. Assist them as necessary.
2. When they have finished, have students exchange their letters with a new partner for feedback on the content.
3. As students work, circulate and skim their writing as time allows, focusing on weaker students and providing assistance as necessary.

V. Proofreading and Refinement (10 minutes)

1. Have students complete their revisions.
2. Have students work in new pairs to carefully proofread their work.

VI. Conclusion (5 minutes)

1. Have students wrap up their work, finishing any remaining details at home. Inform them that the letter should be handed in at the beginning of the next class. (Later, give feedback regarding content, persuasiveness of argument, style and fluency, and accuracy of language use.)
2. Ask students if the writing process helped them. Which parts were most helpful? What might they do differently next time?
3. Congratulate students on a job well done.

HANDOUT 1: PRODUCT PROBLEMS

You recently purchased a product, but after using it for only a short time, it does not work properly. The product cannot be returned to the store, and the representative from the company that made the product has not been very helpful.

Write a business letter to the head office of the company, explaining what is wrong with the product and what you would like them to do about it.

HANDOUT 2: SAMPLE LETTER

Dear Sir or Madam:

I recently purchased one of your beds from Furniture Palace in our town. At first I was excited to try out the bed, but after a week or so, I noticed that the mattress had some serious problems.

First, the mattress began sagging in the middle, and in the mornings I woke up with back pain. Then, a few of the mattress springs began poking me in the back, and the bed became so uncomfortable that I couldn't use it anymore.

The salesperson at Furniture Palace gave me a phone number to contact your company. However, after three calls, I have not received a clear solution to this problem.

Please arrange to have a new bed delivered to my house, or refund my money, as I am not at all satisfied with the quality of this bed.

Sincerely,
George B. Wannasleep

HANDOUT 3: FEEDBACK CHECKLIST

Read your classmate's letter and check the following:

1. Does the letter have a strong introduction that identifies its purpose?
2. Does the letter clearly identify and describe the problem(s), explain any additional details, and suggest a solution?
3. Does each paragraph focus on one main idea? Should some be broken up or combined?
4. Is the letter easy to read overall? Does it sound clear and professional?
5. Are there other ways the letter could be improved?

APPENDIX 12A
Sample Vocabulary Lesson

WORDS FOR BANKING

Lesson Objectives: Students will be able to use common banking terms accurately and naturally in written and spoken English.

Methods: Students will complete the following:
- repeat the correct pronunciation of common banking terms
- complete a worksheet using common banking terms
- complete sentences, orally, using common banking terms
- perform a role play using common banking terms

Materials and Preparation:
- Handouts 1, 2, 3 (one copy of each per student)
- Optional: a good ESL dictionary, along with props such as a bank card, a credit card, a cheque, and a picture of an ATM

Level: Intermediate or high-intermediate
Time: 90 minutes

I. Lead-In and Introduction (5 minutes)
1. Ask students: *Have you ever gone to a bank where people spoke only English? Was it difficult?* Have them share their stories, and then explain to them that in today's class they will learn new vocabulary related to banking.

II. Teach and Clarify Vocabulary (25 minutes)
1. Distribute Handout 1 and ask students to read the first paragraph. Answer any questions they have. Then say the words in bold and have students repeat. Draw attention to pronunciation, including correct word stress.

2. Repeat step 1 for each of the other paragraphs, one at a time.
3. Distribute Handout 2 and read the sentences one by one, having students repeat them. Draw attention to the pronunciation and the common collocations (underlined) of the vocabulary words (in bold), and answer any questions the students may have.

III. Controlled Written Practice (20 minutes)

1. Explain to students that they will complete a story using today's new vocabulary. Distribute Handout 3 and have them complete it individually.
2. When students have finished, have them work in pairs to compare answers.
3. Correct the handout by reading (or by having students take turns reading) the story aloud, pausing to allow students to make corrections. Discuss any difficulties.

IV. Oral Practice (10 minutes)

1. While allowing students to refer to their handouts, read the following hints and have students guess which vocabulary item you are referring to.
    a. I have no cash, so I must go to the _____ to get some.
    b. I have too much cash in my pocket. I should _____ some in the bank.
    c. I don't have enough cash. Maybe I can write a _____.
    d. I want to buy a car. Maybe the bank will give me a _____.
    e. Oh no! The cheque that I wrote last week has _____, and now I will have to pay an extra fee.
    f. The bank mails me a _____ every month to show me a list of my _____.
    g. I like to earn _____ on my account every month.
    h. The ATM is convenient, but I enjoy talking to the friendly _____ inside the bank.
    i. Even when I have no money left, I can still pay my bills with my _____, but then I might have to pay high _____.

2. Have students cover their notes and handouts. Then give the hints again, letting students guess the answer without any written help or reminders.

V. Authentic Practice: Role Play (25 minutes)
1. Have students work in pairs to prepare a role play using at least 10 vocabulary words. Monitor their progress and assist them as necessary.
   - Student 1: *You are a bank teller. You are tired after a difficult day. You have one client left to see, and you hope he leaves quickly, but you also want to answer his questions carefully.*
   - Student 2: *You are a strange person. You usually keep your money under your pillow, but today you want to open a bank account. You don't know anything about banking, and you ask many unusual questions.*
2. Have students perform their role plays without looking at their notes. Keep a list of common errors and go over them as a class when the role plays are finished.

VI. Conclusion (5 minutes)
1. Ask students which words were the most confusing. Clarify meanings as necessary.
2. Ask students which activities were most helpful in learning the new vocabulary.
3. Congratulate students on a job well done.

HANDOUT 1: BANKING WORDS

Read one paragraph at a time. Repeat the words in bold after your teacher, and ask questions to clarify anything you do not understand.

A **bank account** is an agreement between you and a bank. It allows you to **deposit** money (put money into the account) so the bank can keep it safe for you, and to **withdraw** money (take money out of an account) so you can use it.

The bank will give you a **bank card** (sometimes called a **debit card**) that you can use to access your account.

If you want to save money, you should put it into a **savings account** so the bank will pay you **interest** on the money you have saved.

If you want to use your money (to pay bills, and so on), you should put it into a **chequing account**. It pays little or no interest, but it allows you to write cheques. A **cheque** is a special form that is used to make a payment from a bank account. Just be careful that your account has enough money to cover the cheques you write; otherwise a cheque might **bounce**, and you might have to pay extra fees.

When you need to move money from one account to another, you can simply **transfer** it. Transfers, deposits, withdrawals, and other activities in your bank account are called **transactions**, and every month your bank will send you a special form, called a **statement**, that shows all transactions in your account. It also tells you your account **balance**, which is the amount of money in your account.

When you go to a bank, you can go inside and talk to a person, called a **teller**, to make transactions, but sometimes it is easier to go to an **ATM**, also called a **bank machine** or a **cash machine**. Whichever you use, you can get a special form, called a **receipt**, that shows the details of the transactions you made.

Sometimes you want to buy something but you don't have enough money. You might be able to borrow some from the bank. You might get a **loan** to buy a car, or a special loan, called a **mortgage**, to buy a house. If you just want to go shopping, you can use your **credit card** to pay at the store. Be careful, though, because when you have a loan or a mortgage, or use your credit card, you will have to pay interest on the money you borrow.

HANDOUT 2: VOCABULARY IN CONTEXT

Repeat the sentences below after your teacher. Pay particular attention to the pronunciation of new vocabulary words (in bold) and to the common collocations of those words (underlined).

1. After selling my motorcycle to my friend, I **deposited** the money into my **savings account**. I wanted to earn **interest** on the money so that it would grow. Unfortunately, my **bank card** didn't work properly, so I had to see the **teller** inside.
2. I **transferred** $500 from my **savings account** to my **chequing account** because I had written a **cheque** the day before and I didn't want it to **bounce**. Then I **withdrew** $100 from the **cash machine** so that I would have some spending money for the weekend. The machine asked me if I wanted a **receipt**, but I didn't.
3. Last year I got a **loan** to buy a car, and this year I took out a **mortgage** to buy a house. Now I have to **borrow** money from my parents so I can buy some groceries. I need a better job!
4. According to my recent **statements**, I now have a healthy **balance** in my accounts, but I wish I could earn more **interest** on the money in my savings account.

HANDOUT 3: STORY COMPLETION

Choose from the following terms to complete the story below. Each word or phrase can be used only once and may need to be modified (tense, singular/plural, etc.) to suit the story.

- savings account, chequing account, balance
- deposit, withdraw, transfer, borrow, bounce
- loan, mortgage, cheque, receipt, statement, interest
- teller, bank card, debit card, cash machine, bank machine, ATM

Appendix 12A Sample Vocabulary Lesson

After being paid at work last week, I decided to _____ my money in a bank. I went to the bank after work, hoping to meet a friendly _____ who would help me, but the bank was already closed, so I used the _____ instead. I reached into my wallet and pulled out my _____ along with the money I had received from work. After I deposited the money into my savings account, the bank machine gave me a _____.

The next day I had to pay my electric bill, so I wrote a _____ and mailed it. Then I realized that there was not enough money in my _____, so I went back to the bank machine and _____ money from my _____ to my _____ so my cheque wouldn't _____. I also needed some cash, so after checking my account _____ to make sure I had enough money, I _____ $100.

I'm trying to save enough money to buy a car. If I don't have enough by spring, I might try to _____ some from the bank. Then again, I might just save my money instead. Perhaps I will put it into a special account to earn more _____.

A car? Savings? Maybe I'm just dreaming. According to the _____ that the bank sent me in the mail, I probably don't have enough money for anything!

APPENDIX 13A
Verb Tenses in English

simple present	he eats	(normal event; in general; usually is so)
present progressive	he is eating	(happening now; in progress; continuing)
present perfect	he has eaten	(finished before now, at an unspecified time)
present perfect progressive	he has been eating	(happening from past until now, and still happening)
simple past	he ate	(happened at a particular time in the past)
past progressive	he was eating	(in progress at a particular time in the past)
past perfect	he had eaten	(already finished before another event began)
past perfect progressive	he had been eating	(in progress before and when another event began)
simple future	he will eat	(will happen at a particular time in the future)
future progressive	he will be eating	(in progress at a particular time in the future)
future perfect	he will have eaten	(will be finished before another event begins)
future perfect progressive	he will have been eating	(in progress before and when another event begins)

Note that many grammarians and linguists would be quick to point out that English has three tenses (present, past, future) and three aspects (simple, progressive, perfect). However, to avoid confusion, most basic grammar books simply describe the resulting combinations as 12 tenses.

Also note that in English, the grammatical terms *progressive* and *continuous* are used interchangeably whereas some languages differentiate between the two. In Mandarin, for example, *progressive* indicates an ongoing action, while *continuous* indicates an ongoing state.

APPENDIX 14A
Sample Grammar Lesson (Tense)

PRESENT PERFECT TENSE

Lesson Objective: Students will be able to speak and write using the present perfect tense accurately and without excessive hesitation.

Methods: Students will use the present perfect tense to do the following:
- supply the correct tense and form of the verbs in a grammar worksheet
- orally transform simple past statements to present perfect statements
- write the top 10 exciting things they have done
- orally report on the top 10 exciting things their fellow students have done

Materials and Preparation:
- a favourite novel
- Handout 1: Present Perfect Tense Worksheet (one copy per student)
- a list of common verbs on the board—simple present form, simple past form, past participle form

Level: Intermediate
Time: 60 minutes

I. Lead-In/Exposure (10 minutes)

1. Show students the novel. Say: *I read this novel last year.* Then add: *I have read this novel many times.* Write both sentences on the board and ask students how they differ.
2. Clarify for students:
   a. The first sentence is written in the simple past tense. It tells us that something happened at a specific time in the past.
   b. The second sentence is written in the present perfect tense. It tells us about something that happened at an unspecified time in the past. (It is a general truth. The exact time is not important.)

3. Explain: *The present perfect tense is formed by using the present tense form of "to have" with the past participle of the main verb.* (Refer to the list on the board.) Examples: *I have run a marathon. He has run a marathon.*
4. Write the following simple past sentences on the board: *I swallowed a spider. She visited Hawaii. They wrote the language test. I did not swim in the Pacific Ocean.* Then ask students to write the corresponding present perfect sentences and explain the difference in meaning.

II. Controlled Practice, Written (15 minutes)

1. Distribute Handout 1 and have students read the instructions and begin filling in the answers. Monitor students and assist them as necessary.
2. After most students have completed the first four, explain how to form present perfect questions and negative statements, using #5 and #6 as examples.
3. Have students continue; monitor and assist them as necessary. Those who finish first should compare answers in pairs or small groups until the others finish.
4. When everyone has finished, correct the worksheet as a group and clarify any difficulties on the whiteboard.

III. Controlled Practice, Oral (10 minutes)

1. Explain: *I will give you a simple past sentence; give it back to me in present perfect tense. You may need to change "time words" or simply remove them.*
   - Sample prompt: *You didn't do your homework today.*
   - Possible answer: *You haven't done your homework since class began last fall.*

   Use the following prompts, randomly choosing students to answer. Gradually increase the pace if possible. If a student cannot answer, ask other students to help.
   - *John wrote a letter to his grandmother last week.*
   - *Tina ate seven bananas in less than one hour.*
   - *I swam across the river last night.*
   - *Amelia saw the new movie last week.*
   - *The boys next door stayed up all night.*

- I walked downtown today in the middle of the storm.
- My neighbour wrote a novel last year.
- Tina took music lessons for more than 10 years.
- I stood on the mountain and sang Christmas carols.
- We travelled to 14 countries after we graduated from university.

2. When students are doing well, add questions and negative statements:
   - I wasn't absent yesterday.
   - Were you sick recently?
   - Was Sam on vacation last week?
   - I wasn't at school last month.
   - Ahmed didn't arrive yesterday.
   - Did you go to the beach recently?

IV. Authentic Practice, Written (12 minutes)

1. Write on the whiteboard: *Top 10 exciting things I have done in my life.*
2. Ask students to write down their own top 10 lists using the present perfect tense. Monitor and assist them as necessary. Point out any incorrect use of present perfect tense and elicit the correct answer.
3. Students who finish first should compare answers in pairs or small groups.

V. Authentic Practice, Oral (10 minutes)

1. Have all students get into pairs. Then have each student report four items from their partner's list. (If the class is very large, break it into two or three large groups, each working simultaneously.) Students may use their partner's written list, but be sure they use the correct pronoun (*He* or *She*, not *I*) in their reported list.

VI. Closing (3 minutes)

1. Ask students which parts of the lesson were most helpful, and which weren't.
2. Congratulate students on a job well done: *You learned the present perfect tense today, and you <u>have learned</u> it well!*

HANDOUT 1: PRESENT PERFECT TENSE

Complete the following sentences using the simple past tense or the present perfect tense of the verb given in parentheses. (If either tense can be used, be prepared to explain the difference.)

1. Sam _____ (paint) many beautiful pictures of mountains and rivers while he was in New Zealand. He _____ (paint) landscapes all over the world.
2. Jane and Tom enjoy travelling, and they _____ (visit) many countries. Last year, they _____ (visit) New Zealand and Australia.
3. I _____ (eat) raw fish when I was in Japan. I _____ (eat) raw fish many times.
4. We _____ (go) to Newfoundland for our vacation last year. We _____ (go) there many times to relax among the friendly folk in the quiet coastal villages.
5. _____ John _____ (see) the new movie at the cinema last night? No, he _____ (not see) it yet.
6. _____ Tina _____ (see) the movie yet? I _____ (not see) her at the cinema last night.
7. William _____ (not see) the prime minister when he was in Ottawa, but he _____ (meet) him many times since he became a politician.
8. I _____ (not learn) much in calculus class yesterday. In fact, I _____ (not learn) much in that class since it began!
9. Samantha _____ (not wear) her new dress last night. It's strange. She _____ (not wear) it at all since she bought it.
10. You _____ (sit) in the same seat every week since you first came here, but you _____ (not sit) there last week. Why not?

APPENDIX 14B
Sample Grammar Lesson (Conditionals)

CONDITIONALS WITH IF-CLAUSES

Lesson Objectives: Students will be able to accurately speak and write conditional sentences (present, future, and past tenses) using if-clauses.

Methods: Students will complete the following:
- complete written sentences using the conditional present, future, and past
- complete oral sentences using the conditional present, future, and past
- create written sentences using the conditional present, future, and past
- discuss, using if-clauses and conditions, possible reactions to given situations

Materials and Preparation:
- a current lottery ticket (or reasonable facsimile)
- Handouts 1, 2, 3 (one copy of each for each student)
- one hat per three students, each hat containing small slips of paper with prompts (see section V)

Level: High-intermediate or advanced
Time: 90 minutes

I. Lead-In and Introduction (5 minutes)

1. Show students the lottery ticket and ask them what it is. Explain if necessary.
2. Ask students, *What would you do if you won the lottery?* Allow time for three or four answers, helping students with the correct form(s) if necessary. Write a few "I would ..." answers on the board.

3. Give the lottery ticket to a strong student, step back, and ask, *What will you do if you win?* Ask other students for ideas, if necessary. Write a few "I will ..." answers on the board.

II. Teach and Clarify Meaning (15 minutes)
1. Write the following sentences on the board, and ask students how they are different:
    a. *If I won the lottery, I would give money to people in need.*
    b. *If I win the lottery, I will give money to people in need.*
    c. *If I had won the lottery, I would have given money to people in need.*
2. Clarify the difference:
    a. *The first sentence refers to the present/future but is imaginary. (I don't have a ticket.)*
    b. *The second refers to the present/future and implies a real possibility. (I have a ticket.)*
    c. *The third sentence refers to something imaginary in the past. (I didn't actually win.)*
3. Distribute Handout 1. Give students time to go over it and complete the sample sentences. Monitor their progress and assist where necessary.

III. Controlled Written Practice (40 minutes)
1. Distribute Handout 2. Have students complete the exercises and then compare answers with a partner. Monitor progress and have students correct their own errors immediately.
2. Distribute Handout 3. Have students complete the exercises and then compare answers with a partner. Monitor progress and have students correct their own errors immediately.

IV. Controlled Oral Practice (10 minutes)
1. Read the following prompts aloud, choosing students randomly to complete them (orally). If a student makes an error, ask other students to assist.
    a. *If I could sing well ...*
    b. *If [student's name] had an apple ...*

c. If we finish class on time today ...
   d. If [student's name] had been late today ...
   e. If you have free time later this week ...
   f. If we don't eat lunch today ...
   g. If we didn't have an English teacher ...
   h. If it snows tomorrow ...
   i. If we have a day off next week ...
   j. If we had studied harder last week ...
   k. If you have enough money ...
   l. If you had enough money ...
   m. If you had been born in 1800 ...
   n. If [student's name] speaks English at home every day ...

V. Authentic Practice: Small-Group Conversation (15 minutes)

1. Have students form groups of three. Give each group a hat containing the following prompts (and others of your choosing), each written on a small slip of paper: *Your father might buy you a new car. The teacher might let us finish early. We should work hard today. The weather forecast is calling for rain tomorrow. We didn't finish early last week. You probably won't win the lottery, but if you did ...*
2. Have students take turns drawing a slip from the hat and using the prompt to begin a conversation using an if-clause. Encourage others in the group to ask questions and continue the conversation using as many if-clauses as possible.
3. Monitor the groups and assist (with examples and clarification) as necessary.

VI. Conclusion (5 minutes)

1. Ask students which part of the lesson was most confusing.
2. Ask students which activities were most helpful.
3. Congratulate students on a job well done.

HANDOUT 1: CONDITIONALS WITH IF-CLAUSES

Type 1:
- talking about the present or future
- talking about a general truth, a real situation, an expectation, or a real possibility
- usage:
  - use simple present tense for the if-clause
  - use will + [simple form] for the result clause
- Example: *If I win the contest, I will share my prize with you.* (The speaker has a real chance at winning the contest.)

Practice: Complete the following sentences. Be sure to use the correct tense.
1. If you take a fish out of water, it _____.
2. If you don't study hard, you _____ the test.
3. If you go to the beach without sunscreen, you _____.
4. If you eat too much candy, you _____.
5. If you watch movies all night, you _____.

Type 2:
- talking about the present or future
- talking about something untrue, or an unexpected, improbable, or imaginary situation
- usage:
  - use simple past tense for the if-clause
  - use would + [simple form] for the result clause
- Example: *If I won a million dollars, I would travel around the world.* (The speaker does not expect to win a million dollars; it is an imaginary situation.)

Practice: Complete the following sentences. Be sure to use the correct tense.
1. If you took that fish out of water, it _____.
2. If you didn't study hard, you _____ the test.
3. If you went to the beach without sunscreen, you _____.

4. If you ate all that candy now, you _____.
5. If you watched movies all night, you _____.

Type 3:
- talking about the past
- talking about something untrue, or an imaginary situation
- usage:
  - use past perfect tense for the if-clause
  - use would have + past participle for the result clause
- Example: *If I had won a million dollars, I would have travelled around the world.*

Practice: Complete the following sentences. Be sure to use the correct tense.
1. If you had left your fish out of water all night, it _____.
2. If you hadn't studied hard, you _____ the test.
3. If you had gone to the beach without sunscreen, you _____.
4. If you had eaten all that candy, you _____.
5. If you had watched movies all night, you _____.

HANDOUT 2: MIXED PRACTICE I

Write the given verb in the correct form.

1. If they offered me the job, I _____ it. (take)
2. If they offer me the job, I _____ it. (take)
3. If they had offered me the job, I _____ it. (take)
4. If I had sold my car, I _____ much money for it. (not get)
5. If I sold my car, I _____ much money for it. (not get)
6. If I didn't have class today, I _____ with you. (go shopping)
7. If I hadn't had class today, I _____ with you. (go shopping)
8. If the factory _____, a lot of people would be out of work. (close down)

9. If the factory _____, a lot of people will be out of work. (close down)
10. If I _____ my car this weekend, I will buy a new one on Monday. (sell)
11. If I _____ my car this weekend, I would buy a new one on Monday. (sell)
12. I'm sure Jan _____ if you explain the situation to her. (understand)
13. I'm sure Jan _____ if you had explained the situation to her. (understand)
14. I think Amy will lend you the money. I would be very surprised if she _____ (refuse).
15. If I hadn't paid my bills on time, I _____ in a lot of trouble. (be)

HANDOUT 3: MIXED PRACTICE II

Change each of the following sentences into a conditional sentence (using an if-clause and a result clause).

1. I want to write a letter to my friend, but I don't have time.
2. Jim wanted to go to a movie, but he didn't have enough money.
3. Tom wants to buy a CD, but he doesn't have enough money.
4. I will go to the beach tomorrow because the weather will be nice (I think).
5. Jill didn't pass her test because she didn't study.
6. I was late for class today because the bus was late.
7. Tim told everybody the news because Bob hadn't said it was a secret.
8. I didn't do the laundry because I didn't have time.
9. I want to buy a new jacket tomorrow. I think I have enough money.
10. I didn't know about the party because you didn't tell me.
11. We can't have a picnic today because it is raining.
12. I can't go out tonight. I don't want to miss my favourite TV show.
13. I can't lend you a pen because I don't have one.
14. I hope to finish work on time today. I want to meet my friends at the park at 5:00.
15. I didn't win the lottery last week, so I didn't quit my job.

APPENDIX 15A
IPA Vowel Chart for North American English

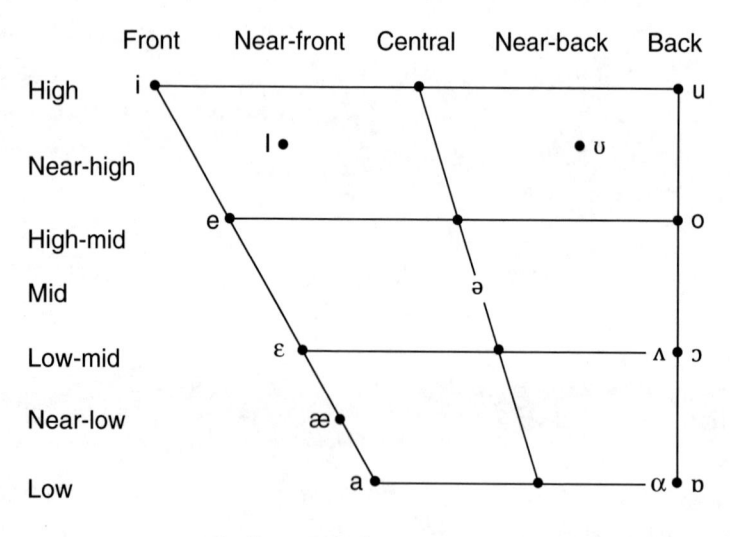

	Front	Near-front	Central	Near-back	Back
High	i				u
Near-high		ɪ		ʊ	
High-mid	e				o
Mid			ə		
Low-mid	ɛ			ʌ	ɔ
Near-low		æ			
Low		a		ɑ	ɒ

unrounded • rounded

APPENDIX 16A
Sound Families for Common North American Vowel Sounds

\multicolumn{4}{c|}{BASIC VOWELS (MAY VARY BY DIALECT)}				
SOUND	**NAME**	\multicolumn{2}{c|}{**SPELLING AND EXAMPLES**}	
[i:]	gr<u>ee</u>n vowel	ea	eat, heat, seat; dream, team; clear, dear; read; speak
		e	be, he, she, me, we; beside; redo
		ee	free, tree; feet, meet; need; keep, sleep; seem; cheek
		ie	belief, believe, chief, thief; fierce, pierce; friend
		ei	ceiling, deceive, receipt, seize, weird
		-y	funny, lady, messy, muddy, pretty, study, ugly, windy
[ɪ]	s<u>i</u>lver vowel	i	bit, it, sit; lip, tip, sip; him, slim, Tim; did, kid, middle
		o	women
[ɛ]	r<u>e</u>d vowel	e	bet, get, set; egg, keg; pen, then, women; bell, fell, tell
		ea	read (past tense)
[æ]	bl<u>a</u>ck vowel	a	bat, bad, apple, sad, sat
[ɑ]	f<u>a</u>ther vowel	a	all, ball, call, fall, mall, tall, salt
		au	aunt, flaunt, autumn, auction
		al	balm, calm, palm
		o	odd, bother, bottle, rock, robot, stop, top, pot
		ou	bought, sought, thought, wrought
		aw	awe, flaw, law, raw, saw, straw
[u:]	bl<u>ue</u> vowel	oo	boot, moon, soon; mood; bloom, room; too, cool
		ue	clue, blue, glue, hue, true
		u-e	cute, flute, brute, mule, prune, fluke
		ew	blew, chew, dew, few, flew, grew, new, stew, threw
		ou	you, route, through
		o	move, to, who, whose
		other	suit, two
[ʊ]	g<u>oo</u>d vowel	oo	book, cook, look, hook, foot, soot, good, stood, wood
		u	put
		oul	could, should, would
[ʌ]	m<u>o</u>ther vowel	u	but, cut, mud, brother, under, run, us; bug, mug; must
		o-e	above, dove, love, shove
[ə]	schwa	\multicolumn{2}{l|}{May occur as any unstressed vowel:}	
		\multicolumn{2}{l|}{<u>a</u>bove, <u>a</u>go, comm<u>a</u>, sod<u>a</u>, cin<u>e</u>ma, fam<u>ou</u>s, butt<u>o</u>n, winn<u>er</u>}	

DIPTHONGS

SOUND	NAME	SPELLING AND EXAMPLES	
[eɪ]	clay vowel	ai	bait, wait; ail, nail; pain, rain, train
		a-e	ate, date, fate, late; game, name, same; bake, cake
		ay	bay, hay, day, hooray, play, pray, stay, way
		ei	eight, freight, sleigh, neighbour, weigh, weight
		ey	they, prey, convey, survey
[aɪ]	high vowel	i-e	bike, like; alive, arrive, drive; bite, write; smile, while
		ie	die, lie, pie, tie
		igh	high, sigh, fight, light, might, night, right, sight, tight
		eigh	height
		-y	by, cry, my, dry, fly, sky, try, why
		ye	bye, dye, rye
		other	buy; I
[aʊ]	loud vowel	ow	brow, brown, cow, how, now, plow
		ou	about, house, mouth, shout, snout, trout
[oʊ]	slow vowel	o	go, no, so, old, cold, fold, sold, told
		oa	oat, boat, coat, float, goat, throat; roam, soap, oak
		o-e	home, rope, poke, wrote, close, nose, stove, drove
		oe	doe, foe, hoe, toe
		ow	blow, crow, low, mow, row, slow, snow, throw, tow
[ɔi]	boy vowel	oy	boy, coy, employ, joy, toy
		oi	oil, noise, join, coin, boil, foil, soil, toil

R-COLOURED VOWELS (MAY VARY WIDELY BY DIALECT)

SOUND	NAME	SPELLING AND EXAMPLES	
[iɹ]	clear vowel	ear	ear, clear, fear, gear, hear, near, rear
		eer	beer, deer
		ere	here, mere, atmosphere
[ɛɹ]	square vowel	air	air, fair, hair, lair
		are	care, dare, mare, square
		ear	bear, tear (v.)
		eir	their
		ere	there
[ɜɹ] or [əɹ]	girl vowel	ir	fir, sir; bird, dirt, flirt, shirt; irk, chirp, girl, whirl
		ur	absurd, burp, hurt, turn
		er	jerk, baker, seller, maker, cover, dinner, supper
		or	word, work, worse, worst
[ɑɹ]	far vowel	ar	arm, bar, car, far, star, start
		are	are
[ʊɹ] [jʊɹ]	pure vowel*	our	tour
		ure	cure, pure
		eur	Europe
[oɹ] or [ɔɹ]	core vowel	ar	war, warm
		or	or, for, nor; force, horse; north; sort, port, storm
		ore	bore, core, more, pore, score, sore, store, tore, wore
		oar	oar, boar, roar; coarse
		oor	door, floor, poor
		our	course, court, four, pour, source

*Note that many dialects use [oɹ] or [joɹ] where others use [ʊɹ] or [jʊɹ].

APPENDIX 16B
Sound Families for Tricky Consonant Sounds

SOUND	SPELLING	EXAMPLES
[k]	c, ck, k, ch	cat, kick, back, school
[f]	f, ff, ph, gh	free, staff, phone, laugh, cough
[dʒ]	j, g, -ge	judge, jump, genius, marriage, carriage
[l]	l, ll, -le	look, ball, table, dribble
[ɹ]	r, wr	read, right, write, wrong
[s]	s, -ss, c, sc, ps	sea, class, princess, cider, cite, science psychology
[ʃ]	sh, ti	she, wish, caution, patient
[ʒ]	s, g	pleasure, television, confusion, beige, rouge
[tʃ]	ch, t	cheap, cheese, watch, culture, fortune
[θ]	th	thin, think, thank, bath, path, cloth
[ð]	th	this, that, these, those, the, them, bathe, clothe
[w]	w, wh	wet, wonder, while, where, what, when, why
[z]	z, s	zoo, poison

GLOSSARY OF KEY TERMS

Note: See also appendix 1A for a description of commonly used acronyms related to language learning and language teaching, and appendix 7A for a list of commonly used language proficiency tests and assessment tools.

accommodation: The adjustment of one's language (accent, complexity, speed, word choice) or expectations (such as cultural) to suit another individual's differences.

accuracy: The degree to which language is used correctly, particularly in terms of grammar, word choice, pronunciation, or spelling.

activate: To put into use, as in students activating language they have previously studied but rarely used.

activity: A unit of instruction that normally includes specific instructions and one or more student tasks working toward a particular objective.

adjacency pair: Two parts of a conversation that require one another, such as question-answer, greeting-response.

allophone: A distinct variation of a language sound caused by the influence of surrounding sounds, such as [p] becoming [pʰ] in *pin*. (Two sounds are allophones if one can replace the other without changing the word. Contrast to *phoneme*.)

approach: A set of principles and assumptions that informs how one teaches.

assessment: The evaluation or estimation of a student's knowledge or ability; see also *formative assessment*, *needs assessment*, and *summative assessment*.

authentic language: Language that approximates that used in real life.

authentic materials: Real-life materials, such as magazine articles, restaurant menus, podcasts, or other items that can be used for practice in a language classroom.

authentic practice: Language practice in which there is a genuine exchange of information, and in which the participants choose what to say and how to say it. (Contrast to *controlled practice*.)

auxiliary verb: A type of verb that is used to determine the tense, mood, or conditions of the main verb.

blog: A website that hosts an online diary, journal, or similar collection of entries that are generally reflective in nature. (Origin: *web* + *log*)

bottom-up listening: Listening for specific components (such as individual sounds or words) in order to construct the overall meaning of the utterance.

clause: A group of grammatically related words containing a subject and a predicate. (See chapter 13.)

cloze: A text in which every nth word is replaced by a blank for students to fill in; alternatively, a "modified cloze" is a text in which the blanks are not random but specifically chosen to achieve a particular objective.

collocation: A phrase made of content words that frequently occur together.

communicative competence: The ability to use language accurately and appropriately in order to communicate effectively.

complex sentence: A sentence made of one independent clause and one or more dependent clauses.

compound sentence: A sentence made of two or more independent clauses and no dependent clauses.

compound-complex sentence: A sentence made of two or more independent clauses and one or more dependent clauses.

comprehensible input: Language, whether spoken or written, that is at or just beyond the students' current level such that they can understand it but with some degree of challenge.

conjunctive adverb: A type of adverb that provides a logical transition between two main clauses.

consonant blend: A group of two or three consonant sounds that blend together in such a way that each individual consonant can be heard in the blend.

content-based instruction: Instruction that is primarily structured around particular content, often academic, rather than around language skills; a content-based lesson or course gives priority to the content material being learned, and focus on language skills is secondary.

content word: A word that names a person, a place, a thing, an action, or a quality and thereby carries meaning, including most nouns, main verbs, adjectives, and some adverbs. (Contrast to *function word*.)

controlled practice: Language practice that is carefully arranged so that there is only one correct answer or very few correct answers; as such, the teacher controls the range of possible answers. (Contrast to *authentic practice*.)

conversation analysis: The study of conversations in order to determine their features and parts.

coordinating conjunction: A word that joins words, phrases, or clauses of equal importance; in English, there are seven coordinating conjunctions: *and, but, for, nor, or, so, yet*.

corpora: Plural of *corpus*.

corpus: A large collection of texts (taken from written works, transcribed conversations, and other authentic sources) that exists as a database that can be searched and analyzed.

countable noun: A word that names a person, place, thing, or idea that can be counted; as such, most countable nouns have a singular form and a plural form.

course goals: The long-term goals toward which a course progresses.

course outline: (informal) A detailed, descriptive list of lessons that make up a particular course; (formal) a document that describes a course and its expectations, topics, schedule, evaluation methods, policies, and other important details; a syllabus.

critical period hypothesis: The suggestion that an individual's ability to learn language declines after a particular age, normally around puberty.

cultural norms: The standards of one's own culture that are thought to be standard or normal, in contrast to those of other cultures.

dependent clause: A group of grammatically related words, containing a subject and a predicate, that cannot stand alone as a sentence but must be attached to an independent clause; also called a *subordinate clause*.

derivational affix: A prefix or suffix used to derive a new word from an existing one.

descriptive grammar: Grammar rules that reflect how the language is actually used rather than prescribing how it should be used. (Contrast to *prescriptive grammar*.)

dictogloss: An activity in which students take brief notes while listening to a text being read aloud, and then try to reconstruct it.

differentiation: The act of giving students different tasks or assignments according to their varying levels or other needs, even if they are in the same class; also called *differentiated instruction*.

diphthong: A speech sound formed by combining two speech sounds into one syllable such that the new sound begins like one and ends like the other.

direct object: A noun phrase that denotes the person or thing that receives the action of the verb.

discourse: Communication of thoughts via speaking or writing.

discourse analysis: The study of discourse in order to determine its features.

discourse marker: A word or phrase used to organize or manage what we say or write.

explicit instruction: Teaching that uses deliberate explanations. (Contrast to *implicit instruction*.)

extensive listening: Listening for longer periods, for pleasure, at a level that is comfortable for the student, normally outside the classroom.

extensive reading: Reading longer texts, for pleasure, at a level that is comfortable for the student, normally outside the classroom.

fairness (of a test): The degree to which a test is free from bias so that no student is disadvantaged because of their age, race, gender, religion, or any other factor that should not affect their performance.

false beginner: A language learner who has previously learned the language to some degree but cannot use it and appears to have forgotten much of it, yet over time begins to recall words, phrases, and basic grammar forms.

feedback: The response given to a student during or after an activity, lesson, class, or course; it generally includes some combination of correction, encouragement, and suggestions for improvement.

fluency: The ability to use language smoothly, without excessive hesitation.

formative assessment: The evaluation of a student's progress used during the learning process in order to facilitate decisions that improve the learning process.

fossilization: The process by which an error becomes habitual to the point that it is very difficult to correct.

four skills: The four skills of language, namely speaking, listening, reading, writing.

free variation: The phenomenon of two phonemes being interchangeable—one can replace the other without changing the meaning of the word.

function word: A word that does not carry substantive meaning but serves a grammatical purpose by establishing the relationship between other words, phrases, or clauses; function words include prepositions, pronouns, and conjunctions. (Contrast to *content word*.)

gerund: A form of a verb that functions like a noun; in English, a gerund is the present participle (-ing) form of a verb that acts like a noun (for example, as a subject or an object).

goals: Desired outcomes for a course.

graded reader: A text, such as a story, that has been simplified to suit a particular language level.

headword: The main word around which a phrase is built.

independent clause: A group of grammatically related words, containing a subject and a predicate, that can stand alone as a sentence; also called a *main clause*.

idiom: An expression or saying that has a special meaning different from the literal meaning of its words, such as *swimming against the tide*.

implicit instruction: Teaching that does not use explanations but relies on examples. (Contrast to *explicit instruction*.)

indirect object: A noun phrase that denotes the person or thing to whom or for whom the action is performed; the recipient of the direct object.

infinitive: The basic form of a verb, sometimes called the dictionary form.

inflection: A property added to a word class; in English, for example, most nouns can be inflected with plural and possessive, many adjectives can be inflected with comparative and superlative, and most verbs can be inflected with (third-person singular) present, present participle, past, and past participle.

information gap: An instance where certain information is missing; in an information-gap activity, students must communicate with each other in order to fill in the gaps in their knowledge.

integrated skills: The use of language skills to communicate meaning or learn content (rather than practicing skills for their own sake).

intercultural communication: Communication that occurs between members of different cultures or social groups.

intercultural competence: The ability to interact and communicate effectively and appropriately with people from other cultures.

interlanguage: The form of language used by a language learner, influenced by the learner's first language as well as by the learner's assumptions about the language being learned.

International Phonetic Alphabet: A set of symbols used to represent human speech sounds.

interrogative adverb: A type of adverb used for asking questions: *how, when, where, why*.

intonation: The pattern of pitch changes in a spoken sentence in order to vary the meaning or attitude of the speaker.

L1: First language, or mother tongue; the language that is most natural and comfortable for an individual.

L2: Second language; other than the first language, it is the language used most by an individual; also used to denote a language being learned in addition to the first language.

language chunk: See *lexical chunk*.

language function: An action that is performed through language, such as apologizing, greeting, making a request, or asking for information.

language learner: An individual who learns a language anywhere and in any way, whether formally (as a student in a class) or informally.

language skills: Speaking, listening, reading, and writing. (Texts that address all skills are often referred to as *four-skill* or *multi-skill*.)

language universals: Language properties or features that are common in the world's languages.

lead-in: A general introduction (to a lesson, for example) that generates interest and activates students' prior knowledge of the topic.

learning style: The manner in which an individual prefers to learn; a visual learner, for example, prefers to have information presented visually as a chart, map, or image.

lesson: A unit of instruction normally covered in one class or period and typically composed of multiple activities that progress toward an overall lesson objective.

lesson objective: The desired outcome toward which the lesson progresses.

lesson plan: A document that describes the objectives, methods, and activities that make up a lesson, including specific instructions for the teacher.

lexical chunk: A group of words that act as a fixed expression that occurs frequently in commonly used language; also called a *lexical phrase*, *lexical unit*, or *prefabricated phrase*.

lexis: Vocabulary, including both single-word and multiple-word units of meaning.

linking verb: A type of verb that does not express action but links the sentence subject to a word or phrase that describes it.

listening fatigue: A feeling of tiredness that occurs after expending significant energy to listen to and comprehend spoken language.

main clause: See *independent clause*.

marked: Different from what is common; for example the English sound [θ] is marked in that it is not common in the world's languages.

markedness: The degree to which a language feature is marked.

markedness differential hypothesis: The supposition that when a property of a target language is different from the equivalent property of the learner's first language, it will be difficult for the learner to acquire only if it is more marked, and the degree of difficulty will correspond to the degree of markedness.

meaning: What is meant by an utterance. (Language activities sometimes focus on the meaning of the text rather than its language features.)

method: A system or way of doing something, such as language teaching.

minimal pair: A pair of words that differ only by a single sound, such as *right/light, bit/bet, leaf/leave*.

modal auxiliary verb: A type of verb that helps determine the conditions of the main verb, such as necessity, ability, advisability, permissibility, possibility, or probability.

monitor (as a learner): To be aware of and evaluate one's own use of language.

monitor (as a teacher): To observe students' work during an in-class activity in order to provide assistance, correction, or other feedback.

morpheme: The smallest part of a word that retains key information about its meaning and/or function, even in different contexts.

morphology: The study of the structure of words (i.e., of how they are made or changed).

multiple intelligences theory: The theory that intelligence takes many forms beyond those stated or implied by the traditional definition, which focuses primarily on linguistic and logical intelligence.

narrative: An utterance, spoken or written, that tells a story.

needs assessment: A tool used to discover the preferences and needs of an individual or group; in a language course, a needs assessment may be written or oral (normally both) and attempts to discover language level, previous experience and education, expectations, and other details that may help in planning the course.

noticing: The act of becoming aware of a particular language feature to the extent of being able to recognize it in the future.

object complement: A noun phrase or adjective phrase that follows a direct object and renames it or modifies it, often telling what it has become.

objective: A desired outcome for an activity or a lesson.

open-ended question: A question that requires a thoughtful answer, not a one-word or yes/no answer.

paced reading: A type of reading activity that measures and aims to gradually increase students' reading speed without sacrificing comprehension.

participle adjective: The present participle or past participle form of a verb that functions as an adjective, as in *the sleeping dog, the tired boy*.

parts of speech: The categories to which words are assigned according to how they behave in phrases, clauses, or sentences. Commonly used categories in English are nouns, pronouns, determiners, adjectives, verbs, adverbs, prepositions, conjunctions, and interjections.

peer feedback: Feedback (correction, evaluation, encouragement) that is given by one's classmates or other peers rather than by the teacher.

phone: A distinct speech sound (or gesture).

phoneme: A distinct speech sound that is critical to the meaning of words; hence two sounds are phonemes if one cannot replace the other without changing the word. (Contrast to *allophone*.)

phonetics: The study of speech sounds and how they are articulated. (This term should not be confused with *phonics*, which is a method of teaching reading and writing by associating written characters with particular sounds.)

phonology: The study of the system of speech sounds, including how they are arranged and modified when used in language.

phrasal verb: A verb that is made up of more than one word yet is a single unit of meaning, such as *turn on, take off,* and *mess up*.

phrase: A group of grammatically related words that is not a clause because it lacks a subject, a verb, or both.

pitch: The degree to which a sound is high or low.

placement test: A form of assessment that determines language level so students can be placed into a suitable class.

portfolio: A collection, built up over time, of a student's work.

power: The position or ability to influence the behaviour of others.

PPP: A class procedure in which the teacher *presents* the new language, the students *practice* it, and the students then *produce* it on their own; some methods of teaching use the terms *introduction, controlled practice,* and *authentic practice* for the same or similar steps.

practicality (of a test): The degree to which a test can be easily and efficiently designed, administered, and graded.

pragmatic competence: The ability to use a language effectively in ways appropriate to the social context.

predicate: The part of the sentence that tells something about the subject, such as what it is or does.

prescriptive grammar: Grammar rules that describe how the language should be used. (Contrast to *descriptive grammar*.)

process writing: A technique that includes various stages of writing, typically including planning, drafting, revising, and proofreading; it often includes feedback at various stages.

productive vocabulary: The vocabulary that an individual can use correctly in speaking and writing.
proficiency test: A test that determines a student's overall language level.

realia: Real-life objects, or toy-like representations of objects.
recasting: A method of correcting a student's spoken error by repeating the corrected form; also known as *reformulating*.
receptive vocabulary: The vocabulary that an individual understands when reading or listening but cannot use in speaking or writing.
register: A style of language used in a particular context and for a particular purpose.
reinforcement: The process of giving students tasks to strengthen knowledge or skills they have already been learning or developing.
relationship oriented: In culture, the tendency to prioritize building relationships over completion of a task.
reliability (of a test): The degree to which the test produces the same results consistently.
rhythm (in a sentence): The overall arrangement or pattern of sounds resulting from stressed and unstressed syllables.
role play: A short skit in which students play the roles and act out the scenario they have been given.
root: The smallest part of a word that contains its core meaning.
rubric: A tool, often in the form of a chart, that lists the criteria used in evaluating students' work.

scaffolding: Support given to students to help them complete the task at hand.
scan: To look over quickly in search of a specific detail. (Contrast to *skim*.)
schwa: In English, a short, weak vowel sound that frequently occurs in an unstressed syllable.
semantics: The study of the meaning of words, phrases, clauses, and sentences.
simple sentence: A sentence made of one independent clause and no dependent clauses.
skim: To look over quickly in search of the gist or overall idea. (Contrast to *scan*.)
social context: The general social situation in which something exists or occurs.
social interactionist theory: The theory that language acquisition is aided by social interaction with others who are more linguistically advanced in the target language and who can thus provide support in language development.
sociolinguistics: The study of language within its social context.

stative verb: A type of verb that expresses a state, not an action, and cannot be used in a progressive tense.

stem: The part of a word, consisting of a root and any derivational affixes, to which inflections are added.

stereotype: An oversimplified perception based on assumptions, not facts, that generally does not recognize exceptions and is often judgmental.

stress (re: words): The emphasis given to a particular syllable in a word or a particular word in a sentence. In English, stressed syllables are said louder, higher, and longer.

student talk time (STT): The time students spend speaking during an activity or a class (in contrast to teacher talk time, or TTT.)

subject: The part of a sentence that tells who or what the sentence is about.

subject complement: A noun phrase, adjective phrase, or prepositional phrase that follows a linking verb and gives more information about the subject of the sentence.

subject movement: The movement of a sentence subject to a position after the auxiliary verb in order to change a statement into a question.

subordinate clause: See *dependent clause*.

subordinating conjunction: A word that introduces a subordinate clause and joins it to a main clause.

subskills (of language): The underlying skills of language: vocabulary, grammar, and pronunciation.

summative assessment: The evaluation of progress used at the end of the learning process.

superordinate: A general term or class that includes numerous subclasses; for example, *animal* is the superordinate of *giraffe, elephant*, and *dog*.

syllabus: See *course outline (formal)*.

syntax: The systematic arrangement of words to create phrases, clauses, and sentences.

target language: The language that is the subject of study, or is otherwise being learned.

task: The part of an activity that students do in order to achieve the objective of the activity.

task-based instruction: Learning that is structured around a particular non-language task; in a task-based activity, the overall objective is to complete the task (which requires use of the target language), and language objectives are secondary.

task oriented: In culture, the tendency to prioritize completion of the task at hand over the building of relationships within the group performing the task.

top-down listening: Listening while drawing from prior knowledge and available context in order to understand the overall meaning of the utterance, even if some details are missed.

topic sentence: The main sentence of a paragraph, usually found at or near the beginning, which gives the topic of the paragraph and to which all other sentences in the paragraph relate.

uncountable noun: A word that names a substance or concept that cannot be counted, such as *evidence, fear, knowledge, sand,* and *water*; also called a *noncount noun* or *mass noun*.

utterance: Anything (a word, phrase, clause, or sentence) that is spoken or written.

validity (of a test): The degree to which a test actually measures what it is intended to measure.

voiced: Made by using the vocal cords.

voiceless: Made without use of the vocal cords.

wh-movement: The movement of an interrogative word or phrase to the beginning of a clause in order to transform a statement into a question.

INDEX

Page numbers in **bold** indicate pages in which the term is defined or its concept is explained or otherwise dealt with substantially. (For formal definitions, see also the glossary in this text.)

accents, 11, 141, 143, 146, 223, 232, 237, 249, 257
accommodation (of differences), **276**–278
accuracy, 36, 39, 43, 47, 48, 49, **84–86**, 104, 135, 204, 205, 216, 217, 240, 241
activate (language), 10, 16, 21, 236
activate (prior knowledge), 13, 93, 146, 217
activities, 23, 81–82
    evaluating, 88–89
    extending, 76
    planning, 83–87
    repurposing, 76
    running, 100–101
adjacency pairs, 269
adjective clauses. *See* relative clauses
adjectives, 186, **188**, 192, 193
adverb clauses, **198**, 289
adverbs, 177, 188, **190**, 192, 194, 195, 244, 259
allophones, **229–230**, 232
approaches, 23, **33–34**, 57, 59, 60, 61, 70
apps, 57, 58, 59, 60, 250
articles (in grammar), **188**, 192, 205, 259, 260, 270, 295
articulation (of sounds), **225–228**, 240
assessment, 28, 91, **111–125**, 145
assisted writing, 166
audio, 58, 59, 75, 116, 136, 146, 148–149, 182, 248, 283
Audio-Lingual Method (ALM), 34, **37–38**, 60, 61, 62, 215, 299–302
authentic language, 22, 41, 43, 44, 45, 54, 209
authentic practice, 45, 181, 215, 216, 217
auxiliary verbs, 189, 196, 206, 244

blogs, 4, 57, 58, 59, 167, 284
bottom-up listening, 141
business English, 12, 69, 73, 78, 209

CDs, 58, 148, 149, 182, 248
class management, 27, 37, **95–110**
clauses, 184, 185, 187, 190, 191, 192, **194–200**, 206, 246
cloud storage, 58
cloze, 48, 54, 157, 158
collocations, **53**, 177–178, 180, 241
Common European Framework (CEFR), 288, 311
communicative competence, **41**, 68
Communicative Language Teaching (CLT), 34, **41–45**, 60, 91, 209, 303–306
Community Language Learning (CLL), 56
comparative, **186**, 188, 205, 289
comprehensible input, **51**, 53
computers, 57, 58, 59, 115, 149
confidence, 17, 51, 105, 128, 129, 130, 132, 160
conjunctions, 190, **191**, 198, 199, 244, 260, 289
consonant blends, **229**, 230, 232, 233, 256
consonant sounds, **225–228**, 229, 231, 234, 345
content words, **53**, 244, 247
Content-Based Instruction (CBI), 34, **47–50**, 62, 70, 73, 91, 92, 131, 147, 161, 171, 181, 218, 281, 282, 307–309
contrastive stress, 244
controlled practice, 34, 44, 72, 333
conversation analysis, 268
conversational English, 44, 60, 128, 203, 204
Cooperative Learning, 34, **57**
corpus, corpora, 208
countable, 187, 289
course goals, **67–68**, 78, 81
course outline, 78, 79
course planning, 66–80
critical period hypothesis, 26

dependent clauses, **198**–200
derivational affixes, 185, **186**, 258
Desuggestopedia, 56–57
determiners, **188**, 192, 193, 194, 197, 244, 260, 270, 289
dictation, 29, 40, 119, 239, 244, 245, 290
dictionaries, 58, 154, 177, 179, 221, 238
dictogloss, 48, 308
differentiation, 97
diphthongs, 222, **224**, 232
Direct Method, 34, **40–41**, 60, 61
direct objects, **194**, 195, 196, 197, 199, 205, 206
discourse, 92
discourse analysis, 267
discourse markers, 136, 269, 312
drills, 37, 38, 39, 60, 61, 76, 132, 215, 264, 299–302
DVDs, 58

eliciting, 100, 109, 121, 179, 283
English as an Additional Language (EAL), 12, 286
English as a Foreign Language (EFL), 12, 286
English as a Second Language (ESL), 12, 286
English for Academic Purposes (EAP), 12, 70, 73, 286
English for Speakers of Other Languages (ESOL), 286
English for Specific Purposes (ESP), 12, 286
errors (dealing with), 103–106
expectations (of students), 27, 28, 97, 272, **273–274**, 290
explanations (giving), 100, 109
exposure (to language), 34, 51, 136, 239, 248
extensive listening, 54, 58, 136, **148–149**, 182, 245, 248, 249, 282, 283
extensive reading, 54, 154, **160**, 182, 283

facilitating, 7, 12, 13, 47, 95, 112, 136, 137, 159–160, 238, 283
false beginners, **21**, 29, 30, 74
feedback, 86, 93, 101, 103–107, 112, 113, 114, 116, 117, 122, 124, 260, 283
    on grammar, 215, 216, 217
    on listening, 149

    on pronunciation, 240, 248, 249–250
    on speaking, 130, 138
    on writing, 166, 169, 170–171
flashcards, 179
fluency, 39, 43, 44, 47, 49, 55, 70, 73, 74, **84–87**, 92, 103, 128, 129, 130, 131, 162, 165, 203, 204, 216, 217
formality, 12, 135, 136, 209, 270, 273
formative assessment, 112–114
fossilization, 253
free variation, **230**, 232
free writing, 45, **165–166**, 168
function words, 244

gist, 145, 147, 154, 158
graded readers, **148**, 182, 248
Grammar-Translation Method (GTM), 34, **35–37**, 295, 296, 298
grouping (students), 21, 42, **96–97**, 137

headwords, 193
high-context cultures, 271

idioms, **53**, 174, 177, 178, 260
IELTS, 115, 311
indirect objects, **194–195**, 196, 197, 206
inflection, 206, **185–186**, 258, 260
instructions (giving), 100, 283
integrated skills, 10, **11**, 92, 138, 147, 161, 171, 181, 218, 248
intensive reading, 154, **156–158**
intercultural communication, 263–278
intercultural competence, 276
interlanguage, 252–254
International Phonetic Alphabet (IPA), **221**–223, 342
Internet, 58, 59, 148, 155, 175, 284
intonation, 141, 206, **245**–246, 249

jobs, 284–285

language acquisition, 22, 23, **25–27**, 51, 129, **252–261**
language chunks, 53, 54, 55, 61, 160, 177–178, 182, 247, 310. *See also* lexical chunks

language counsellor, 57, 129, 160
language functions, **41**–**45**, 61, 70, 71, 72–73, 91, 92, 128, 135, 181, 267, 303–304
language learners, 10, 15–31, 140, 141
    and grammar, 205–207
    and pronunciation, 231–234
    and semantics, 175–177
language levels, 20–21
language skills, 10–11
language transfer, 232, **254**, 256, 257, 258, 259, 260
language universals, **254**–255
lead-in, 44, 49, **91**, 93, 100, 132, 138, 146, 159, 168, 217, 283, 303, 307, 317, 321, 325, 332, 336
learning styles, 24
lesson objectives, **81**–**83**, 84, 93, 119, 303, 307, 317, 321, 325, 332, 336
lesson plans, **90**–93, 179–181, 158–159
Lexical Approach, 34, **53**–**56**, 61, 310
lexical chunks, **53**, 54, 55. *See also* language chunks
lexis, 174
listening comprehension, 58, 140–149, 174, 249
listening fatigue, 23
low-context cultures, 271

main clauses, 189, 191, **197**, 198
markedness, **254**–256, 257, 258
matching, 36, 120, 179, 180
minimal pairs/sets, **238**, 239, 240
modal verbs, **189**, 209, 216, 289, 306
monitoring, 8, 13, 23, 91, 101, 111, 112, 113
morphemes, **185**–187, 258, 259, 260
morphology, 184–187, 258
motivation, 19, 23, 25, 26, 28, 43, 46, 48, 51, 98, 151, 156, 166, 167, 168, 170, 203, 282
multiple choice, 118, 120, 121, 157, 158
multiple intelligences theory, 24

Natural Approach, 34, 50–51
needs assessment, **28**–29, 79, 116, 290–294
non-verbal communication, 271, 274–275
noticing, 44, 72, 303
noun clauses, 56, **199**–200, 289

noun phrases, **193**, 194, 195, 197
nouns, 174, 186, **187**, 192, 194, 195, 205

object complement, **195**, 196, 206
objectives. *See* lesson objectives
open-ended questions, 91, 108, 109, 135
oral reading, 130, 160, 249

paced reading, 161
Participatory Approach, 34, **50**, 62
participle, 186, 187, 332
participle adjectives, **188**, 192, 195, 289
parts of speech, **187**, 191, 192
passive, 165, 185, 189, 289
peer assessment, 113
peer feedback, 169
phonemes, **229**–230, 232
phones, 220, 240
phonology, **229**, 252, 257
phrasal verbs, **53**, 174, 205, 289
phrases, 192–193
placement test, 21, 29
podcasts, 43, 58, 143, 148
politeness, 136, 209, 272–273
portfolio, 59, 115–117
PPP Method, 34, **39**
pragmatic competence, 41
predicate, **194**, 195, 197
prefabricated phrases, 53
prefixes, 186
prepositional phrases, 190, **193**
prepositions, 53, **190**, 191, 192, 193, 206, 207, 259
prescriptive grammar, 207
process writing, 167–170
productive vocabulary, 175
proficiency, 20, 22, 55, 112, **114**, 115, 288, 290
proficiency test, 21, 59, 311
pronouns, 186, **188**–**189**, 192, 205
pronunciation, 11, 12, 20, 26, 38, 76, 119, 130, **220**–**250**

qualifications (for teaching), 284

reading strategies, 153–155
recasting, 105

receptive vocabulary, 175
registers, 270
relationship-oriented cultures, 271, 272
relative clauses, 189, **198**, 199, 289
repetition, 37, 240, 243, 244
rhythm, 25, 243
role plays, 43, 45, 47, 104, 105, **134**, 138, 215
rubric, 113, 116, **122**–124

scaffolding, 8
scanning, **154**, 155
schwa, **224**, 241, 343
semantics, **175**–177, 260
sentence stress, **243**–244
sentence transformation, 36, 38, 120, 215, 301
sentences (types), 200
short-answer questions, 121–122, 158
similes, 53
simulation, 134, 313
skimming, **154**, 155, 157, 158
smart phones, 58, 60, 116, 149, 250
social context, 41, **42**, 43, 145, 178, 208, 267, 303
social interactionist theory, 27
social media, 57, 59
sociolinguistics, 265, 267
speech sounds, 220–234
spelling (influence on pronunciation), 233
stative verbs, 189
stems, 185, 186
stereotypes, 275–276
student talk, 23, 283
students (defined), 18. *See also* language learners
subject (of a clause), 189, **194**, 195, 196, 197, 198, 199, 206, 255, 258, 259
subject complement, **195**, 199
subject movement, **196**, 206, 260
subskills, **11**, 70, 91, 119, 135, 136
substitution (of sounds), **231**–232, 233, 257
suffixes, 185, 186, 187
summative assessment, 114, 117
superordinates, 260
supplementing textbooks, **75**–**77**, 87, 282
syllabus, 51, 55, 78

syntax, 184, 252, 258

Task-Based Instruction (TBI), 34, **45**–**47**, 85, 147, 161, 216
task-oriented cultures, 271–272
teacher development, 107–108
teacher talk, 6, 23
technology, 9, 33, 57–60
TESOL (Teaching English to Speakers of Other Languages), 284, 285, 286
testing. *See* assessment
textbooks, 29, 35, 36, 44, 68–75, 208, 214, 282, 289
thought groups, **246**–248
TOEFL (Test of English as a Foreign Language), 115, 311
TOEIC (Test of English for International Communication), 115, 311
top-down listening, 141
Total Physical Response (TPR), 34, **51**–**52**, 61, 62
translators, 58, 59

uncountable, 187, 207, 289

verb phrases, **193**, 194, 197
verbs, 3, 179, 186, **189**, 192, 205, 206, 209, 211, 243, 244, 259, 263, 289
video, 43, 46, 58, 59, 108, 113, 116, 136, 143, 146, 148, 149, 247, 281, 283
video chat, 59
vocal cords, 223, 225
voiced, voiceless, 222, 223, **225**–226, 227, 228, 230, 232, 233, 255, 256
vowel sounds, 222, **223**–225, 231, 233, 240, 241, 242, 243–244

websites, 43, 46, 57, 58, 59, 108, 134, 214, 247, 282, 284, 285
whiteboards, 59, 100, 109, 283
wh-movement, **196**, 206, 255, 258, 260
word processors, 58, 59
word roots, 178, **185**
word stress, 141, 179, **242**–243, 257